TROILUS AND CRISEYDE

GEOFFREY CHAUCER (*c*.1343–1400), the son of a well-to-do London wine-merchant with court connections, began his career as a page in the household of Elizabeth, Countess of Ulster, wife of Edward III's son Lionel, Duke of Clarence. As a squire serving in Edward III's army when the king invaded France in 1359, he was captured at the siege of Rheims, and subsequently ransomed. A few years later he married Philippa de Roet, a lady-in-waiting to Constance of Castile, the second wife of John of Gaunt, Duke of Lancaster. It was to commemorate John of Gaunt's first wife, Blanche, that Chaucer composed in 1368 *The Book of the Duchess*, the earliest work that can confidently be attributed to him. He served in various campaigns in France and Spain, and twice visited Italy as a negotiator on important diplomatic missions. By the age of 31 he had been appointed Controller of Customs and Subsidy of Wools, Skins, and Hides in the port of London, a very responsible post which he held for twelve years. During this period he found time to write such major and innovatory works as *The House of Fame*, *The Parliament of Fowls*, and *Troilus and Criseyde*. In 1386 he became a Justice of the Peace and Knight of the Shire to represent Kent in Parliament. Soon afterwards his wife died, and he devoted the rest of his life to composing *The Canterbury Tales*, a project that was never completed. He died in 1400 and was buried in Westminster Abbey.

BARRY WINDEATT is a Fellow of Emmanuel College Cambridge, and Reader in Medieval Literature in the University of Cambridge. His books include a critical introduction to *Troilus and Criseyde* in the Oxford Guides to Chaucer, and an edition of Chaucer's poem in parallel with its chief inspiration, Boccaccio's *Il Filostrato*. He has also edited an anthology, *English Mystics of the Middle Ages*, and translated *The Book of Margery Kempe*.

OXFORD WORLD'S CLASSICS

*For almost 100 years Oxford World's Classics have brought
readers closer to the world's great literature. Now with over 700
titles—from the 4,000-year-old myths of Mesopotamia to the
twentieth century's greatest novels—the series makes available
lesser-known as well as celebrated writing.*

*The pocket-sized hardbacks of the early years contained
introductions by Virginia Woolf, T. S. Eliot, Graham Greene,
and other literary figures which enriched the experience of reading.
Today the series is recognized for its fine scholarship and
reliability in texts that span world literature, drama and poetry,
religion, philosophy and politics. Each edition includes perceptive
commentary and essential background information to meet the
changing needs of readers.*

OXFORD WORLD'S CLASSICS

GEOFFREY CHAUCER

Troilus and Criseyde
A New Translation

Translated with an Introduction and Notes by
BARRY WINDEATT

Oxford   New York
OXFORD UNIVERSITY PRESS
1998

Oxford University Press, Great Clarendon Street, Oxford OX2 6DP

Oxford New York

Athens Auckland Bangkok Bogota Bombay Buenos Aires
Calcutta Cape Town Dar es Salaam Delhi Florence Hong Kong Istanbul
Karachi Kuala Lumpur Madras Madrid Melbourne Mexico City
Nairobi Paris Singapore Taipei Tokyo Toronto Warsaw
and associated companies in
Berlin Ibadan

Oxford is a trade mark of Oxford University Press

First published as an Oxford World's Classics Paperback 1998

British Library Cataloguing in Publication Data

Data available

Library of Congress Cataloging in Publication Data
Chaucer, Geoffrey, d. 1400.
Troilus and Criseyde : a new translation / Geoffrey Chaucer;
translated with an introduction and notes by Barry Windeatt.
(Oxford world's classics)
Includes bibliographical references and index.
1. Troilus (Legendary character)—Poetry. 2. Cressida (Fictitious
character)—Poetry. 3. Princes—Troy (Extinct city)—Poetry.
4. Women—Troy (Extinct city)—Poetry. 5. Epic poetry, English
(Middle). 6. Trojan War—Poetry. I. Windeatt, B. A. (Barry A.),
1950- . II. Title. III. Series: Oxford world's classics (Oxford
University Press)
PR1895.W7 1998 821'.1—dc21 97–34380
ISBN 0–19–283290–5

1 3 5 7 9 10 8 6 4 2

Typeset by Graphicraft Typesetters Ltd., Hong Kong
Printed in Great Britain by
Caledonian International Book Manufacturing Ltd.
Glasgow

For Ruth Morse

CONTENTS

CONTENTS

INTRODUCTION

TROILUS AND CRISEYDE is Chaucer's greatest single achievement, a masterpiece 'unmatched by anyone between Dante and Shakespeare',[1] and one of the finest narrative poems in the English language. Set during the siege of Troy, it tells the story of how Troilus, son of King Priam, falls in love for the first time with a beautiful widow, Criseyde. Aided by Criseyde's uncle, Pandarus, Troilus becomes Criseyde's lover, only to lose her to the Greek leader Diomede. Although the tale of Criseyde's infidelity had first been told centuries before in several Continental sources and was well known in England, this tale is the subject of only the latter part of Chaucer's narrative. In his *Troilus and Criseyde* Chaucer has prefaced the familiar story of how the love affair ended with a longer account of how love began and came to fulfilment. Although the outcome of the plot was already familiar, Chaucer's insight into human character, his flair for comedy and drama, and his exploration of the philosophical and spiritual dimensions of his narrative make his version of the whole story profoundly original in both form and content, and give it a unique place in his own writings.

In sheer craftsmanship and design *Troilus and Criseyde* is Chaucer's supreme technical accomplishment. The verse—1,177 seven-line stanzas, divided into five books—is supple and varied, and shaped into a symmetrical structure that reflects the fundamental pattern in the poem's action, the rise and fall of Troilus' fortunes, with the lovers' union occurring at the centre of the total number of lines in the poem. The formal structure presents the poem within a self-consciously dignified layout which was almost unknown as yet in works written in English. Chaucer's skill in making his seven-line stanza work as a fluent narrative medium is an art that conceals art; his very success means that the stanza becomes a flexible vehicle for all the poem's brilliant range of style and register, containing high style and colloquial interchange equally naturally and effectively. It is especially through his ability to catch the accents of speech in vivid dialogue, and to match patterns of speech to individual character,

[1] George Kane, *Chaucer*, Past Masters (Oxford, 1984), 65.

that Chaucer's poem still speaks most directly to the modern reader of its concerns.

The poem's theme is announced at the outset as the 'double sorrow' of Troilus' fortunes in love. Its narrative represents an exploration of the potential and limits of human love, and also of the freedom of the individual will in a world seemingly governed by destiny or chance. This is a poem that creates and contains a world, a world that for its characters is re-made by love and then un-made by time and change, and by betrayal. For Chaucer, in concluding, the poem can be termed 'my little tragedy', yet this is a narrative that endows its old love story with so many new dimensions and such abundance of implication as to pass not only beyond romance but perhaps beyond any other single generic definition. What had begun as a story about an ending fittingly becomes in Chaucer's version a poem that includes a troubled response to the story's end within its own problematic close. A sense of an ending in the last hundred or so lines of *Troilus and Criseyde* is promoted through an acute sense of difficulty, denial, and displacement, medieval in accent but still strikingly immediate.

In Chaucer's own development, *Troilus* stands unsurpassed artistically and unrepeated thematically in the middle years of his poetic career, by far his longest completed single poem. On the evidence of his surviving works—from the dream poems, such as *The Book of the Duchess* or *The Parliament of Fowls*, to many of the individual *Canterbury Tales*—Chaucer was repeatedly drawn to rather brief narrative forms and showed some disinclination to finish what he began, so that the sheer scale and scope of *Troilus* stands out all the more remarkably among his writings. A narrative poem so ambitious in conception and form allowed Chaucer to achieve things he had not attempted before and which he evidently would not feel driven to do again. Before *Troilus* Chaucer wrote elegant short poems, often in a French manner; afterwards he worked on a collection of brief, thematically linked narratives in his *Legend of Good Women*, before moving on to his dynamic experiment with framed narratives spoken by different tellers in *The Canterbury Tales*. Individual tales, such as *The Knight's Tale* or *The Franklin's Tale*, may treat comparable themes with comparable insight, generosity, and compassion, but nowhere else in his work does Chaucer expose his reader so fully and directly to the action and to his characters as he does in *Troilus*, in a sustained exploration of private life and inward feeling that challenges comparison with the novel.

For some centuries after Chaucer's death it was not so much *The Canterbury Tales* as *Troilus and Criseyde* which was prized as his central achievement, prompting a range of allusion and rewriting. In *The Testament of Cresseid* (*c*.1475) the Scottish poet Robert Henryson imagined what happened to Criseyde after she fades from Chaucer's narrative. It offers an alternative or supplement to Chaucer's ending, not unlike modern sequels to well-known stories. Included in sixteenth-century printed editions of Chaucer's works as an unattributed pendant or sequel to *Troilus and Criseyde*, Henryson's *Testament* pervasively influenced the reception of the original poem and its heroine. To the view of Criseyde as a type of the faithless woman, familiar from the earliest versions of her story, there was now added a tradition which typecast and punished her. It is in the context of these accumulated traditions that Shakespeare wrote his play *Troilus and Cressida* (1602) which—despite its very different light on the story and characters, and its few close verbal parallels with *Troilus and Criseyde*—cannot but address and challenge disturbingly Chaucer's poem on the same theme. After Chaucer's poem and Shakespeare's play, it is perhaps unsurprising that the story of Troilus and Criseyde goes little further as a subject in English literature, and there are relatively few references until the story finds an echo and a revival of interest among modern readers:

> Troilus
> Patrols the Stygian banks, eager to cross,
> But the value is not on the further side of the river,
> The value lies in his eagerness. No communion
> In sex or elsewhere can be reached and kept
> Perfectly or forever. . . .
>
> Louis MacNeice, 'The Stygian Banks', vii. 10–15[2]

DATES AND CONTEXTS

Troilus and Criseyde was probably composed during the early and middle years of the 1380s and finished by early 1387. Chaucer's friend

---

[2] *The Collected Poems of Louis MacNeice*, ed. E. R. Dodds (London, 1966), 266 7. Dryden rewrote Shakespeare's play into his *Troilus and Cressida, or Truth Found Too Late* (1679); Wordsworth made a verse translation of Chaucer's *Troilus*, Book V, lines 519 686 (see *Poetical Works*, ed. E. de Selincourt (Oxford, 1966), iv 231); William Walton's opera *Troilus and Cressida* (1954; revised 1976) has a libretto by Christopher Hassall.

Ralph Strode—the London lawyer to whom *Troilus* is co-dedicated and submitted with a request for correction—died in 1387, and Thomas Usk, who was executed for treason on 4 March 1388, had shown a close familiarity with the text of *Troilus* in his prose work *The Testament of Love*, his allegorical figure of Love referring to Chaucer as 'the noble philosophical poete in Englissh', because of the 'tretis that he made of my servant Troilus'.[3] If the statement early in *Troilus* that 'our first letter is now an A' is indeed an allusion to the fact that 'now' (following the marriage of Richard II to Anne of Bohemia on 14 January 1382) the initial of the Queen of England was an 'A', this may indicate when Chaucer was working on *Troilus*. The synchronizing of the union of Troilus and Criseyde in Book III with a conjunction of Jupiter, Saturn, and the moon in the sign of Cancer, a rare and portentous conjunction that occurred in June 1385 for the first time since AD 769, may also date *Troilus*, although the conjunction would not necessarily need to have taken place for someone as interested in astrology as Chaucer to be mindful of it when writing his poem set at the siege of Troy. Trojan connections were made much of in London at the time Chaucer was writing: by tradition, Britain had been founded after the sack of Troy by a Trojan noble, Brutus, who gave the land his name and built London as his capital with the name of 'New Troy'. In the mid-1380s Nicholas Brembre (several times mayor of London, and Chaucer's associate in the Customs service) was reported to be planning to change the name of London to 'Little Troy'. Trojans may seem distant, but they are both ancestors and contemporaries, they are us.

As the 'tretis' of a 'noble philosophical poete', *Troilus and Criseyde* comes as the culmination of Chaucer's earlier writings and interpretations. It was evidently composed after Chaucer's translation into English prose of *De consolatione philosophiae* (The Consolation of Philosophy) by the late Roman writer Boethius, for Boethian ideas, images, and language suffuse the poem,[4] just as Chaucer's encounters in the 1370s with the works of Dante, Petrarch, and Boccaccio find their supreme expression in *Troilus*. From them Chaucer could

---

[3] Thomas Usk, *The Testament of Love*, in W. W. Skeat (ed.), *Chaucerian and Other Pieces* (Oxford, 1897), 123.

[4] The recurrent imagery in *Troilus* of navigation, of the stars, seas, and winds, of light and darkness, and of binding and constraint, all find significant parallels in Boethius' work.

derive an exalted sense of what it meant to be a poet, a confidence in the potential for writing in the vernacular, and an interest in the pagan past of antiquity. When Chaucer bids his *Troilus* follow and kiss the footsteps of Virgil, Ovid, Homer, Lucan, and Statius (v. 1791–2, p. 152), there is in that humility a proud claim that could be made for no contemporary English poem.

Chaucer's sense of himself as the poet of *Troilus* is fictionalized in his next poem, the *Prologue to the Legend of Good Women* (thought to date from 1386–8), where the God of Love rebukes the poet for his translation into English of the *Roman de la rose* (which 'makest wise folk fro me withdrawe' (F 331)), and for writing what he pleases about Criseyde ('That maketh men to wommen lasse triste' (F 333)), and imposes upon him the punishment of writing the *Legend*. In his defence, the poet—assuming the humble guise of mere translator—protests that whatever his source may have meant, his own intention in writing was to further and cherish fidelity in love, and to warn against unfaithfulness and wrong by the example of his writing (F 466–74). Chaucer's next poem is thus presented as arising out of contemporary response to the ambiguity of *Troilus* and its challengingly many-sided approach to the history of Criseyde.

The *Prologue* imagines Chaucer defended against an angry God of Love by Queen Alcestis, epitome of devoted wives in classical mythology, who evidently refers to the offending poem by the title of 'Creseyde' (F 441; G 443); Chaucer himself refers elsewhere to his poem as 'Troilus' or 'The Book of Troilus' (in *Adam Scriveyn*, his grumpy short poem to his careless scribe, and in the *Retractions* at the close of *The Canterbury Tales* (x. 1086)). A title for the poem is not specified within the text; the final explicit 'Here ends the Book of Troilus and Criseyde' is attested by half the manuscripts extant at that point but may not be authorial, and the title *Troilus and Criseyde* is first recorded in the early fifteenth century, after Chaucer's death. Although it may seem unthinkable now not to call Chaucer's poem by the names of both the lovers, such a title would have been less appropriate for the works in which their story had earlier appeared.

BOOKS OF TROILUS AND CRISEYDE

The figure of Troilus, a son of Priam who fought at the siege of Troy, is passingly mentioned in Homer's *Iliad* and Virgil's *Aeneid* ('unfortunate youth and ill-matched in conflict with Achilles', 1.475),

and in scattered brief references by other classical authors.[5] The figure
of Troilus was an emblem of early death, and the fate of Troy was
linked with his: there was a tradition that if Troilus reached 20 Troy
could not be overthrown, and that his death would be a sign of Troy's
downfall.[6] His role as one of the most important Trojan warriors
grew in the sixth-century Latin *De excidio Troiae historia* (The Fall
of Troy, A History) by Dares Phrygius, often linked with the fourth-
century *Ephemeridos belli Troiani libri* (A Journal of the Trojan War)
by Dictys Cretensis.[7] Although Dares does not develop Troilus as a
character in love, he does present him as the most pre-eminent Trojan
warrior after the death of Hector. Dares also provides a series of
descriptions of the main Trojan and Greek characters, including
Troilus, Diomedes, and Briseis (the concubine of Achilles). That Dares
describes Briseis more fully than Helen of Troy—with no apparent
reason, for she plays no part in his narrative—may perhaps have
prompted the later invention of a story about her. Readers of *Troilus*
who wish to read more about the Trojan War are referred to the
accounts in Homer, Dares, and Dictys (i. 146, p. 5) and later urged
to read Dares (v. 1771, p. 152), but Chaucer himself probably relied
on the fuller reworking of Dares, the *Daretis Phrygii Ilias* (The Iliad
of Dares the Phrygian) by the Anglo-Latin poet Joseph of Exeter
(*c.*1185).[8] At least, Chaucer's portraits of Diomede, Criseyde, and
Troilus in Book V of *Troilus* are drawn from Joseph's text, and by
including those portraits Chaucer collects and incorporates some of
the early sources and documents for the story.

The figure of Criseyde first appeared in a twelfth-century French
romance, for it is in *Le Roman de Troie* (*c.*1155–60) by Benoît de
Sainte-Maure, that the story of the love of Troilus for 'Briseida' and
his displacement by Diomede is first found, as one of a series of love

[5] Callimachus, fragment 363; Cicero, *Tusculan Disputations*, 1.39.93; Horace, *Odes*, 2.9.13–
16; Hyginus, *Fabulae*, 113.3; Seneca, *Agamemnon*, 784; Quintus Smyrnaeus, *Fall of Troy*,
4. 430–1. See also A. C. Pearson (ed.), *The Fragments of Sophocles* (Cambridge, 1917), ii.

[6] Plautus, *Bacchides*, 953–5; G. H. Bode (ed.), *Scriptores rerum mythicarum Latini* (Celle,
1834), 210, p. 66.

[7] F. Meister (ed.), *Daretis Phrygii de excidio Troiae historia* (Leipzig, 1873); W. Eisenhut
(ed.), *Dictys Cretensis ephemeridos belli Troiani libri* (Leipzig, 1958); R. M. Frazer, jun.
(trans.), *The Chronicles of Dictys of Crete and Dares the Phrygian* (Bloomington, Ind., and
London, 1966). Both works are thought to derive from Greek originals written in the
first century AD.

[8] Joseph of Exeter, *Daretis Phrygii Ilias*, in L. Gompf (ed.), *Briefe und Werke* (Leyden
and Cologne, 1970); G. Roberts (trans.), *The Iliad of Dares Phrygius* (Cape Town, 1970).

stories interwoven with a narrative of the Trojan War.⁹ Benoît's nar-
rative of the affair only begins at the point when Briseida is about
to be sent from Troy to the Greek camp, and so corresponds to the
events of Chaucer's fifth and last book. There is no account of how
Troilus had previously won and enjoyed the love of Briseida, and
Benoît's focus is at least as much on Briseida's developing involve-
ment with Diomede as on her abandonment of Troilus. From its
earliest extant appearance the story of the love between Troilus and
Criseyde is hence presented within the context of its painful disap-
pointment and ending. Benoît's gift for contriving courtly but nat-
ural and graceful speech is at its best in presenting the grief of Troilus
and Briseida at their parting, the wooing speeches of Diomede, and
the reflective soliloquies of Briseida in her isolated predicament, upon
all of which Chaucer has drawn closely in Book V of *Troilus*.

In inventing his story, Benoît effectively assigned Briseida her
original Homeric role of a woman passed involuntarily from one
man to another. Benoît evidently did not understand 'Briseida' in
Dares' list of portraits as a patronymic of Hippodamia, daughter of
Brises, the slave girl whom Agamemnon took from Achilles. Dares
does not include the story of Hippodamia, whom he names only as
'Briseida'. Benoît apparently did not recognize that Hippodamia
(whose story he borrowed from Dictys) was that 'Briseida' whom he
found described in Dares, and so felt free to make Briseida the object
of that rivalry between Troilus and Diomede already suggested in
Dares. Benoît perceived the interest in an enigmatic combination of
admirable qualities with changeability in his heroine, and created the
circumstances in which her constancy would be most cruelly tested
by insecurity. Chaucer sets aside Benoît's explicitly anti-feminist cri-
tique, but absorbs the lessons available from the *Roman de Troie* in
presenting the heroine at once sympathetically and critically.

Benoît's 'Romance of Troy' was subsequently translated and
paraphrased into Latin prose as *Historia destructionis Troiae* (The
History of the Destruction of Troy) by the Sicilian judge Guido
de Columnis of Messina (1287).¹⁰ In his moralizing 'history' (which

⁹ L. Constans (ed.), *Le Roman de Troie*, Société d'anciens textes français, 6 vols.
(Paris, 1904–12). For extracts, see R. K. Gordon (trans.), *The Story of Troilus* (London,
1934), and N. Havely (trans.), *Chaucer's Boccaccio* (Cambridge, 1980).
¹⁰ N. E. Griffin (ed.), *Historia destructionis Troiae* (Cambridge, Mass., 1936); M. E.
Meek (trans.), *Historia destructionis Troiae* (Bloomington, Ind., 1974).

enjoyed greater influence than the *Roman de Troie*), Guido takes an unsympathetic attitude to the experience of Briseida and her lovers; he demotes the motivation of romantic love in the *Roman de Troie* into lechery and lust, and it reflects Guido's harsher view of women's inconstancy that Briseida's affections change away from Troilus on the very day of her arrival in the Greek camp. Chaucer's more direct debt is to Benoît—he uses passages in the *Roman* which Guido omitted or abbreviated unsympathetically—and Guido's significance for *Troilus* is more for the *Historia*'s baleful influence on the heroine's reputation, for when Criseyde foresees that 'these books will ruin me' (v. 1060, p. 139), she could be speaking of the *Historia*.

Following the works of Benoît and Guido, other references to the lovers' story began to appear, and (*c*.1335) Giovanni Boccaccio made the love affair of Troilus and 'Criseida' the subject of his early narrative poem *Il Filostrato* (The One Overwhelmed by Love).[11] As the title suggests, the focus is centred on the hero's feelings in his affair with Criseida, who is here a widow, not the unattached girl of the earlier stories. Boccaccio's originality included his making the Troilus and Criseyde story the sole subject of an extended independent work, inventing the story of how their love started and developed until their enforced separation, the point at which earlier accounts had begun. As *Filostrato* was probably little known in England when Chaucer made it his main narrative source for *Troilus*, there was all the more novelty in an account of the whole love affair from beginning to end. A copy of *Filostrato* was evidently in front of Chaucer as he worked: he often matches it stanza for stanza, and Boccaccio's scene structure underlies Chaucer's narrative. These scenes—with one or other of the lovers alone, or with Pandarus, or occasionally together—allow for much quasi-dramatic exchange of dialogue and lyrical expression in soliloquies, lamentations, letters, and songs. In drawing on *Filostrato*, Chaucer constantly adapts and deepens Boccaccio's characterization, and he also goes back to the older texts to supplement his own version of the story.

Although Chaucer drew on such a variety of sources, he acknowledges none directly but instead twice claims for his source an author,

[11] *Il Filostrato*, ed. V. Branca, in *Tutte le opere di Giovanni Boccaccio*, ed. V. Branca, ii (Verona, 1964). For a translation, see N. Havely (trans.), *Chaucer's Boccaccio*; for the text of *Troilus and Criseyde* in parallel with that of *Il Filostrato*, see B. A. Windeatt (ed.), *Troilus and Criseyde: A New Edition of 'The Book of Troilus'* (London, 1984; 2nd edn., 1990).

Lollius, who almost certainly never existed, and the proem to Book II insists—contrary to the truth—that *Troilus* is being translated from a Latin source.[12] Who did Chaucer think Lollius was? Among the historians and poets who bear up the fame of Troy in Chaucer's *House of Fame* (1465–72)—a poem usually thought to pre-date *Troilus*—Lollius is included along with such authorities as Homer, Dares, Dictys, and Guido de Columnis, which suggests that Chaucer believed there was an ancient authority on Trojan history called Lollius. Through textual corruption and misconstruing, a line in an epistle by the Roman poet Horace could be understood to address his friend Maximus Lollius as 'the greatest writer about Troy', yet Chaucer cannot have believed the Italian poem on his desk was by the ancient author Lollius, although he may have thought *Filostrato* was based on his work. What Chaucer had indeed discovered in *Filostrato* was an original modern offshoot from the Troilus story, but the unfamiliarity of *Filostrato*'s vernacular account of Troilus and Criseyde could be the measure both of its authenticity as a rediscovered ancient text and of its lack of that traditional authority which medieval poets craved for their own writings. Boccaccio is Chaucer's principal source for three of his major poems set in pagan times—*The Knight's Tale, The Franklin's Tale*, and *Troilus*—yet Chaucer never mentions Boccaccio's name nor acknowledges his indebtedness to this near-contemporary author. By contrast, Chaucer and his early readers could well have believed in the existence of an early authority called Lollius, but no one had ever seen or read a copy of his work, and to present *Troilus* as a translation of Lollius (if not something of a joke) ostensibly amounts to a claim to be making available a major literary discovery of a lost work.

ROMANCE AND TRAGEDY

That in *Troilus* Chaucer is among the first writers to use such terms as 'tragedy' and 'comedy' in English underlines his sense of innovation and experiment. Treatments of the story of Troilus before Chaucer fall into particular generic categories, whereas Chaucer's poem achieves a distinctive conjoining of genres through use of diverse source elements. From Dares, or Joseph of Exeter, Chaucer's first readers might have been aware of the martial and epic role of Troilus,

[12] For a fuller discussion of 'Lollius', see Barry Windeatt, *Troilus and Criseyde*, The Oxford Guides to Chaucer (Oxford, 1992; repr. 1995).

and, from the *Roman de Troie*, of the story as romance and of Troilus as a lover. In Guido's *Historia*, with its imitations in various 'Troy Books', the story existed as part of a history. In *Filostrato*, Boccaccio's invention of an 'ascending' action climaxing in the lovers' union creates a rise-and-fall pattern that Chaucer could associate with tragedy. From medieval commentaries on Seneca's tragedies Chaucer may also have developed an interest in dramatic dialogue and monologue, as also in the models of philosophical dialogue and debate in Boethius. *Filostrato* already offered the model of an essentially lyric narrative with much direct speech, but Chaucer has extended and built on its example of a lyric narrative with inset lyrics. Counterpointing and energizing everything else is a comic sense, in what develops into a distinctively tragicomic variation on a romance theme.

Troilus has often been termed a 'romance' (although Chaucer never refers to it as such). There are no quests, magic, or enchantments, yet the all-possessing nature of Troilus' experience in love makes that experience for him a kind of inward equivalent of adventure, just as the new strangeness of love, and that force of idealization which he brings to his experience, give it the momentum of a quest and the quality of a marvel. *Troilus* develops a kind of referential relation to romance, less through its use of romance motifs than through its use of language, convention, and representation of behaviour. It is self-consciously literary, too, in developing the role of Pandarus, who becomes the author of the affair; he shapes the romance of the lovers' successful experience in the first three books, invents a plot by prompting correspondence and stage-managing meetings, and, having brought the lovers together, retires to the fire as if to look over 'an olde romaunce', although it is not altogether clear whether he is reading or watching (iii. 980, p. 75).

Yet by such reference to romance *Troilus* draws together material from different layers in the development of a romance tradition: its main narrative source in *Filostrato* has already reached the stage of a post-romance, the single undigressive narrative of a novella, achieved in part by excluding some generic features and subjects of romance. This is a tale of the hero's affair with a not unwilling widow, presented in an essentially urban, domestic setting, with no place for quests or marvels, or for much that is idealizing. Chaucer accepts Boccaccio's singularly co-ordinated structure but not the exclusions of subject and mood which helped create it. *Filostrato*'s powerful drive away from romance still moves beneath *Troilus*, which thus develops in an uneasy relation to traditional romance and comes to question the presuppositions with which romances typically begin and end, not least by following the hero both up to and beyond death, and hence beyond the normal boundaries of romance narrative. *Troilus* works through a process of disillusionment with the idealization of romance, although the disillusionment is dependent upon—and so in a sense lesser than—the idealization. The unsustainable nature of human idealisms both draws Chaucer to include the characteristic experience of romance but also necessarily leads him to an untypical conclusion in an intensity of disappointment that invites comparison with tragedy.

A link between the genre of tragedy and the subject of love is made explicit by Ovid in the *Tristia* (2. 381–4, 407–8) and in the stories of unfortunate love in his *Heroides* and *Metamorphoses*, but for Chaucer, the term 'tragedy' was most likely to recall that definition which Philosophy represents Fortune as giving to Boethius in *The Consolation of Philosophy*, translated into English by Chaucer in his *Boece* (2.pr.2.67–72). Here Chaucer could find Fortune asking what tragedies lament, other than that Fortune with an unexpected stroke overturns noble kingdoms (to which is added a gloss that tragedy is a composition on the subject of happiness that lasts for a while and ends in unhappiness). To this would be added recollections of the 'Falls of Princes', as in Boccaccio's *De casibus virorum illustrium* (The Falls of Illustrious Men) and *De claris mulieribus* (Concerning Famous Women), and works like Chaucer's *Monk's Tale* which are modelled upon this tradition. Chaucer's Monk defines tragedy as a story 'Of hym that stood in greet prosperitee, | And ys yfallen out of heigh degree | Into myserie, and endeth wrecchedly' (vii. 1975–7), a definition which in his own misery Troilus evidently applies to himself (iv. 271–2, pp. 95–6). But as the outlook of Chaucer's worldly Monk, or as Philosophy's impersonation of Fortune's self-defence against men's complaints, both these definitions of tragedy elsewhere in Chaucer's works are qualified by their contexts and suggest the irrelevance of tragedy to those who can learn to view this world with proper detachment, and with faith in God's dispensations. At key moments in a pointedly symmetrical structure *Troilus* incorporates some of the motifs of a tragedy of fortune, of rise and fall, yet differences from the Monk's definition of tragedy point to the specialness of what Chaucer is doing. If Troilus' love starts as a fall from pride, this is the beginning, not the climax, of the action and initiates a process in which Troilus learns and develops in humility, and in which the main focus is on the hero's career as a lover, his emotional rise and fall, re-created as a narrative shape of psychological, inward significance. Nor does the story's end fit well with a tragedy of fortune: the loss that Troilus suffers in Criseyde's infidelity is not like the loss of worldly prosperity or dominion; the end of Troilus' trust in Criseyde does not coincide with the end of his life; his love for Criseyde is never described as having an end; and long before the poem's end the evaded tragedy of the lovers' lucky avoidance of a double suicide in Book IV is an anti-tragic, anticlimactic moment, unlikely to be succeeded by another tragic climax.

If it is the nature of the ending that defined a medieval tragedy of fortune, it is in its relation of beginning and ending that *Troilus* explores a distinctive reading of tragedy, for the accumulating sense of multiple points of view and the absence of any single dominating perspective work against that simple, omniscient judgement characteristic of medieval tragedies. Troilus and Criseyde do not have tragic flaws, and for all the fullness of attention to the characters in *Troilus*, or perhaps because of it, the paradoxes and strains which prompt a sense of tragedy lie in the nature of earthly experience itself. Tragedy is in the pattern of the poem's action as a whole, rather than in Troilus or Criseyde, and the last two books, in their pathos, their intense sense of the pity of what they relate, embody the Boethian understanding of tragedy as an art of complaint and lamentation.

A further dimension to tragedy in *Troilus* is in the way that Chaucer's narrative follows its slain hero beyond the earthly end of death, in his ascent to the spheres. To show the spirit of the slain hero not only looking back on life from the other side of death, but contemning the world and even laughing at those he sees lamenting his death, can only be a tragedy in a way that invokes tragedy but does not let it stand alone, in order to redefine the idea by relating it to a perspective which is that of divine comedy, as Troilus' ascent succeeds and supplants tragedy in the hero's experience (and in the poet's, as he looks forward to following *Troilus* with 'some comedy').

NARRATIVE AND AUDIENCE

The concluding section of *Troilus*, with its literary allusions and writerly concerns, forms an apt conclusion to the distinctive narrative form of the work. Through the sheer amplitude of *Troilus* Chaucer exposes his readers to the flow and texture of his characters' speeches and thoughts in a way that he does in no other work. Framing and mediating this account of his characters, however, is Chaucer's most sophisticated development of a self-conscious narrative form which recurrently challenges and educates its readers' assumptions.

Most of those first encountering *Troilus* in Chaucer's time would have heard it rather than read it, but *Troilus* presents a concurrence of identities and deliveries. It refers to itself as both the written pages of a book, which the poet is still in the midst of composing at his desk, and as the script of a performance which is in the act of being presented to an audience, in a distinctive stylization into permanent form of the ephemeralness and mobility of actual delivery, although as the book grows larger, the sense of performance gives way somewhat to that of composition, and in Book V *Troilus* addresses itself for the first time to an imagined 'You, reader' (v. 270, p. 125). This double sense of the text as product of both a scholar and an entertainer lends the narrative its combination of ambitious, pondered, bookish form with a conversational ease, immediacy, and open-endedness.

In *Troilus* the customary authority of the writer is abdicated, or a game is made of abdicating, so that the narrating voice presents himself as writing without any personal experience of his subject; he invokes Clio, muse of history, implying that his own role is confined merely to translating into English and putting into rhyme the historical matter in his source. Throughout, *Troilus* maintains the fiction of itself as the slavishly close rendering of an ancient author, implying its subjection to its source on over twenty occasions (often when Chaucer is actually writing independently of *Filostrato*). The fiction of such dependence on sources also includes a useful helplessness in the face of their supposed gaps and shortcomings, as when it is claimed (not altogether accurately) that no authority reveals how long it was before Criseyde succumbed to Diomede's advances, and the reader is challenged to check in his own books (v. 1086–90, p. 139). So, similarly, the source supposedly does not reveal whether Criseyde had children (i. 132–3, p. 5), although actually *Filostrato* expressly says she did not (1.15); Criseyde's age, it is claimed, cannot be known (v. 826, p. 135), although *Filostrato* had variously described her as young. The supposed reticence of the source on what Criseyde really thought about the assurance that Troilus would not be at Pandarus' house if she went there (iii. 575–8, p. 67) only draws attention to the crucial nature of some intriguing information which the text is not providing. Nor can the author of *Troilus* be blamed (he protests) if his source has already made editorial decisions not to include certain documents, like the lost letter mentioned in Book III (iii. 500–4, p. 66). Different contexts produce different claims: although the narrator claims, on unrevealed authority, to be somehow providing the very words of Troilus' first song, where Lollius gave only the gist (i. 393–9, pp. 9–10), he later makes a point of rejecting the idea that a narrative like his could be other than a selective abridgement of the experience and time-span it depicts (iii. 491–5, p. 66).

Troilus insistently fictionalizes its dependence on its source so as to foreground the question of authority, sometimes casting itself in the role of responding to imagined objections to its procedures. A slightly blustering tone colours the gallant protestation that Criseyde certainly did not fall in love with any indecent haste, as some ill-intentioned person might suppose (ii. 666–79, p. 35). But the defence—that only the beginning can be shown of what was a lengthy process—again draws attention to the match between narrative form and the subject it is depicting. In Book III the impossibility of providing a full transcript of the lovers' every word and look is dismissed in a squashing response to some imagined objection from a member of the audience (iii. 495–9, p. 66). The proem to Book II reminds us that customs and language in love change over time, as if addressing itself to an audience of contemporary lovers perplexed by the poem's picture of Trojan ways in love (ii. 22–46, p. 23), and the implied audience that *Troilus* projects is a significant aspect of how its narrative is presented.

It is an audience of lovers that the poem ostensibly addresses, as if present in the same place where the poet is reciting, their knowledgeability flattered by a narrator who casts himself as excluded from their experience. In the story of a secret love, to hear is to overhear: the narrative addresses its audience as if imparting confidences, sharing secrets in a way that at times assumes the reader or listener is an accomplice in the action ('the only thing we are lacking is . . .', iii. 531, p. 66). Since the implied audience has special expertise in the poem's subject of love, the poet can submit the language of his composition for their expert appraisal (iii. 1324–36, p. 81), and this allows any actual audience or readers to locate themselves in relation to that implied audience, and hence to the experience the poem presents. It is a poised and witty fiction that heightens awareness of the match or mismatch between matter, form, and style, for the poet who prays at the close that no scribe miscopy his text, and who submits his work for correction to a learned poet and a philosopher, is not actually inviting any self-appointed lover-critic to adapt the language of Book III in the light of his experience. Nor does the fiction of an audience of lovers remain unchallenged by the unfolding of the narrative, for the closing stages of *Troilus* witness an altered address to audiences of women and of young people, both 'he and she'.

GAMES OF LOVE

In *Troilus* a narrator professedly inexperienced in love himself writes (with fond partiality) about a hero's very first experience of love. For Troilus everything is being done for the first time. His experience is unique, unparalleled, wholly possessing. That Troilus has no previous experience to tell him what to do allows for a vast deal of talking and thinking about how he feels and how he is to act. This lends the poem that discursive dimension by which it becomes so much more of a consideration of love than simply the story of its hero and heroine, and so much like an old romance that the conventions by which love is heightened and idealized are ultimately used to question and explore the love they express. As players, lovers are seen as a sect apart, and love is an art and craft to be practised by them, whether through composing complaints, songs, or letters, or in composing their behaviour. Much of the affair is carried on through the medium of the traditional 'game of love',[13] with all its fictions and play as the secret life of the lovers, for it is through these very games and fictions that human aspirations and uncertainties can be formulated. Within the conventions of love as 'service', Troilus is presented as committed to the feudal 'service' of his 'lady' Criseyde, who, when she accepts Troilus as her servant in love, makes a point

---

[13] J. Stevens, *Music and Poetry in the Early Tudor Court* (London, 1961), ch. 9, 'The "Game of Love"'. The notion of 'courtly love' in medieval texts as a monolithic set of regulations for love affairs, a 'code' of behaviour solemnly and universally observed, is almost certainly a modern misinterpretation of the availability of courtly styles, idioms, and conventions to be read in a range of literal, playful, and ironic ways, depending on context.

of setting aside within the private world of their relationship his princely rank in society (iii. 169–75, p. 60). While such language of humble service and devotion remains a fiction and play of the lovers' private life and imagination—Troilus does not really relinquish his royal rank (i. 432–4, p. 10)—it can articulate the linked striving and commitment he pours into his emotional life. For Troilus loving and serving, loving as serving, are inseparable, for service gives expression to devotion, and Chaucer explores through such rhetoric of feudal service both the self-sacrificing and expectant aspects of love. In principle, love service is to be accepted as an open-ended commitment, a privilege in itself, but there is also a sense that serving implies deserving, and that love's fulfilment may be seen as an earned reward after suffering, in the tradition of love as a sickness or even madness for the lover ('What is this strange illness? I die . . .', sings Troilus (i. 419–20, p. 10)). It is a sickness to which the lady—as a kind of physician—may bring healing and cure, and from the beginning of Troilus' love until the lovers' union this allows for much play with the ironies of illnesses feigned and real, although always veined with seriousness, since some medieval medical writings did indeed recognize the lover's malady as a form of illness. That a man might die for love could be treated as an established erotic fiction, part of the serio-comic verbal extravagance in playing the game of love.

The parallel between love and illness provides a potent metaphor for the suspense and disturbance of the lover's state, waiting to be cured, with patience or restlessness. The notion that Troilus might actually die for love is one means by which Pandarus puts pressure on Criseyde to make concessions, and the intensity of the most important emotional transitions and experiences is throughout associated with the extremity of death. Yet Pandarus as well as Troilus and Criseyde all pay lip-service to the belief that lovers can indeed die for love, and the devotion of the lover to his lady becomes the practice of a quasi-religious devotion. Having undergone conversion, confessed, and repented, the lover identifies with an order of lovers and looks forward to salvation. This is at the disposition of his lady, determined by her rather than by his desert, and by extension the relation of the lover with the lady is presented in terms of the Christian theology of grace, while the attainment of sexual fulfilment can be set about with references to heaven. The familiar structures and aims of religious devotion in this way act as a correlative to the devotion

within the love affair, lending it the force and value of religious asso-
ciations, yet thereby perhaps also suggesting how experience of love
in this life must fall short of all that religious language portends.

To all this there is a further perspective, for there cannot but
be comedy where there is so much solemnity. To Pandarus, at least
part of the time, all these roles and fictions are aspects of courtship
played as a kind of game: he can expound the principle of endless
love-service to Troilus in Book I as well as teasing the lord kneel-
ing to his lady in Book III; he can toy with the fictions of the lover
as sick or dying, as well as taking them at face value; and he can liken
love to religious observance in a long series of knowing allusions.
What Troilus will take solemnly and literally can be for Pandarus a
manner of speaking and a means to an end (although he too has his
romantic side, his moments of faith). In this game of love Criseyde
is a player responding to the gambits of others, not unversed in the
rules and conventions, and it is these differences between the char-
acters that fuel the poem's analysis of the ways love is conceptual-
ized and valued.

CHARACTERS

Troilus

It is the double sorrow of Troilus in love which the poem announces
as its subject, and Troilus is the figure whose emotional life raises
the poem's central questions. At the close of each of the five books
the focus settles squarely on him. His end is the end of the narrative,
which ignores the subsequent lives of other characters. Troilus is the
hero of the poem, but one in whom the endeavour and venturing
associated with a hero is translated by his exceptional capacity to
feel. His characteristic expression is apostrophe, song, complaint, or
prayer. Troilus is a hero by virtue of being in love—and he sees his
experience of love in some metaphysical dimension—but he is also
an ancient pagan of moral worth, not wise in the ways of the world,
but acting generously to others and doing no mean thing himself. In
earlier texts—except *Filostrato*—Troilus had been a hero by dint of
heroism in feats of arms, a young and spirited warrior. Chaucer emphas-
izes more the fearful dread of the hero in love, so that Troilus' sta-
tus as hero of the narrative must be newly defined: in his passivity,
his idealism, he is a study in a literary archetype taken to the brink

of absurdity, but perhaps all the more admirable. The whole conduct of the affair through a go-between—the supposedly 'accidental' meetings, the hero's entering his lady's bed by being thrown into it in an unconscious state—allow Troilus to be brought together with his lady with the minimum of active initiative or direct responsibility on his part. For Troilus the role of petitioner and supplicant in love lends ritual form to a naturally passive disposition, albeit taken to exceptional and eccentric extremes, and this prepares for his role in the traditional story of the lovers' separation, where he does not intervene to prevent Criseyde's departure. In what seems a natural extension of his character all along, he now submits to what he sees as the inevitability of the exchange.

Such an exploration of behaviour which is not conventionally masculine raises questions about the values of traditional sexual stereotypes. There is no uncertainty in the outward, public role of Troilus as a soldier, but in the private world Troilus is acted upon by his feelings in ways that do not conform to manhood. His fainting is reproved both by Pandarus and by Criseyde, and the prince, who at his first appearance is accustomed to lead a group of young men as they confidently subject women to the male gaze, is by the midpoint of the poem being chastened and admonished by his lady as if he were a child. Sexual possession comes only after the man's moment of humiliation and humility. His swoon is the extreme instance of all that setting aside of conventional masculine initiative and assertiveness that has characterized Troilus as a lover: male fear and shame trigger sexual consequences here, rather than a male advance. His subsequent call on Criseyde to submit to him sexually, or the likening of the male lover to the sparrowhawk taking the lark, can now only be reassertions of the archetypal masculine role in a newly qualified context. His rapt exploration of the woman's body comes only after his own unconscious body has been undressed by the woman's uncle and then variously rubbed, wetted, and kissed, in their attempts to revive him, by Criseyde and Pandarus. As a deflation of male stereotypes of sexual conquest and mastery, the swoon is both comic yet also an endorsement of value in Troilus. Lack of experience does not mean lack of desire, which both burns and grips him (and increases and feels different after his first night with Criseyde) but is always subject to his self-control, for the lovers' pleasure in their union is described as springing from a mutual obedience to each other's desire.

To Pandarus, it seemed that by manly self-assertion Troilus could shape the world to his wishes by abducting Criseyde, but Troilus' restraint is a more difficult course than conventional conformity to male assertiveness. In Troilus manhood is associated with discretion and self-control, and the poem's exceptional understanding of the nature of Criseyde as a woman is complemented by the way that her lover is understood to be a better man because his 'manhood' includes some of the qualities of 'womanhood'.

Yet Troilus may still seem—by comparison with Criseyde or Pandarus—a relatively simple character, for there is little withheld or unknowable about him. He is recurrently praised as second only to Hector, but such praise is inseparable from an implicit qualification. He is given the rhetoric and the lyrical artistry to invest a value in human love which experience will test, and in this he may seem heroic or misguided, or both. In one view Troilus is a character of some moral worth, a virtuous pagan, both philosopher and lover; in another view, he may be seen as given to wilful self-enslavement, irrational self-delusion, and subjection to the senses. His capacity for idealization may seem either admirably high-minded or naïve and impractical. His humble passivity may seem a reflection of gentleness and modesty, but it may appear either comically or tiresomely ineffectual. His decision not to abduct Criseyde may be seen as moral responsibility or as weakness. His unchanging loyalty may be read as consistency and steadfastness, or as rigidity and obsession. The contrast between his brutally abrupt end and the privilege of his soul's ascent beyond death does suggest a virtue in the spirit of Troilus, that merits such an altered level of perception after death, and gives a larger worth to his experience of a loss which can stand to represent the failure of any human attachment or ideal.

Criseyde

Chaucer's 'Book of Troilus' becomes the story of Criseyde as well, and the two stories modify each other. Her fascination challenges but eludes any single explanation of her nature, not least because Criseyde is a character who comes with a history, already a familiar figure identified with an act of infidelity. During most of *Troilus* Criseyde's past infidelity is still to come, but that unchangeable end to the traditional story poses questions about the development, consistency, and predictability of character. Was Criseyde's change of heart part of her character all along? In the narrative of a secret love affair, presented with such narratorial chivalry about a lady much concerned with her honour, the extent of Criseyde's knowledge and desires, and hence her responsibility, remains tantalizingly beyond our power to determine. Is this the narrative of a seduction or of a pretence of being seduced? Is there innocence or calculation in Criseyde's character, or an ambiguous mixture of both? To pose alternatives about Criseyde is usually to see that the text allows no exclusive interpretation as one thing or the other. A narrative, which at points takes us so close to Criseyde's consciousness, moves us outside her at critical moments; a sense of knowing Criseyde is always accompanied by a sense of what is unknown. In Book III Criseyde retorts to Troilus that, if she had not already yielded, she would not be there (iii. 1210–11, p. 79), but this decisive moment has never been depicted. This is in keeping with the earlier presentation of Criseyde in Book II, which approaches so closely to her very consciousness, the ebb and flow of her mood, yet describes no moment of conscious decision. By preserving some mystery about what Criseyde knows, Chaucer preserves for her an autonomy, an independence both of other characters in the poem and of the poet and reader. We know, as she ostensibly does not, how so much that happens to her in Books II and III is manipulated. Does Criseyde realize exactly what is afoot, happy to let herself appear to be manœuvred into what she really wants while preserving appearances, which allow her to seem innocent of what is happening? She shows every sign both of quick intelligence and of a kind of shrewd prudence. Yet her self-possession coexists intriguingly with other signs of a nature easily frightened but also easily soothed, while what her outward appearance is taken to reveal are a quintessentially female nature and attributes. The focus on womanly nature is thematically central, and the conversations between Pandarus and Criseyde in Book II, and her subsequent reflections alone, are couched with alertness to the position of women, for just as Chaucer has added to his source almost all mention and qualification of masculinity, so too, and interrelatedly, he has added much of the reference to women's qualities and nature.

Chaucer does not evade the question of his Criseyde's sexuality, which is accepted without embarrassment and uncensoriously as part of her make-up, even if obliquely presented. When Pandarus goes too far too quickly in anticipating the lovers' union ('then the ruby's well set in the ring . . .'), Criseyde quickly censors his innuendo but adds ambiguously 'You're ruining everything!' (ii. 585–90, p. 34). Yet Chaucer suggests she is aroused soon afterwards by the sight of Troilus as he rides back from battle past her window, a triumphant young warrior but a modest one: she is attracted by the thought of his qualities and the glimpse of his physique, prowess, and vigour— and the new knowledge that he has already admitted his love for her, and thus his subjection. She blushes at her own thought (ii. 652, p. 35). Consciously, Criseyde may think up reasons against an affair —all that upheaval, so disruptive and constricting, is it worth it? —but set against that is the unconscious: her dream of an eagle (emblem of royalty, but white, perhaps for purity) tearing her heart from her breast and inserting his own, a kind of stylized penetration by a male creature which, we hear, neither frightened nor hurt her. Chaucer may have adapted this from a later dream in *Filostrato* (7.23– 4), much changed in *Troilus*, where Troiolo sees the boar (emblem of Diomede) tearing out Criseida's heart with his tusks, to her apparent pleasure. Both Criseyde's lovers are identified with fierce male animals, just as her attraction to the warrior Troilus returning from battle is matched by her later attraction to the wounded, bleeding body of Diomede, injured by Troilus. When she visits Troilus in his sickroom, Criseyde can contemplate her lover from a position of advantage, calmly and approvingly observing his blushing, tongue-tied confusion which, like the farcical comedy before the consummation, redraws the bounds between the roles of men and women. That accommodation is celebrated in the mutual pleasure and considera-tion of the consummation and becomes part of the lovers' continu-ing life together. Other people's sympathy misses the point about separation ('they gave her about as much relief with that as one gets from a headache by being scratched on the heel!', iv. 726–8, pp. 103–4), and it is Criseyde who suggests to Troilus, after she has recovered from her faint, that they talk over their problems in bed together, where love-making, along with arguing, is seen as part of the pat-tern and texture of shared life. Once aware of her miscalculation in coming to the Greek camp, Criseyde's chief worry about trying to return to Troy is her understandable fear of being raped if caught crossing enemy lines (v. 704–6, p. 133).

Is fear the key to understanding Criseyde? She is frightened by her father's defection, Pandarus' threats and his news of an admirer, the dangerous predicament of Troy and her own isolation, played upon by Diomede. She is said to be the most fearful person there might be, and her fearfulness disposes her to see all the drawbacks in any new turn of events. She is both flattered by the attentions of a prince and nervous of possible consequences in refusing them. Both Pandarus' stratagems play in turn on Criseyde's fears, first of the lawsuit and then of what Troilus might do in jealous despair, but fearfulness is an understandable reaction from a woman without power in a world she cannot control and can only propitiate. As Criseyde remarks, pagan religion was thought to be founded on fear (iv. 1408, p. 115), yet this observation is part of a larger scepticism and confidence. Her pivotal decision—her plan to comply with her exchange and then return—stems from an unjustifiable self-confidence in her power to deceive the seer Calchas. Fearfulness does not explain this crucial moment, but to highlight any single quality as the key to Criseyde's character is contrary to the mixture of attributes which the text accumulates. Timidity is one part of an impressionable side to Criseyde's character which enables Chaucer to show her responding to so many suggestions and possibilities without also revealing the depth, effect, and interrelation of all the impressions she receives.

Chaucer inherited Criseyde's precarious position as the daughter of a known traitor to Troy, but he gave her a much higher social status than her prototypes: she is mistress of a palatial household, and enjoys the grandest social connections. With her highly respectable social station comes a keen concern for what society will say of her, for her honour and good name. Criseyde remains an essentially social creature, and her inner self is never wholly independent of her environment, just as honour here constitutes a public reading of something intimately related to the woman's body. Criseyde is concerned to conform with whatever the person she is with expects her to be, although, by trying to please everyone, she eventually loses everything. There is poignancy in the way Chaucer shows Criseyde internalizing and accepting the values of the world made by men.

In his account of her infidelity Chaucer gives Criseyde belated self-knowledge: she acknowledges her self-delusion in coming to the Greek camp, laments the necessities driving her to be unfaithful, accommodates herself to the idea of abandoning Troilus. In allowing for her change of heart the narrative fractures normal chronology as if in denial of Criseyde's betrayal, disparaging as hearsay her reported infidelity, which it then proceeds to report Criseyde regretting and lamenting, albeit at some unspecified future time (v. 1050, 1069–71, p. 139). The matchlessly beautiful woman (i. 101–5, 171–2, pp. 4, 5), of gaiety and accomplishment (iv. 866, v. 565–80, pp. 106, 130–1), who once seemed so near, slips ever further out of focus, known only through a disingenuous letter which we see Troilus reading but not Criseyde writing, and which in its empty flourishes, evasions, and insinuations of bad faith against Troilus painfully suggests a disintegrating personality. Neither the hero nor audience can altogether understand what has happened to Criseyde, and a reader's baffled sense of losing Criseyde in the narrative shares in the bafflement and pain of Troilus himself.

Pandarus

Chaucer catches the essence of Pandarus' nature as a friend: he is simply superb company, a man of inexhaustible wit, vivacity, and charm, the most talkative character in the poem, full of gaiety and sly good humour, affably ready to help and to sympathize, a devoted friend who wishes the happiness of his friends. Such is his exuberance that the whole pulse of action quickens whenever he makes his entrance. The intelligence of Pandarus is of a quite different order from that of other characters in the text. He takes advantage of life as it passes and has an exceptional power to extemporize. He is the essence of initiative and resourcefulness; he generates action and shapes it. A performance tuned to the highest pitch, it is also gracefully urbane and seemingly effortless. A figure with such control shows an inventiveness in making things happen which parallels (even rivals) the inventive power of the narrative that presents him. Not for nothing is the god Janus invoked to guide him, and, like his conversation, Pandarus is protean, mobile, shifting—and his consistency is in so being. He is revealed—characteristically—to have 'connections', to be on good terms with the royal family and spend whole days with the king. But what does he look like? The poem offers no description of his physical appearance, while presenting full portraits of the three other main characters. He is Criseyde's uncle (rather than her cousin, as in *Filostrato*), which may imply that he is in a different generation from Troilus, although without apparent effect on his extraordinary vitality and relish for life, nor on his own interest in love. Like Troilus' successful career as a warrior, Pandarus' unsuccessful life as a lover is something off-stage to Chaucer's narrative, and the explanation for his lack of success is never enlarged upon, although Pandarus becomes architect and stage-manager for others of a love affair which, granted the character of both lovers, could scarcely have begun without him. His role requires him to be both a highly practical fixer and a theoretician about love—and about life in general. Interest in love notwithstanding, Pandarus is the antithesis of all that tends to the spiritual and idealizing in the lovers. He is consistently this-worldly, and through his conversation down-to-earth lore, adage, proverb, and colloquial expression enter the text. Indeed, his speech is characterized by a stream of proverbs and proverbial-sounding expressions, many of which are first recorded in English here (but which may be misinterpreted nowadays, when sententiousness is hardly appreciated).[14] Pandarus' use of proverbs fittingly gives voice to his characteristic outlook that all human experience repeats itself and so falls into the predictable patterns and formulas that proverbs express. Not that Pandarus is predictable, for his inventive speech always has the potential to surprise: his conversation makes a range of connections and allusions, from geometry to dream theory and philosophy, so that his talk seems the outcome of a range of observation and reading, from folk wisdom to bookish allusion. Yet while full of arguments for doing things, he is not shown in any kind of reflection; he has no lyrics, monologues, or introspective debates. An opportunist, he always tries to seize the time, but in seizing it he serves it too.

Pandarus does so much, but why he does it—other than because of a ready sympathy for his friend—is never explained. His characteristic activity is a foil to the lovers' inaction, and in his dealings with Troilus he is often given the comic character's privilege of voicing an audience's censored exasperation. He is always impatient with inaction, wasting time, or not trying. Urgent, undignified, physical actions and gestures are the role of this friend, yet the directness of his outward movements only emphasizes how indirectly he prefers to move events. If the conduct of life is play and game, Pandarus is a cunning player whose moves stay exultantly far ahead of others, and whose own feelings and motives can barely be separated from his zest for the game. The two stratagems by which Pandarus brings

[14] The incidence of proverbs in the poem is recorded in the Index of Proverbs (see pp. 191–4). Pandarus is by far the most frequent user of proverbs; Criseyde also utters them quite often, but Troilus uses them infrequently.

the lovers together, first at the house of Deiphebus and then at his own home, are in his terms triumphs of manipulated events. But they also involve so many apparently unneeded risks as to amount to a kind of virtuoso performance in the art of delusion, and all to gain his kinswoman as the sexual partner of his closest friend—he and Troilus often call each other 'brother'. Is there perhaps something unsavoury or suspicious in such manipulation of the intimate lives of others, however much it is prompted by the inexperience of Chaucer's lovers? He knows what he is doing could be called procuring, although Troilus prefers a fancier name (iii. 253–6, 395–406, pp. 62, 64). Pandarus seems to anticipate that three people rather than two will be made happy by his activities (i. 994, p. 20), and his intimacy with both lovers may point to a voyeuristic interest in their sexual fulfilment. It is unclear whether he ever leaves the lovers' bedroom, and his visit to his niece before she has got up next morning is not without innuendo. Yet Chaucer's narrative leaves it to the reader to define an ulterior motive for Pandarus, just as it leaves us to decide why, if Pandarus is a voyeur, we are not equally so ourselves.

In the first three books Pandarus embodies a genial humour which casts its spell as long as the lovers' happiness lasts, but he is not well placed to help them once Fortune's wheel turns. Pandarus assumes that human love is inseparable from the presence of the body and cannot survive separation and absence, for new experience will supplant old. His characterizing speech and bustle now lose their relevance, no longer initiating and shaping actions but responding to events. It is the aptest end to his role as talker and fixer that Pandarus' last words in the poem are an admission of speechlessness.

Diomede

Diomede is positively created to be the least complicated of the principal characters. His intentions are unambiguous, while in pursuing them with Criseyde he is consistently disingenuous. There is no mystery about what motivates Diomede: he is always completely self-serving and wholly self-confident. Diomede is aggressively competitive and assertive, and Chaucer establishes an impression of physical and temperamental masculinity. The principal image of Diomede is his portrait in the set taken from Joseph of Exeter, describing tersely the powerful frame and forceful qualities of a warrior. It is a study in power, which will express itself in the will to sexual possession for its own sake. He is stressed to be characteristically bold, but, in approaching Criseyde, his is a nicely calculated boldness. He is called impetuous, but he shows an excellent sense of pace. He has the cunning necessary to the successful huntsman or fisherman, interested in netting or hooking his prey. There is a symbolism in Diomede's taking of the rein and bridle of Criseyde's horse to lead her away from Troy and from Troilus, and Diomede refers back to this act as if it represents a prior claim on her. Diomede sets the pace by forcing it: he takes Criseyde's hand when they have only just met; he later takes Criseyde's glove, and, as Chaucer summarizes events, the emphasis is on Criseyde's gifts to Diomede. There is no answering sense that Diomede gives anything of himself in return, and Troilus' dream of Criseyde lavishing her kisses on a sleeping and unresponsive boar is an image of the imbalance between give and take in the union of Criseyde and Diomede.

Where Chaucer allows us into Diomede's thoughts, he is planning what we then see him putting successfully into effect as a skilful operator, and the visit on the tenth day follows extended premeditation. The first thing noticed about Diomede is his perceptiveness as to how things stand between Troilus and Criseyde; on that he acts as an adventurer, who feels he may as well try to exploit his opportunity with Criseyde. His insincere rehearsal to Criseyde of the language of feudal service is a feigned humility, in which the supposed will to serve is actually in the service of a will to master, and the traditional claim to be helplessly in the power of love is belied by the very efficient manner in which the claim is pressed. Chaucer replaces all evidence in his sources that Diomede is motivated by love; his thoughts are wholly given over to calculation, and he is not shown to act under any impress of feeling, in marked contrast with Troilus. Diomede is motivated above all by the desire to gain, to win, to conquer. His repeated references to the comparative merits of Greeks and Trojans as lovers reflect an individual male competitiveness, as well as his identification of winning Criseyde from her Trojan lover with the larger war over a woman between the Greeks and Trojans. For Diomede, the man who wins Criseyde could call himself a 'conqueror'—of the lady, and of another man, her present lover.

Yet it is not the character of the seducer who holds the attention, but his victim, and there is sadness in watching Diomede's palpably insincere gambits received by Criseyde with a meek, apparently unsuspecting politeness, which is then to merge with accommodatingness, and eventually with concession. Both an enemy warrior and her lover, Diomede's proffers of love come with menacing assurances of the utter destruction of Troy and its citizens. The text need not enter into detail to convey that Diomede has already won what he set out to win, but Cassandra will put it bluntly: 'This Diomede's in, and you're out!' (v. 1519, p. 147).

'THE NOBLE PHILOSOPHICAL POETE IN ENGLISSH'

In *Troilus*, Chaucer's retelling of an inherited story of disappointment and betrayal in love is inseparable from larger questions posed by the narrative about any human commitment or ideal in a world subject to time and change. His analysis of human love—how it may seem everything, how it may fall short—has all the more timeless force because the claims of that love are realized in all their power. The absence from some *Troilus* manuscripts of Troilus' soliloquy on free will, his soul's ascent to the spheres, and his song in Book III on love as the binding force of all things—these passages were probably added at a late stage of composition—points to Chaucer's concern to stress with urgent, bold strokes the metaphysical and philosophical dimensions to his narrative, in what develops into at once a celebration and a critique of human love.

   In the lengthy process leading to the lovers' union, and in what later happens to that love, there is so much discussion and reflection on the nature, conception, and value of loving that *Troilus* comes to constitute a form of debate about love. The context for this debate is an approach to his story by Chaucer which allows love to be progressively redefined. In the *Roman de Troie* Diomede looks forward to the time when he will sleep with Briseida, and he duly supplants Troilus in possession of her. In *Filostrato* the physical nature of the satisfaction Troiolo seeks for his love is as clear all along to the reader as it is to Criseida. In *Troilus*, by contrast, all that protracted process of talking and thinking is only retrospectively seen to have led towards physical consummation. Sexual union comes aptly at the poem's centre, with the bodily nature of love frankly and exultantly acknowledged, celebrating the joy of sexual fulfilment in its moment. The passivity of Chaucer's lovers and the delegation of all arrangements to Pandarus mean that Troilus and Criseyde arrive in bed together and on the verge of physical union, having made no direct sexual initiative to each other. The outcome of this separation of means from end is that, when sexual fulfilment does come, it is paradoxically a physical experience that seems miraculous and transcendent. The effect is that love has unfolded as a discovery for the lovers and as an exploration for the reader of the questions posed by their experience of love.

To summarize those passages where questions arise about love is to review many of the principal scenes and episodes. Questions are explicitly raised about the nature of love (morally improving, but anyway irresistible . . .) in the excursus after Troilus is struck by Love's arrow; in Troilus' first song on the paradoxical quality of love; in the first interviews between Pandarus and Troilus (no one uninclined to love, either heavenly or earthly . . .), between Pandarus and Criseyde, and in her monologue on the pros and cons of love; in Antigone's song on the transformative effects of love; and in the exchanges in Book III. Questions are also implied by many other contexts: the prayer which forms the first proem; Troilus' responses to love after returning from the temple in Book I; the richly ambiguous invocation to Venus in the third proem, matched by Troilus' Boethian song at the close of Book III, both associating the famously mutable love of Troilus and Criseyde with that enduring power of love which unifies and orders all things; the various addresses in Book III expressing the hero's transcendent view of what love comprehends; and the whole presentation of the disintegration of love and understanding in the later part of the poem, against the backdrop of the Trojan War. The poem's painstaking setting in that pagan world frees Chaucer to present an example of the universal experience of love, but outside the contemporary moral context in which such love would be judged in his own time. *Troilus* presents the natural love of pagans in a pre-Christian world (allowing for mythological allusions to stories of love as violence, oppression, obsession, and betrayal), and sets that love in a comparative relation to Christian discriminations between loves in a way that sharpens analysis of what earthly love can be.

That analysis of love includes questions about the freedom of the individual will, for the characters are disposed to interpret their lives in terms of destiny, fortune, and chance. Narrative events are recurrently cast as chance events (although what constitutes chance depends on the point of view), and paralleled with the movement of the heavenly bodies, with their potential influence over human life. Chaucer's characters have the fatalistic opinions that (in medieval understanding) were typical of pagan belief and distinct from the orthodox Christian view that the agency of fortune functioned within the larger frame of providence, and that God's omniscience—divinely unconstrained by our humanly linear conception of time—did not predetermine our free actions. That Troilus is himself disposed to see whatever happens to him as predestined, and makes strongly fatalistic speeches, does not mean that the poem as a whole offers a sternly predestinarian reading of its story. Troilus' soliloquy on free will in Book IV (borrowed from Boethius) has a continuity in theme, and perhaps even in character, with Troilus earlier in the poem. There is irony in the depiction of an individual freely arguing away the freedom he actually possesses, but stylistically the very awkwardness of the soliloquy aptly expresses the hero's sense of hopelessness. This strongly predestinarian monologue—and the failure to include as part of Troilus' awareness anything of the rebuttal of Boethius' speech by Philosophy in the original, proving the compatibility of divine prescience and human free will—serves by its very one-sidedness to underline how the characters' declarations about fortune and freedom are to be seen as partial. It is Troilus' dilemma over whether or not to act to prevent Criseyde's departure which proves the moral pivot of the poem in its exploration of the lovers' freedom. Chaucer shows Troilus declining to exercise the possible choices that are available to him, declining to request Criseyde openly, and submitting to the will of his lady a decision on whether to abduct her. His prowess as a soldier suggests Troilus could intervene successfully to prevent the exchange by military action. This option he has, but chooses not to take. The courtly observance of this is stressed, so that a freely and deliberately chosen inaction becomes very much the expression of the hero's devotion to the ideal of service in love. Troilus refuses to exercise dominion over his lady; his refusal happens to be fatal. Despite all the fatalistic rhetoric which casts Troilus as helpless before external forces, Chaucer carefully shows Troilus giving up choice and freedom (rather than never possessing it) and analyses Criseyde's freedom and its constraints with comparable care. Intensely concerned with how her freedom of action will be affected by a love affair, manipulated and taken advantage of, Criseyde retains an impressive initiative and control. Determined not to go along with Troilus' plans for escape, she instead argues for evading seeming necessity by stratagem and ingenuity, and her confidence here in the effectiveness of the human will contrasts poignantly with her later recognitions of necessity in the Greek camp. In turn, the tendency of the characters to see their lives in relation to the operation of fortune is framed by the way in which the narrative exemplifies in itself the question of freedom and predestination. A form of predestination is being illustrated through the narrator's own claims to be subject to his sources, and his narrative dramatizes the debate in Troilus' soliloquy as to whether knowing a thing to be true necessitates its happening. The lovers' future in the end of the old story is foreknown and, as it were, predestined. That the reader knows (as past) what to the characters is future (and therefore unknown) effectively puts the reader in God's place.

Translated to the skies, it is a perspective from the heavens that Troilus—and with him the reader—gains only after the close of a narrative that has educated its audience that there can be no single fixed point of view in this world. The combination of the soul's flight with the inward laugh of Troilus—he who has so rarely laughed or smiled—is a striking emblem of transition and relinquishing at the close of a poem that has promoted a kind of multiconsciousness, in which any interpretation must necessarily be offset by its opposite or contain its contrary within itself, and where unity is understood more by including than by excluding, more in process than in product. If 'the end is the strong point of every tale' as Pandarus declares (ii. 260, p. 28), the particular strength of the ending of *Troilus* lies in its continuing capacity to invite questions about itself and the poem it concludes. The ending is implicit through a complex structure of ironies in the narrative, yet when it comes it retains a power to surprise. However conventional many of its materials and sentiments, it makes, in its context, no conventional effect. The problem was to furnish a conclusion not only to a story that ends in anticlimax, but also to all that abundance of implication with which Chaucer had invested his narrative. If the *story* had no climax, could there be a climax to the *poem*, a climax of interpretation? Through the performative quality of his conclusion, Chaucer dramatizes the problematic process of making an ending, deploying what seems as many closing devices and formulas as could be thought of, with shifts and turns, flurries of apology and anxiety, renunciation and rejection, in a way that emphasizes the necessary artificiality of a made conclusion to the narrative. It becomes a series of closures, both an attempt at comprehensiveness and an accumulation of alternatives, addressed to various audiences. Here ends the Book of Criseyde, with apologies to women, but with warnings too against men's betrayal. Here ends the Book of Troilus, with its hero in the heavens, and all he loved in ruins. In closing, the text includes (how could it not?) a momentary sense of its own art as an illusion and a futility, along with the love which that art has celebrated and made to live again, and the sense of strain in the ending reflects an acute awareness of change and difference between the beginning, middle, and end of the narrative. A promise of lasting happiness in human life and sexuality was not the pattern in the old tale of Troilus and Criseyde, and the wisdom of Chaucer's vision of their story lies in realizing both its climax and the ensuing anticlimax with such intensity of joy and pain that any reader will still feel challenged to make sense of relating them, and may not succeed.

TRANSLATOR'S NOTE

As early as *c.*1630 the first three books of *Troilus and Criseyde* were modernized into an English verse paraphrase, as the title-page says: 'For the satisfaction of those | Who either cannot, or will not, take ye paines to understand | The excellent Authors | Farr more Exquisite and significant Expressions | Though now growen obsolete, and | out of use.'[1] A more rigorous satisfaction was offered by the publication in 1635 of Sir Francis Kinaston's translation of the first two books of *Troilus* into the timeless medium of Latin verse, set in parallel with a text of the poem reprinted from Speght's 1598 edition of Chaucer, and with a preface promising a complete translation with explanatory commentary.[2] Following these early translations have come various modernizations of *Troilus and Criseyde*, each responding to the sense of a widening gap between Chaucer's poem and contemporary English.

The present translation has been made with the aim of assisting modern readers' understanding of the sense of the original, and therefore offers a rendering into modern English prose. Speech is set out according to modern conventions. Paragraphing is editorial, and although paragraphs in the translation coincide not infrequently with breaks between stanzas in the poem, the original's division of material into stanzas is not otherwise retained in the form of the translation. References to the line numbers of the poem are given in square brackets at suitable intervals in the translation. The Latin rubrics of the books, proems, songs, and letters have been translated into English. It has sometimes been necessary to re-order material and unravel complex syntax within stanzas, in order to achieve something that reads more clearly. The translation endeavours to be as faithful to Chaucer's original as is compatible with producing an idiomatic and readable version in modern English.

The translation is followed by Explanatory Notes, and an asterisk in the text indicates the presence of a note. All translations in the notes are mine, unless otherwise stated. All references to *Troilus and*

[1] H. G. Wright (ed.), *A Seventeenth-Century Modernisation of the First Three Books of Chaucer's 'Troilus and Criseyde'* (Berne, 1960).

[2] *Amorum Troili et Creseidae libri duo priores Anglico-Latini* (Oxford, 1635).

Criseyde are to the book and line number of the poem, followed by the page number in this translation (iv. 1009–10, p. 108). All references to Chaucer's works are to *The Riverside Chaucer*, general editor Larry D. Benson (Oxford, 1988); all references to Boccaccio's works are to *Tutte le opere di Giovanni Boccaccio*, general editor V. Branca (Verona, 1964–). References to classical authors are to the relevant volumes in the Loeb Classical Library; the *Roman de la rose* is cited from the edition of E. Langlois (Société d'anciens textes français, 5 vols., Paris, 1914–24).

This translation of *Troilus and Criseyde* is based upon a fresh edition of the text from all extant manuscripts of Chaucer's poem. The work of the editors and translators cited in the Select Bibliography has been of the greatest interest and help in the preparation of this book.

SELECT BIBLIOGRAPHY

EDITIONS

Baugh, A. C., *Chaucer's Major Poetry* (Englewood Cliffs, NJ, 1963).

Benson, L. D., *The Riverside Chaucer* (Boston, 1987; Oxford, 1988); the edition of *Troilus and Criseyde* is by Stephen A. Barney.

Donaldson, E. T., *Chaucer's Poetry: An Anthology for the Modern Reader* (2nd edn., New York, 1975).

Fisher, J. H., *The Complete Poetry and Prose of Geoffrey Chaucer* (New York, 1977).

Robinson, F. N., *The Works of Geoffrey Chaucer* (Boston, 1957).

Root, R. K., *The Book of Troilus and Criseyde by Geoffrey Chaucer* (Princeton, 1926).

Shoaf, R. A., *Troilus and Criseyde* (East Lansing, Mich., 1989).

Skeat, W. W., *The Complete Works of Geoffrey Chaucer*, 7 vols. (Oxford, 1894–7).

Windeatt, B. A., *Troilus and Criseyde: A New Edition of 'The Book of Troilus'* (London, 1984; 2nd edn., 1990).

MODERNIZATIONS

Coghill, N., *Troilus and Criseyde* (Harmondsworth, 1971).

Krapp, G. P., *Troilus and Criseyde, Englished Anew* (New York, 1932).

MacKaye, P., and Tatlock, J. S. P., *The Complete Poetical Works of Geoffrey Chaucer* (London, 1912).

Stanley-Wrench, M., *Troilus and Criseyde* (London, 1965).

CRITICISM

Aers, D., *Chaucer, Langland, and the Creative Imagination* (London, 1980), ch. 5.

—— *Community, Gender and Individual Identity* (London, 1988), ch. 3.

Barney, S. A. (ed.), *Chaucer's 'Troilus': Essays in Criticism* (London, 1980).

Benson, C. D., *Chaucer's 'Troilus and Criseyde'* (London, 1990).

—— (ed.), *Critical Essays on Chaucer's 'Troilus and Criseyde' and his Major Early Poems* (Milton Keynes, 1991).

Bishop, I., *Chaucer's 'Troilus and Criseyde': A Critical Study* (Bristol, 1981).

Boitani, P. (ed.), *Chaucer and the Italian Trecento* (Cambridge, 1983).

—— (ed.), *The European Tragedy of Troilus* (Oxford, 1989).

—— and Mann, J. (eds.), *The Cambridge Chaucer Companion* (Cambridge, 1986), chs. 2, 4, 5, 13.

Davenport, W. A., *Chaucer: Complaint and Narrative* (Cambridge, 1988), ch. 6.

David, A., *The Strumpet Muse: Art and Morals in Chaucer's Poetry* (London, 1976), ch. 2.

Dinshaw, C., *Chaucer's Sexual Poetics* (Madison, 1989), ch. 1.

Donaldson, E. T., *Speaking of Chaucer* (London, 1970), chs. 4, 5, 6.

Gordon, I., *The Double Sorrow of Troilus* (Oxford, 1970).

Hansen, E. T., *Chaucer and the Fictions of Gender* (Los Angeles, 1992), ch. 6.

Havely, N. (trans.), *Chaucer's Boccaccio* (Cambridge, 1980).

Kean, P. M., *Chaucer and the Making of English Poetry* (London, 1972), ch. 4.

Kelly, H. A., *Love and Marriage in the Age of Chaucer* (Ithaca, NY, 1975).

—— *Ideas and Forms of Tragedy from Aristotle to the Middle Ages* (Cambridge, 1993).

—— *Chaucerian Tragedy* (Cambridge, 1997).

Knight, S., *Geoffrey Chaucer* (Oxford, 1986), ch. 2.

Lawton, D., *Chaucer's Narrators* (Cambridge, 1985), ch. 4.

Lewis, C. S., *The Allegory of Love* (Oxford, 1936), ch. 4.

McAlpine, M. E., *The Genre of 'Troilus and Criseyde'* (Ithaca, NY, 1978).

Mann, J., *Geoffrey Chaucer* (Hemel Hempstead, 1991).

Margherita, G., *The Romance of Origins: Language and Sexual Difference in Middle English Literature* (Philadelphia, 1994), ch. 5.

Martin, P., *Chaucer's Women: Nuns, Wives and Amazons* (2nd edn., Basingstoke, 1996), ch. 9.

Mehl, D., *Geoffrey Chaucer: An Introduction to his Narrative Poetry* (Cambridge, 1986), ch. 6.

Mieszkowski, G., *The Reputation of Criseyde 1155–1500* (New Haven, 1971).

Minnis, A. J., *Chaucer and Pagan Antiquity* (Cambridge, 1982), ch. 3.

Muscatine, C., *Chaucer and the French Tradition* (Berkeley, 1957), ch. V.

Nolan, B., *Chaucer and the Tradition of the Roman Antique* (Cambridge, 1992).

North, J. D., *Chaucer's Universe* (Oxford, 1988).

Norton-Smith, J., *Geoffrey Chaucer* (London, 1974), ch. 6.

Patterson, L., *Chaucer and the Subject of History* (London, 1991), ch. 2.

Salter, E., *English and International: Studies in the Literature, Art and Patronage of Medieval England*, ed. D. Pearsall and N. Zeeman (Cambridge, 1988), chs. 10, 11, 15.

Salu, M. (ed.), *Essays on 'Troilus and Criseyde'* (Cambridge, 1979).

Schoeck, R. J., and Taylor, J. (eds.), *Chaucer Criticism*, ii. *'Troilus and Criseyde' and the Minor Poems* (Notre Dame, Ind., 1961).

Shoaf, R. A. (ed.), *Chaucer's 'Troilus and Criseyde': "Subgit to alle Poesye": Essays in Criticism* (Binghamton, NY, 1992).

Spearing, A. C., *'Troilus and Criseyde'* (London, 1976).

—— *Readings in Medieval Poetry* (Cambridge, 1987), ch. 5.

Steadman, J. M., *Disembodied Laughter: Troilus and the Apotheosis Tradition* (Berkeley, 1972).

Stillinger, T. C., *The Song of Troilus* (Philadelphia, 1992).

Strohm, P., *Social Chaucer* (Cambridge, Mass., 1989).

Taylor, K., *Chaucer reads 'The Divine Comedy'* (Stanford, Calif., 1989), chs. 2, 3.

Wallace, D., *Chaucer and the Early Writings of Boccaccio* (Cambridge, 1985).

Wetherbee, W., *Chaucer and the Poets: An Essay on 'Troilus and Criseyde'* (Ithaca, NY, 1984).

Wimsatt, J. I., *Chaucer and his French Contemporaries* (Toronto, 1991).

Windeatt, B., *The Oxford Guides to Chaucer: 'Troilus and Criseyde'* (Oxford, 1992; repr. 1995).

A CHRONOLOGY OF GEOFFREY CHAUCER

*c.*1343   Born in London, son of John Chaucer, vintner, and Agnes de Copton

1357   Entered as a page in the household of Elizabeth, Countess of Ulster, wife of Lionel, Duke of Clarence, son of Edward III

1359   Goes as a squire to France with Edward III's army of invasion, and is captured by the French at the siege of Rheims

1360   Ransomed on 1 March for £16 and employed as a messenger carrying letters from Calais to England

*c.*1366   Marries Philippa de Roet, daughter of Sir Paon de Roet, a lady-in-waiting to Queen Philippa of Hainault, wife of Edward III

1368   His wife Philippa Chaucer becomes lady-in-waiting to Constance of Castile, wife of Edward III's son John of Gaunt, Duke of Lancaster. Chaucer accompanies Edward, Prince of Wales (the Black Prince), to Spain and is appointed an Esquire of the King's Household. Composes *The Book of the Duchess*

1369   Campaigns in France in the service of John of Gaunt

1372   Visits Italy as one of three commissioners to negotiate with the Duke of Genoa. Visits Florence

1374   Acquires house above Aldgate and is appointed Controller of Customs and Subsidy of Wools, Skins, and Hides in the Port of London

1377   In France 'on the king's secret affairs'. Death of Edward III; Richard II becomes king

1378   Visits Italy in the retinue of Sir Edward de Berkeley to negotiate with Bernabo Visconti, Duke of Milan

*c.*1379   Composes *The House of Fame*

1381   Peasants' Revolt and death of Wat Tyler

1382   Appointed Controller of Petty Customs on Wines

*c.*1382–6   Probable date of composition of *Troilus and Criseyde*

1386   Relinquishes posts of Controller of Customs and moves to Greenwich. Appointed Justice of the Peace and Knight of the Shire to represent Kent in Parliament

*c.*1387   Death of Philippa Chaucer. *The Canterbury Tales* begun

1389   Appointed Clerk of the King's Works

1390   Commissioned to supervise repairs to St George's Chapel,
         Windsor, and the erection of scaffolding for tournaments at
         Smithfield. He is assaulted and robbed

1391   Replaced as Clerk of the Works and appointed Deputy Keeper
         of the Royal Forest of North Petherton

1399   Richard II deposed by Henry IV

1400   Dies 25 October and is buried in Westminster Abbey

c.1478   William Caxton brings out the first printed edition of *The
         Canterbury Tales*

c.1483   William Caxton brings out the first printed edition of *Troilus
         and Criseyde*

TROILUS AND CRISEYDE

BOOK ONE

Before I part from you, my purpose is to tell of the double sorrow*
of Troilus, son of King Priam of Troy—how his fortunes in love rose
and fell* from misery to joy, then afterwards out of joy. Tisiphone,*
help me to compose these sorrowful verses, that weep even as I write
them! I call on you, goddess of torment, cruel Fury, ever sorrowing
in pain: help me, who am the sorrowful instrument that, as best I
can, helps lovers to lament. For, to tell the truth, a sad companion
best suits a sorrowful person, and a sad expression a sorrowful
tale.* For I, serving the servants* of the God of Love, do not dare
(because of my own unsuitability) to pray to Love for success—though
I die for it—I am so far removed from his help, in darkness. But
yet if this may bring happiness to any lover and further his cause,
let him have the thanks due to me, and let mine be this labour!

You lovers, who bask in happiness, if there be any drop of pity
in you, remember the sadness you have felt in the past, and the adver-
sities of other people, and think how you have felt when Love dared
displease you, or you have won it too easily. And pray for those*
who are in Troilus' plight, as you can afterwards hear, that Love
bring them to joy in heaven; and also pray for me to dear God, that
I have the power to express in some way, in Troilus' luckless mis-
fortune, such pain and misery as Love's people endure. And also
pray for those who are in despair* in love and will never recover,
and also for those who are unjustly injured by malicious tell-tales,*
whether male or female; and so pray to God, of his goodness, to
grant those who are in despair of Love's grace to pass soon out of
this world. And also pray for those in contentment, that God grant
them long continuance always, and send them the power so to please
their ladies that it be honour and delight to Love. For so I hope to
advance my own soul best, by praying for those who are servants of
Love, and writing of their unhappiness, and living in charity, and
by having compassion on them, as though I were their own dear
brother! Now listen with good will, as I go straight to my subject-
matter, in which you may hear the double sorrows of Troilus in his
love for Criseyde, and how she forsook him before she died. [56]

It is well known how the Greeks, strongly armed, went to Troy with a thousand ships, and long besieged the city, for nearly ten years* before they stopped; and in diverse ways but with a single purpose, they devoted all their efforts to avenge Paris' ravishment of Helen.* Now it so happened that there was living in the town a lord of great authority, a great soothsayer called Calchas,* who was so expert in his learned art that from the replies of his god, who was called Lord Phoebus or Delphic Apollo,* he knew that Troy should be destroyed. So when Calchas knew by calculations, and also by reply from Apollo, that the Greeks should bring such an army, through which Troy must be ruined, he at once planned to leave the city, for he well knew by the casting of lots* that Troy should be destroyed—yes, whether anyone wished it or not! Therefore this wise and foreseeing man resolved to leave quietly, and he straightaway stole very secretly to the Greek host, and they in courteous fashion showed him honour and service, trusting that he had the skill to advise them in every danger there was to fear. [84]

A clamour arose throughout the town when this was first discovered, and it was said everywhere that Calchas had fled like a traitor and allied himself with the Greeks, and they determined to be avenged on him, who had so treacherously broken faith, and said he and all his family deserved to be burned at once, skin and bones! Now in this unfortunate situation—quite unaware of this treacherous and wicked act—Calchas had left behind his daughter, who suffered a great deal: she feared dreadfully for her life, not knowing what was the best advice, for she was both a widow and alone, without any friend* to whom she dared to bemoan her sorrow. Criseyde was this lady's name, indeed. In my opinion there was none so beautiful in the whole city of Troy, for, so angelic and surpassing all others was her innate beauty, that she seemed like something immortal, as does a heavenly, perfect creature, sent down to earth to put nature to scorn. [105]

This lady, who was continually hearing of her father's dishonour, his treachery and treason, was very nearly out of her mind for sorrow and fear. In a widow's flowing garment of dark silk she fell down on her knees before Hector* to excuse herself and, in a piteous voice and weeping tenderly, she begged for his mercy. Now Hector was compassionate by nature, and saw that she was overwhelmed by unhappiness, and that she was so beautiful a creature. Out of his goodness he comforted her at once and said:

'Put your father's treason out of your mind. Bad luck to him! And you yourself, stay here with us in Troy for as long as you like. And you shall have all the honour that people can accord you, as much as when your father lived here. And, as far as I'm able to learn or hear anything about it, no one will lay a finger on you.'

She thanked him with a very humble demeanour, and would have thanked him more often if he had let her, and took her leave, and went home and lived quietly. She remained in her house with such household as it was necessary for her honour to maintain. And while she was living in the city she lived appropriately to her station, was beloved by both young and old, and people spoke well of her. But I cannot find in my source whether or not she had children,* and so I pass over that. [133]

Things often happened, as they do in war, between the Trojans and Greeks, for one day the Trojans had the worst of it, and another time the Greeks did not find the Trojans at all yielding. And so, all the while they continued at odds, Fortune wheeled them both round on her wheel,* now up above, and now down underneath again, after her fashion. But it is no part of my purpose to relate how this city came to its destruction, for it would be a lengthy digression from my subject-matter and would detain you too long. But for the Trojan events as they happened—whoever is able to, can read of them as they are written about in Homer, or in Dares, or in Dictys.*

Yet though the Greeks penned the Trojans in and besieged their city all around, the Trojans would not discontinue their ancient practice of honouring their most sacred gods; and without doubt they honoured most of all a relic called Palladium,* which they put their trust in more than anything. It so happened, when April time had come, when the meadow is clothed with new greenery at the beginning of delightful springtime, and white and red flowers smell sweetly, the people of Troy performed in various ways, as I read, their ancient ceremonies, in order to observe the festival of Palladium. Many people went in a body to the temple,* in their very best fashion, to listen to the service of the Palladium, and especially many a vigorous knight, and many a blooming lady and radiant maiden, very well dressed, the highest, middling, and lowest in rank—yes, in honour of both the season and the festival! [168]

Among other people was Criseyde, in her black widow's attire. But nevertheless, just as our first letter is now an A,* so she stood first in beauty, matchless. Her lovely looks gladdened all the crowd.

Never yet was anything seen that was to be praised more highly, nor so bright a star under a black cloud as was Criseyde—as everyone said who saw her in her black clothing. Yet she stood very humbly and quietly on her own, in a little space behind other people, and near the door, always in dread of being put to shame, simply dressed and gracious in expression, and quite composed in look and manner. [182]

Like someone accustomed to guiding his young knights about, this Troilus* was leading them up and down throughout that spacious temple, always quizzing the ladies of the city, now here, now there, for he had no devotion to any of them to deprive him of his rest, but praised and found fault with whichever he pleased. And as he walked, he was watching closely if any knight or squire of his group began to sigh or let his eye feast on any woman that he could see. He would smile, and consider it folly, and speak to him, like this:

'God knows, she sleeps comfortably for love of you while you're tossing and turning! I've heard tell, by God, of your way of life, you lovers, and your foolish observances, and what an effort people have in obtaining love and what uncertainties in keeping it—and when your prey is lost, misery and suffering! O true fools, you are silly and blind! There's not one of you that can take warning from another's example.'

irony

And with those words he raised an eyebrow, as if to say:

'You see! Wasn't that wisely spoken?'

At which the God of Love began to glower with resentment, and determined to be revenged. He showed at once his bow was not broken, for he suddenly hit him squarely—and even to this day he can still pluck as proud a peacock!* [210]

O blind world!* O blindness of purpose! How often quite the opposite outcome happens from arrogance and vile presumptuousness, for caught are the proud and caught are the meek! Troilus has climbed on the stair and little supposes that he must come down—but fools' expectations are disappointed all the time. It is like proud Bayard* the horse, who begins to skip out of the way, feeling his oats, until he gets a lash from the long whip, and then he thinks:

'Though I prance in front, the first horse in the team, quite plump and freshly groomed, I am still only a horse and must endure horse's law and pull with my fellows.'

So it happened with this fierce and proud knight. Although he might be a noble king's son and supposed nothing had such power that it could move his heart against his will, yet with one look his heart was set on fire, so that he who a moment before was most proudly superior suddenly became most subject to love. [231]

Therefore, all you wise, proud, and noble folk, learn from the example of this man about scorning Love, which can so soon enslave the freedom of your hearts. For it was always so, and it will always happen, that Love can bind everything,* because no man may abolish the law of nature. This has been proved to be true, and is still being so proved. I believe you know this, one and all: people read of none that have greater intelligence* than those who have been most taken with love; the strongest* have been overcome, and the noblest and highest in rank. This was and is so, and people will see it yet.* And it is truly very fitting that it should be so, for the wisest of all have been pleased by love; and those who have been most of all in misery have been most comforted and relieved. Love has often appeased the cruel heart, made noble folk nobler in repute, and causes most people to fear wrong and disgrace.* Now since it can hardly be resisted, and is a thing so virtuous in its nature, do not refuse to be enslaved to Love, since it may bind you as it pleases. The sapling that will bow and bend is better than the one that breaks, and I therefore advise you to follow love, which can give you such a lead. [259]

But to continue particularly about this king's son of whom I was telling, and leave aside other subsidiary matters, I mean to continue my tale about him, both of his happiness and his chilling miseries. And because I began to tell of it, I will return to the subject of how he behaved.

This Troilus went about inside the temple, making fun at the expense of everyone around, looking now at this lady and now at that, whether she were from the city or from out of town. And by chance it happened that his look pierced through a crowd and went so deep that it hit upon Criseyde, and there it stopped. And at that he suddenly grew astounded and looked at her more closely and carefully.

'O mercy, God,' he thought, 'where have you been living, who are so lovely and pleasing to look at?'

With that his heart began to swell and feel exalted, and he sighed softly in case anyone might hear him, and recaptured his former playful air. [280]

In height she was not among the shortest,* but all her limbs corresponded so well with everything womanly that no creature was

ever less mannish in appearance; and also her very way of moving
showed that in her one could suppose honour, rank, and a womanly
nobility of character. Troilus was simply wonderfully well pleased
with the way she moved and with her manner, which was somewhat
haughty, for she let fall a sidelong glance, as if to say: 'What! May
I not stand here?' After that her look brightened, so that it seemed
to him he had never seen so fine a sight. And from her looks there
began to arise in him so great a desire and such affection that his
fixed and deep impression of her pierced to the bottom of his heart.*
If before this he had gazed intently in all directions, now he was glad
to draw in his horns: he scarcely knew whether to keep his eyes shut
or open. See! He who considered himself so knowledgeable, who
scorned those who suffer the pains of love, was quite unaware that
Love dwelt within the ethereal beams of her eyes,* so that it sud-
denly seemed to him that, just with her look, he felt the vital spirit*
in his heart die. Blessed be Love, that can convert people like this!
[308]

Troilus stood looking at her, this woman in black, who pleased
him above everything else. He neither revealed by his expression,
nor said a word about, his desire or why he was standing there like
that. But from a distance, in order to maintain his usual manner, he
sometimes directed his look at other things and then back at her
again, while the service lasted. And after this, not absolutely in con-
fusion, he slowly left the temple, regretting that he had ever made
fun of Love's devotees, in case the weight of scorn came down fully
on himself. But whatever he thought, he dissembled and hid his unhap-
piness, lest it were known in any way. [322]

When he had left the temple like this, he returned immediately
to his palace, shot through and pierced by her very look, although
he pretended that he was continuing his life of pleasure; he also bur-
nished up all his manner and talk; and, in order to cover up for him-
self, he was always smiling at the servants of Love all the while, and
said:

'Lord, how you lovers all live in bliss! For the cleverest of you,
who serves best and most diligently, experiences setbacks as often
as advantages from that. Your service is repaid you, yes, God knows
how! Not by one good for another, but by scorn for good service. In
faith, your "order" has a very good "rule"!* All your observances are
without any certainty, unless in a few insignificant details. Nothing

requires dedication as great as does your devotion, and that you all know. But that's not the worst of it, bless me! I believe that if I told you the worst thing—even though I were telling the truth—you'd be offended with me. Just think about this: what you lovers often avoid doing, or else do with good intentions, your lady will very often misconstrue and judge harmful. And yet if she's angry for another reason, you'll soon have a scolding. Lord, how lucky he is who can be one of you!'

But despite all this, when he saw his time he held his peace—no other remedy was of any help to him—for love began so to lime his feathers* that he could scarcely even pretend to his household that other pressing needs preoccupied him. He was so unhappy that he did not know what to do, but told his people to go where they pleased. [357]

And when he was alone in his room, he sat down at the foot of his bed and first he began to sigh and likewise to groan. He thought about her so continually without ceasing that, as he sat there wide awake, his spirit dreamed that he saw her in the temple, and pondered afresh the whole manner of her look. So he began to make a mirror out of his mind,* in which he saw her person completely. He could certainly find it in his heart to grant that it was a great good fortune for him to love such a one and, if he did his best to serve her, he might yet win her favour, or else pass for one of her servants. He imagined that neither effort nor suffering could be wasted for such an excellent creature as she was, nor any shame on him for his desire, even if it became known, but that he would be esteemed and exalted by all lovers much more than before—so he reasoned at the beginning, quite unaware of his unhappiness to come. He thus decided to pursue the art of love, and thought he would work secretly, at first hiding away his desire in secret from absolutely every living being, unless he could benefit in any other way, remembering that love made widely known yields bitter fruit, though sweet seed be sown. In addition to all this, he thought a great deal more still about what to say and what to hold back, and he sought for a way to induce her to love. He immediately started on a song, and he began to get the better of his sorrow* out loud, for with high hope he fully assented to love Criseyde and not regret it. [392]

I make bold to give not only the gist of his song (as my author, called Lollius,* writes), but in full, save for the difference in our languages. Look! Here is what Troilus sang, in its entirety, every word exactly like this. And whoever wishes to hear it, see! he may find it in the following lines:

Troilus' Song*

'If there is no love, O God, why do I feel like this? And if love exists, what kind of thing is it? If love be good, where does my unhappiness come from? If it be bad, it seems a marvel to me, when every torment and adversity that comes from love can seem pleasant to me, for I thirst continually, the more that I drink of it.

'And if I am burning at my own desire, where do my wailing and my lamentation come from? If harm is agreeable to me,* why do I lament? I do not know, nor why, without being weary, I grow faint! O living death, O sweet harm so strange, how can there be such a quantity of you within me, unless I consent that it be so?

'And if I consent, I am surely lamenting wrongfully? So, tossed to and fro, I am in a rudderless boat in the midst of the sea, and between two winds that are perpetually contrary to each other. Alas, what is this strange illness? I die of cold when I have a fever, and of a fever when I am cold!'* [420]

And to the God of Love he said in a piteous voice:

'O Lord, now my spirit is yours, which ought to be yours! I thank you, Lord, who have brought me to this. I don't know whether she be goddess or woman,* indeed, whom you make me serve. But as her man I'll live and die. In her eyes you stand very high, as in a place worthy of your excellence. Therefore, Lord, if my service or I may please you, be gracious to me. For I here resign my royal position into her hand, as my dear lady, and in humblest manner become her man.' [434]

The fire of love—from which God protect me!—did not deign to spare the blood royal in him, nor spared him in any way, despite all his virtue and excellent prowess, but kept him like a humble slave in distress, and constantly burned him so in differing ways that he lost colour sixty times a day. So much, day by day, did his own thoughts quicken and increase, out of desire for her, that he took no account of every other responsibility. Very often, therefore, in order to put an end to his hot fire, he pressed to see her pleasing looks, for he supposed he would get relief from that, and always, the nearer he was, the more he burned. For always, the nearer the fire, the hotter it is*—this whole company knows that, I believe—but whether he were near or far, I dare say this: by night or day, for wisdom or folly, his heart (which is the eye of his breast) was always set upon her, who was more beautiful to see than Helen or Polyxena* ever were. Nor did there pass an hour of the day that he did not say to himself a thousand times:

'My good, my beauty, to whom I am a servant and for whom I labour to serve, as best I can—now would to God, Criseyde, you would have pity on me before I died! My dear heart, alas, my health, and looks, and life are lost, unless you will have pity on me!' [462]

All other fears were fled from him, both of the siege and for his own safety, nor did desire breed in him any other offspring than arguments to this end: that she would have compassion on him, and he would become her man while he lasted. See! Here was his life, and his cure from death! On that account, the fierce and terrible assaults, the proof of arms, that Hector or his other brothers undertook, left him unmoved. And yet, wherever men rode or walked, he was found the very best, and to have remained the longest time where there was danger. He did such great feats of arms that it was a marvel to think of it. But it was neither because of any hatred he had for the Greeks, nor the rescue of the city, that made him rage in battle like this, but only, you see, for this purpose: to please her the better because of his renown. From day to day he succeeded so well at arms that the Greeks dreaded him like death. [483]

Then from this time onwards love deprived him of his sleep, and made his food his enemy; his sorrow was also multiplying, so that—if anyone noticed—it showed in his colour* both in the evening and morning. He therefore mentioned the name of another illness, in case people imagined that the hot fire of love was burning him, and said he had a fever and felt unwell. But how it was, for certain, I cannot say: whether his lady did not understand this, or pretended that she did not know, one or the other. But I read, indeed, that in no way did it seem that she cared about him or his pain, or whatever he was thinking. But then Troilus felt such unhappiness that he was very nearly mad, for his fear was always this: that she so loved someone else that she would never pay any attention to him. Because of that it seemed to him he felt his heart bleed; nor did he dare begin to tell her of his unhappiness, for all the world. [504]

t when he had a respite from his sorrows, he often lamented
nself in this way, saying:

'O fool, now you're in the snare, you who once mocked at love's
pain! Now you're caught, now gnaw your own chain! You were always
accustomed to reproach each lover for something you can't defend
yourself against. What will every lover now say about you, if this
becomes known, but always laugh scornfully behind your back and
say: "Look! There he goes, the man of such great wisdom, who held
us lovers in the lowest esteem. Now, thanks be to God, he can join
in the dance* of those whom Love wishes to make only feeble pro-
gress!" But O, you unhappy Troilus, since you must love because
of your destiny, would to God that you were bestowed on someone
that knew about all your unhappiness, even if she lacked pity! But
your lady is as cold towards you in love as frost beneath a winter
moon, and you are done for, as snow soon is in fire! Would to God
I had arrived in the port of death, to which my sorrow will lead
me! Ah, Lord, it would be a great comfort to me! Then I would be
free of languishing in uncertainty. For if my hidden sorrow should
be widely talked about, I shall be mocked a thousand times more
than that fool* whose folly men make rhymes about! But now help,
God, and you, sweet one, because of whom I lament, I in captivity
—indeed, never a man so firmly! O mercy, dear heart, and save me
from death, for, while my life may last, I will love you more than
myself until my death. Cheer me with a friendly look, my sweet,
though you should never promise me anything more!' [539]

He spoke these words and very many others too, and continually
called out her name in his lamentation, in order to tell her of his
unhappiness, until he nearly drowned in salt tears.* All was in vain.
She did not hear his lamenting. And when he reflected on the folly
of that, his unhappiness multiplied a thousandfold.

While he was bewailing alone like this in his room, a friend of his
called Pandarus* came in unexpectedly, heard him groan, and saw
his friend in this distress and sorrow.

'Alas,' said he, 'who's the cause of all this to-do? O mercy, God!*
What misfortune can this mean? Have the Greeks made you lose
weight so soon? Or do you have some remorseful fit of conscience,
and are now at your devotions? . . . And are wailing for your sins and
your transgression? . . . And have been frightened into some mild con-
trition? God save those who have besieged our town, who can shelve
our cheerfulness like this and turn our gallant folk to religion!'

He said all these words on purpose, so that he might make him angry with such things and, through anger, make him temporarily less miserable and rouse his spirit. But he well knew, as was reported far and wide, that there was not a man of greater daring, nor one who desired honour more. [567]

'What chance or destiny,' said Troilus, 'has brought you here to see me suffering, who am universally rejected? But for the love of God, go away from here, I ask you; because seeing me die will certainly distress you, and I've got to die. So go away then—there's no more to say. If you suppose I'm ill like this because I'm frightened, it's not the case—so spare me your sneers! There's something else I care about much more than anything the Greeks have yet done, which will be the death of me for sorrow and grief. But don't be angry if I don't want to tell you about it now—I'm hiding it for the best.'

This Pandarus, who was nearly melting for sorrow and pity, often asked:

'Alas, what can the matter be? Now, friend,' he went on, 'if there's ever been, or is, love and loyalty between you and me, never do so cruel a thing as to hide so great a trouble from your friend! Can't you see it is I, Pandarus? If I can't bring you any comfort, I'll share all your suffering with you, as it's a friend's right, to tell the truth, to share unhappiness as well as pleasure. In right and wrong I've loved you all my life and will do, whatever people say, true or false. Don't hide your unhappiness from me, but tell me what it is quickly.' [595]

Then this sorrowful Troilus began to sigh, and spoke to him like this:

'God grant it be my best course to tell you about it, for since it pleases you I'll tell it then, even though it breaks my heart. I know very well that you can't bring me any peace. But in case you think I don't trust you . . . Now, listen, friend, because this is how things stand with me. Love—against which whoever defends himself most, does himself least good of all—attacks me so sadly with despair that my heart is sailing straight towards death. At the same time, I'm feeling an attack of such burning desire that it would be a greater happiness to me to be killed than to be king of Greece and Troy! I've said enough, my firm friend Pandarus, because now you know why I'm unhappy. And for the love of God, keep my chill misery a secret— I've never told it to others, because more than a few misfortunes might ensue if it were known about. But be happy, yourself, and let me die of my unhappiness in secret!' [616]

'How have you kept this from me so cruelly and so long, you fool?' said Pandarus. 'You may perhaps be longing for just such a person where my advice can help us right away.'

'That'd be a miracle,' said Troilus. 'You could never manage your own love affairs. How the devil* can you bring me to bliss?'

'Yes, Troilus, now listen,' said Pandarus, 'though I may be foolish,* it often happens like this, that someone whom an excess of feeling makes get on badly himself, can keep his friend from that by good advice. I've seen myself a blind man walk safely where someone with good eyesight fell over. Also, a fool can often guide a wise man, and a whetstone is no cutting instrument, yet it sharpens cutting tools.* And where you know I've gone wrong in any way, avoid that yourself, because such a thing can be a lesson to you. So wise men often take warning from the example of what happens to fools.* If you do so, you'll be using your head. Everything is known for what it is by its opposite.* For how could sweetness ever have been known to him who never tasted bitterness?* Nor can any man be completely happy, I believe, who was never in some distress or sorrow. Also, white by black, nobility beside disgrace—each thing set beside the other shows up more because of the other, as people can see, and so the wise judge it. Since there's one lesson to be learned from two contraries like this, I, who have so often experienced hardships in love, should be all the more able to advise you on what you're so dismayed about. And you oughtn't to be displeased, though I long to carry your heavy burden with you, because it will do you less harm. I'm well aware that I'm in the same situation as a shepherdess called Oenone, who wrote a lament* about her sorrow to your brother Paris—you saw the letter she wrote, I suppose?'

'No, not as yet, actually,' said Troilus. [657]

'Well, listen,' said Pandarus, 'it went like this: "It was Phoebus who first invented the art of medicine," she said, "and knew the remedy and best advice for the care of every patient through herbs he knew thoroughly, and yet his knowledge was worthless to himself, because love for King Admetus' daughter had so bound him in a snare that all his skill could not cure his sorrows".* With me it's just the same, unfortunately for me! I love one person best, and that gives me a lot of pain. And yet, perhaps, I can advise you, and not myself. Don't reproach me anymore. I've no reason, I'm well aware, to soar up like a hawk that wants to play. But I can still say something to help you. And you can be very sure of one thing: that I'll certainly never give you away, even if I died under torture. Nor, upon my word, do I care about restraining you from your love, even though I knew it were your brother's wife, Helen. Love her as you please, whoever she may be! So trust in me absolutely as a friend, and tell me bluntly now what's the reason for, and ultimate cause of, the sorrow you're going through. For don't be afraid: I've no intention of reproaching you now, for no one can stop a man from loving until he wants to stop. [686]

'And do understand that both things are faults: either to mistrust everyone or else believe everyone.* But I know very well that the mean between these two extremes is not a fault, for to trust someone is a proof of loyalty, and therefore I would gladly remove your wrong opinion, and make you trust someone enough to tell him your sorrow. Do tell me, if you will. The wise man says: "Woe to him that is alone, for if he fall, he has no one to help him rise";* and since you do have a friend, tell him what's making you unhappy. For as wise folk teach us, this isn't the most direct way to win love— to wallow and weep like Queen Niobe,* whose tears can still be seen in marble!

'Leave off your weeping and your gloom, and let's give a lift to your unhappiness by talking about other things. That way, your unhappy time may seem shorter. Don't take pleasure in seeking out misery,* as do these fools who increase their sorrows with other sorrow when they have misfortune, and don't want to seek any other cure for themselves. People say: "To a miserable person it's consolation to have a companion in his pain." That ought indeed to be our opinion, for both you and I complain about love. I'm so full of sorrow, to tell the truth, that certainly no more bad luck can perch on me, because there's no more room!* God willing, you aren't afraid of me, in case I trick you out of your lady! You know yourself, by God, whom I've loved, as best I can, for a long time now. And since you know I'm not doing it out of any guile, and you say I'm the one you most trust, tell me something about it, since you know about all my unhappiness.' [721]

Yet in spite of all this Troilus did not say a word, but lay for a long time as still as if he were dead; and after this he started up with a sigh, and lent an ear to Pandarus' voice, and rolled his eyes, so that Pandarus was afraid he would fall into a frenzy, or else soon die; and shouted:

'Wake up!' surprisingly loudly and sharply. 'What! Are you sleeping as if in a sleeping sickness?* Or are you like a donkey at the sound of a harp,* that hears the sound when the strings are plucked, but no such melody from that can penetrate his mind to make him happy, because his animal nature makes him so dull-witted?' [735]

And with that Pandarus stopped speaking; and Troilus still did not say anything to him in reply, because it was not his intention ever to tell anyone on whose account he was behaving like this. For it is said: 'A man often makes a rod for his own back in various ways' (as these learned people say), and especially in telling one's own counsel in matters concerning love that ought to be secret, for it will come to light of itself soon enough, unless it is the better controlled. It is also sometimes expedient to seem to flee from a thing which actually is being hunted eagerly*—all this Troilus thought over in his heart. But nevertheless, when he heard him shout 'Wake up!' he heaved an incredibly deep sigh and said:

'Friend, though I'm lying still, I'm not deaf! Now be quiet, and stop shouting, for I've heard what you've said, and your advice. But let me bemoan my misfortune, because your proverbs can't help me. Nor can you come up with any other cure for me, and I won't be cured. I shall die. What do I know about Queen Niobe? Give your old examples a rest, I ask you!' [760]

'No,' said Pandarus, 'that's why I say it's fools' delight to weep like this over their unhappiness, but they don't care to seek a cure. Now I know you're losing your reason. But tell me: if I knew who she was—for whom you're so unfortunately stricken like this—would you dare let me whisper something in her ear about your unhappiness (since you don't dare to yourself out of fear), and beg her to have some pity on you?'

'Why, no,' said he, 'by God and on my oath!'

'What?' said Pandarus, 'not if I did it as zealously as though my own life depended on this affair?'

'Certainly not, brother!'* said Troilus.

'And why's that?'

'Because you'd never succeed.'

'You're sure of that?'

'Yes, beyond a doubt,' said Troilus. 'In spite of anything you might be able to do, she won't be won over to such a wretched creature as I am.' [777]

'Alas!' said Pandarus. 'How can this happen—that you've despaired like this without cause? What! Isn't your lady alive, bless us? How do you know that you're not in favour? Such troubles aren't always without remedy. Why, don't assume your cure is impossible like this, since things to come are often uncertain! I admit that you're enduring misery as sharp as Tityus* does in hell, whose stomach the birds called vultures tear out eternally, as books tell us. But I can't bear to have you maintain so unreasonable an opinion as that there's no cure for your misery. Won't you even once—because of your coward's heart, and because of your temper and foolish wilfulness and distrust—tell me about your painful sorrows, or make an effort to help yourself at least as much as to utter one reason more or less? Instead you lie there like someone who doesn't want to care about anything. What woman could love such a wretch? What else can she think about your death—if you die like this, and she doesn't know why it is—but that you've given up the ghost out of fear, because the Greeks are besieging us? Lord, what sort of thanks will you then get for that! This is what she'll say, and so will the whole town at the same time: "The wretch is dead—the devil have his bones!" [805]

'You can weep and cry out and kneel here alone—but love a woman who doesn't know about it, and she'll pay you back in ways you won't feel! Unknown is unkissed, and what's unsought for is lost. What! Many a man has paid very dearly over twenty winters for a love his lady did know of, and never yet has he kissed his lady's mouth!* What? Should he fall into despair about that, or admit defeat because of his own vexation, or kill himself, even though his lady be beautiful? No, no, but be always fresh and eager to serve and love the dear queen of his heart, and think that to serve her is a reward a thousand times greater than he can deserve!'*

Troilus heeded those words, and immediately thought what a foolish situation he was in, how Pandarus was telling him the truth, and that he would not gain anything by killing himself but commit both an unmanly action and a sin. His lady would not be to blame for his death, for, God knows, she knew very little of his unhappiness. And with that thought he heaved a heavy sigh and said:

'Alas! What's the best thing for me to do?'

'The best thing,' Pandarus replied to him, 'is that you tell me all your unhappiness, if you will. And here's my pledge: unless you find I am a help to you before too much time has passed, have me drawn in pieces and then hanged!' [833]

'Yes, so you say,' said Troilus then, 'alas! But God knows, it won't happen any sooner. It would be very hard to help in this case, for I find indeed that Fortune is my enemy, and all the men that can ride or walk cannot withstand the harm done by her cruel wheel, for she toys with everyone as she pleases, whether free or slave.'

'Then you're blaming Fortune because you're angry,' said Pandarus. 'Yes, now I see it for the first time. Don't you know that to some degree Fortune is common* to every sort of person? And yet you do have this comfort, you see, that as her joys must pass away, so must all her sorrows. For if her wheel were to stop turning, then she would immediately cease to be Fortune. Now since her wheel may in no way stop, how do you know if her changeableness won't do in your case exactly as you wish yourself, or that she may not be far from helping you? Perhaps you have good reason to sing! And so do you know what I'm asking you? Give up your misery and your down-cast looks. For whoever wants to be healed by his doctor must first uncover his wound.* May I be bound to Cerberus* in hell forever, but even though all your sorrow were for my sister,* she should be all yours tomorrow, if my wishes had anything to do with it! Look up, I say, and tell me at once who she is, so that I may go about your business. Do I know her? For love of me, tell me! Then I'd hope to succeed sooner.' [865]

Then a vein in Troilus began to bleed, for he was hit, and he went all red for shame.

'Aha!' said Pandarus. 'Now the fun begins!'

And with those words he started to shake him and said:

'You thief! You've got to tell her name!'

But then poor Troilus began to tremble, as though he were being led into hell, and said:

'Alas, my sweet enemy, then, the source of all my unhappiness, is called . . . Criseyde!—' and with the word he very nearly died of fright.

And when Pandarus heard her name pronounced, Lord! he was glad and said:

'My dear friend, all success to you now, by Jove's name in heaven! Love has bestowed you well. Be in good spirits! For she has sufficient good name, and wisdom, and manners, and nobility too—you know yourself if she's beautiful, I suppose! I never saw a more generous person in her position, nor a more cheerful one, nor friendlier in her talk, nor better disposed to do well, nor who had less need to seek what to do. And to make all this even better: in matters of honour, as far as she's concerned, a king's heart seems like that of a wretch in comparison with hers. And so mind you take heart! For indeed, in a noble and well-ordered nature the most important thing is for a man to be at peace with himself.* So ought you to be, for there's nothing but good in loving well* and in a worthy place. You oughtn't to call it chance but grace. Think too—and cheer yourself up with the thought—that since your lady is altogether virtuous, then it follows that there is some pity amongst all these other virtues* in general. So see that you particularly ask for nothing that is contrary to her good name, for virtue does not stretch so far as to include anything shameful. [903]

'I'm happy I was ever born, to see you settled in such a good place. Upon my word, I'd have dared to swear that such good luck in love as this would never have come your way. And do you know why? Because you used to attack Love scornfully, and as an insult to call him "Saint Idiot, lord of all these fools". How often have you made your foolish jokes, and said that out of foolishness all Love's servants were just born fools; and how some would munch their food alone, lying in bed and groaning; and one, you said, had a love-sickness,* and you prayed to God that he should never recover! And how some of them, on account of feeling the cold, pulled over them more than enough clothes, so you very often said. And how some have often pretended, and told how they remain awake when they sleep soundly. And so they thought to have come out on top, but nevertheless were unsuccessful in the end. So you said, and joked fast and furiously. You also said that these lovers would mostly speak in general terms, and thought it was a sure method against lack of success to try everywhere.* (Now I can make fun of you, if I want!) But nevertheless, even though I should die for it, I dare say you were never one of those. Now beat your breast* and say to the God of Love: "Grant me your grace, Lord! I repent if I said anything wrong, for now I am in love myself." Say this with all your heart, in good intent.'

'Ah, Lord! I submit,' said Troilus, 'and pray you to forgive my jokes, and I will never make any more as long as I live.' [938]

'Well said,' said Pandarus, 'and now I hope that you've completely appeased the god's wrath. And since you have wept many a teardrop and said such things as are pleasing to your god, now would to God that you'll be comforted! And think indeed, that she from whom all your unhappiness arises may hereafter be your comfort too. For that same ground that bears noxious weeds also bears health-giving herbs, just as very often next to the coarse nettle, rough and thick, grows the rose, sweet and smooth and soft; and beside the valley is the hill above; and after the dark night the glad morning; and also joy is nearest to the end of sorrow.*

'Rein yourself in with moderation and, for the best, always be patient until the right time, or else all our work is in vain. He hastens well who can wait prudently. Be diligent and faithful, and always be discreet. Be cheerful, generous, persevering in your service, and all is well if you act in this way. He that is divided between many places is nowhere whole,* as those wise scholars write. What wonder is it, though such a person have no luck? You also know how it goes with some love-service, like planting a tree or herb in various ways, and next morning pull it up right away! No wonder it never thrives!* And since the God of Love has bestowed you in a place worthy of your own worth, stand fast, for you have rowed to a good port. And, despite any unhappiness, always be hopeful in yourself. For unless low spirits or overhastiness spoil both our efforts, I hope to make a good end of this. [973]

'Do you know why I'm the less afraid to discuss this matter with my niece? Because I've heard this said by the wise and learned:* no man or woman was ever yet begotten who wasn't disposed to suffer the heat of love, either heavenly love or else natural love. So I hope to find some favour in her. And speaking of her particularly: considering her beauty and her youth, it doesn't suit her as yet to turn to heavenly love, even though she both would and could. But truly, it would certainly be very appropriate for her right now to love and cherish an excellent knight, and unless she does so I consider it a fault. And so I am, and will be, always ready to exert myself to do you this service, for in this way I hope to please both of you in time to come, for you are both prudent and can keep it secret in such a way that no one shall be any the wiser about it. And so all three of us can be made happy!

'Upon my word, I have a fine notion about you in my mind right now, as I suppose, and now I want you to see what it is. I think, since

Love, out of his goodness, has converted you from wickedness, that
you will be the best pillar of his whole religion, I believe, and do most
harm to his enemies! For example: consider these wise scholars who
err most of all against a law and are converted from their wicked
deeds through the grace of God, who is pleased to draw them to him
—these are people who are then most in awe of God, and strongest
in the faith, I understand, and can best of all withstand a mistaken
belief.' [1008]

When Troilus had heard how Pandarus agreed to help him in his
loving of Criseyde, he became (as one might say) untormented by
his unhappiness, but his love grew hotter and he spoke like this, with
a sober expression although his heart was light:

'Now blessed Venus grant that I may deserve some thanks from
you, Pandarus, before I die! But, dear friend, how shall my unhap-
piness be any less until this is done? And, good friend, tell me this
too: how will you speak of me and my distress, in case she be angry—
this is what I'm most afraid of, indeed—or won't hear or believe
how it is? I'm afraid of all this, and also that, for appearances' sake,
she won't hear of any such thing from you, her uncle.'*

'You're worrying a lot in case the Man in the Moon* fall out
. . . !' said Pandarus. 'Why, Lord! I hate your foolish behaviour! Will
you just concern yourself with what you've got to do? Do me a favour,
I ask you, for the love of God; just leave me alone, and that'll be
the best thing for you!'

'Why, friend,' said he, 'now do just as you please. But listen,
Pandarus, one word more, because I wouldn't have you think me
so very foolish as to desire from my lady anything involving wrong
or any dishonour. For without a doubt, I'd rather die than have her
believe anything of me except what might tend towards good.' [1036]

Then Pandarus laughed and replied at once:

'And with me as your surety? Pooh! No one does anything else!
I wouldn't care though she stood here and heard how you're talk-
ing! But farewell, I'll be going. Goodbye! Cheer up! God speed to
us both! Give me this work and this task, and may all the sweetness
of my success be yours!'

Then Troilus fell down on his knees, and clasped Pandarus tightly
in his arms and said:

'Now, I scorn all the Greeks! Indeed, in the end God will help
us yet! And without a doubt, I swear before God that, if my life may
last, some of them will feel pain . . . and yet I regret that this boast

escaped my lips! Now Pandarus, I can say no more but (you being wise) you know, you can do, you are everything! My life, my death, I lay entirely in your hands. Help me now!'

'Yes, upon my word, I shall!' said he.

'God reward you, my friend, and particularly for this,' said Troilus, 'that you commend me to her who can command me to my death.'

Eager to serve his close friend, Pandarus then spoke like this:

'Goodbye, and think that I will be deserving of your thanks! You will indeed be hearing about that, and you have my word!'—and he went on his way thinking about this matter, and how he might best beseech her for her favour, and find a time and a place for it. [1064]

For everyone who has a house to build does not rush to begin the work with hasty hand, but will wait a while and send out his heart's line from within, in order to achieve his design first of all.* All this Pandarus thought in his heart, and planned his work very wisely before he acted.

But then Troilus no longer lay down, but was up at once on his bay steed, and acted the lion on the field of battle. Woe to that Greek who crossed his path by day! And in the city from that time on his manner was always so pleasant, and won him so much favour, that everyone loved him who but looked upon his face. For he became the friendliest person, the noblest and also the most generous, the most admirable, and the very best knight that there was or could be in his time. Gone were his jokes and his cruelty, his lofty bearing and distant manner, and each of those changed into a virtue.

Now let us stop talking of Troilus for a while, who behaves like a man who is seriously hurt, and who is somewhat relieved from the aching of his wound but no nearer being healed and, like a compliant patient, awaits the advice of the one who goes about curing him. And so Troilus continues to endure his lot. [1092]

Here ends the first book.

BOOK TWO

TROILUS AND CRISEYDE

Here ends the proem of the second book.

Here begins the second book.

In May, the mother of happy months, when the fresh flowers killed off by winter are quickened by the warmth, all blue and white and red—and every meadow overflows with dainty happiness, and which

Here begins the proem of the second book.

O wind, O wind, the weather begins to clear, to sail out of these black waves, for in this sea the ship of my skill* has such difficulty that I can scarcely steer it! This sea I call the tumultuous subject of despair that Troilus was in; but now begin the first days of hope.* O my lady, whose name is Clio,* from henceforth may you be my Muse and my help, to put this book into good rhyme until I have finished. I do not need to practise any other art here. I therefore excuse myself to every lover, because I do not compose this out of any personal feeling* but am translating it into my language from Latin.* For that reason I want neither thanks nor blame for all this work but humbly beg you to excuse me if any word be lame, for just as my author said, so say I! It is no wonder if I speak about love unfeelingly, for there is nothing new in that: a blind man cannot judge well between colours. You also know that over a thousand years there is change in the forms of speech,* and words that were current then now seem amazingly silly and strange to us, and yet they spoke them like that and got on as well in love as people do now. To win love in different times and different places, customs differ. And so if it should happen somehow that there be any lover here in this place who listens (as the story will tell) to how Troilus gained his lady's favour, and thinks 'I wouldn't set about winning love like that', or marvels at Troilus' way of talking or behaving—I don't know, but it's no surprise to me! For every person who travels to Rome does not keep to one route or always to one way,* and in some countries the whole game would be ruined if they behaved in love as people do here, as, for example, in public conduct and appearance, in visiting formally, or delivering their speeches. Therefore, people say: 'Each country has its own rules.' And there are scarcely three people here present who have said and done exactly the same thing in love, for this may suit you for your purposes, and you not at all. Yet everything is said, or will be; and it happens some people carve in wood, and some in stone. But, since I have begun, I shall follow my author if I can. [49]

Here ends the proem of the second book.

Here begins the second book.

In May, the mother of happy months, when the fresh flowers killed off by winter are quickened into life again—all blue and white and red—and every meadow overflows with balmy fragrance, and when Phoebus spreads his bright beams in the sign of Taurus, the white Bull*—it so happened (as I shall sing) on the third day of May* that Pandarus too, despite his wise talk, felt his share of love's sharp arrows, so that, even though he could preach ever so well about loving, it still made him go green repeatedly during the day. It so happened that some unhappiness in love befell him that day, and because of that he went to bed in misery and often tossed and turned before it was day.

When morning came, the swallow Procne,* with a sorrowful song, began to lament how she had been metamorphosed into a bird. And all the while Pandarus lay in bed half asleep, until she made her twittering so near him—how Tereus abducted her sister—that he woke up at the sound of her, and called, and prepared to get up, remembering that he had an errand to do for Troilus, and his great undertaking as well. When he worked out an astrological forecast* and discovered that the moon was in a favourable position for venturing, he made his way very soon to his niece's palace nearby. Now Janus,* god of entrances, may you guide him! [77]

When he came to his niece's palace he asked her people: 'Where's my lady?'

And they told him, so he went on in, and found her and two other ladies seated in a paved parlour,* listening as they pleased, the three of them, to a young girl reading them the story of the siege of Thebes.*

'My lady, may God watch over you with your book and everyone here!' said Pandarus.

'Ah, uncle, welcome indeed,' she said; and getting up she quickly took him tightly by the hand and said: 'Three times last night I dreamt of you—I hope something good comes of it!' And so saying, she had him sit down on a bench. [91]

'Yes, niece—you'll certainly be better off the whole year, God willing,' said Pandarus. 'But I'm sorry I've stopped you from listening to your book that you praise so. For the love of God, what does it say? Tell us! Is it about love? Oh, teach me something useful!'

'Uncle,' she said, 'your mistress isn't here.'

With that they laughed, and then she said:

'This romance that we're reading is about Thebes, and we've heard how King Laius died through his son Oedipus,* and that whole affair; and we've stopped here at this rubric*—how Bishop Amphiaraus,* as the book describes, sank through the ground into hell!'

'I know about all this myself,' said Pandarus, 'and the whole siege of Thebes and its sorrow; for there are twelve books written about it. But leave this be now, and tell me how you are. Put away your veil,* and let your bare face show! Put away your book—get up, and let's dance and honour the month of May!' [112]

'Oh, God forbid!' she said. 'Are you mad? Is that any life for a widow,* God save you? By God, you're really frightening me! You're acting so wildly, it seems as if you're raving. It'd be much more suitable for me to be always praying and reading holy saints' lives in a cave. Let girls go dancing, and young wives.'

'I swear,' said Pandarus, 'I could still tell you something to make you happy.'

'Now, dear uncle,' she said, 'tell it us, for the love for God! Is the siege lifted then? I'm frightened to death of Greeks.'

'No, no,' he said, 'I swear, it's something a lot better than five such pieces of news.'

'Oh, God in heaven!' she said. 'What thing can that be? What! Better than five such pieces of news? Ah! No, indeed! I can't tell what it could be, for all the world. I think this is some joke; and unless you tell us what it is, my brains are just not up to working it out. God help me, I don't know what you mean.' [133]

'You can take my word for it: you'll never hear this thing from me—I swear it!'

'And why's that, uncle? Why's that?' she said.

'By God,' he said, 'I'll tell you that straightaway! Because there'd be no prouder woman alive, if you but knew it, in the whole city of Troy. I'm not joking—as I hope to be happy!'

Then she began to wonder a thousand times more than before, and looked down; for never, since the day she was born, did she long to know anything so much; and with a sigh she said to him at last:

'Now, uncle, I won't displease you, nor ask anything more that may upset you.'

So, after this, with many cheerful words and friendly talk and in buoyant mood, they bantered over this and that, and went on to talk about many an out of the way, pleasing, and deep subject, as friends do when they meet, until she asked him how Hector was faring, who was like a wall to the city and scourge of the Greeks. [154]

'Very well, thank God, except that he has a little wound in his arm,' Pandarus said. 'And likewise his young brother Troilus, that wise and excellent second Hector,* who's so full of every excellent quality—such as faithfulness and nobility of every kind, wisdom, honour, magnanimity, and worthiness.'

'Indeed, uncle,' she said, 'I'm so glad they're doing well—God save them both! For truly, I think it's most honourable for a king's son to do well in battle and to show fine qualities of character as well. For great power and moral virtue are seldom seen here together* in the same person.'

'Indeed, that's true,' Pandarus said. 'But, upon my word, the king has two sons—that's to say, Hector and Troilus—and certainly, though I should die, they're as free of faults, I dare say, as any men now alive: their strength is widely known, and what they're capable of. About Hector there's no need to say more. In all this world there's not a better knight than he is—he's the very fountainhead of nobility itself—and he has even more moral excellence than physical strength. Many a wise and worthy person knows this. I'd say just the same about Troilus. God help me, I don't know such another pair.' [182]

'By God,' she said, 'that's true of Hector. I believe the same to be true of Troilus. For undoubtedly, people say he does so bravely in battle day by day, and behaves here at home so considerately to everyone, that he receives all praise from those people by whom I'd most like to be praised myself.'

'What you say is very true, indeed,' Pandarus said. 'Anyone who had been with him yesterday might have marvelled at Troilus, because so thick a swarm of bees* never yet flew the way those Greeks fled on account of him, and all over the battlefield the only cry everyone heard was: "There goes Troilus!" Now here!—now there!—he hunted them so fast that there was nothing but Greeks' blood—and Troilus! Now these he wounded!—and those he unhorsed altogether! Wherever he went, it turned out like this: he was death to them—and shield and life for us!—so that no one dared resist that day while he held his bloody sword in his hand! Yet he's also the friendliest man of high rank that I ever saw in my life, and, when he wants, knows how to show the greatest friendliness to those he thinks deserve to succeed.' [207]

And having said that, Pandarus then took his leave at once and said:

'I must be going.'

'No, then I'd be at fault, uncle,' she then said. 'What's the matter with you—to be tired like this so soon, and especially of women? Are you serious? No, sit down! By God, before you go I've some business to talk to you about—to discuss what it would be sensible to do.'

And everyone who was round them then, and heard that, went and stood at a distance* while the two of them transacted whatever business they wished.

When their conversation—about her position and the management of her affairs—was quite brought to an end, Pandarus said:

'Now it's time for me to go. But I still say: get up, let's dance, and throw your widow's weeds away—good riddance to them! Why do you want to make yourself look ugly like this, since such good luck has come your way?'

'Ah, that subject again! For the love of God,' she said, 'am I not to know what you mean by this?'

'No, this thing needs time,' he then said, 'and also I'd regret it very much indeed, if I revealed it and you took it wrongly. It'd be better to hold my tongue than say something true that went against your inclinations. For, niece—by the goddess Minerva,* and by Jupiter who makes the thunder ring out, and by the blessed Venus whom I serve!—you are the woman now living in this world (not including mistresses,* as far as I know), whom I love best and am most reluctant to upset. And that, I believe, you know quite well yourself.' [238]

'Indeed, uncle,' she said, 'thank you! I've always found you a friend. I'm beholden to no one, truly, as much as to you and have given so little in return. With God's grace, I'll never intentionally displease you by any fault of mine; and if I have before now, I'll make amends. But for the love of God I beg you—as you're the man I most love and trust—do drop this distant way of speaking to me and tell me, your niece, what you want.'

And when she said that, her uncle immediately kissed her and said:

'Gladly, my dear, dear niece! What I'm now going to say to you—do try and take it well!'

With that she lowered her gaze, and Pandarus cleared his throat a little and said:

'You see, niece, however much some people take pleasure in embellishing their conversation with subtle artifice, still, in spite of all that, in their intentions their talk is always entirely directed towards some end, after all. And since the end is the strong point of every tale,* and this matter is so important, why should I colour my tale or spin it out at length to you who are so loyally my friend?'

And so saying, he observed her very closely and looked into her face and said:

'Good fortune come to such a mirror!'

Then he thought in this way:

'If I put what I've to say at all complicatedly, or make some elaborate story of it for any length of time, she won't enjoy that very much at all and will think I'm out to deceive her. For sensitive minds imagine it's all trickery* in any case where they can't completely understand. So I'll try and adapt what I say to her intelligence.' [273]

And he looked at her intently, and she was aware that he was observing her like that and said:

'Lord! How you do stare at me! Haven't you ever seen me before? What do you say? No?'

'Yes, yes,' he said, 'and will do better before I go! But, on my word, I was thinking just now whether you were going to be fortunate, for now we'll see. Because some lucky break comes everyone's way at some point, if he knows how to take it. But if he'll pay no attention to it when it comes but wilfully let it pass by—well! neither chance nor fortune deceives him, but just his sheer idleness and wretched dullness. Such a person is to be blamed, I believe. O my lovely niece, you've found good fortune very easily, if you know how to take it. And for the love of God—and of me too—seize it at once, in case opportunity passes you by! Why should I make a long rigmarole about it? Give me your hand, for—if you want—there's no one in this world in such a happy situation. And since I speak from good intentions, as I've said to you before, indeed, and love your honour and good name as well as anyone in this world, by all the oaths that I've sworn to you—if you should be angry because of this or think I'm lying, I'll never set eyes on you again! Don't be afraid!

Don't tremble so! Why should you? Don't go so pale with fright! For certainly, the worst part of this is over and, though what I've said may be new to you now, you can always rely on it that you'll find me loyal. If it were anything I thought unsuitable, I wouldn't bring it up with you.' [308]

'Now, dear uncle, for the love of God, I beg you,' she said, 'hurry up and tell me what it is! For I'm both afraid of what you'll say, and I'm also longing to know what it is, to be sure. For whether it's for better or worse, do tell me—don't let me remain in this state of fright.'

'So I will! Now listen! I'll tell you. Now, my niece, the king's dear son—that good, wise, excellent, lively, generous man, who always behaves well—the noble Troilus—loves you so much that, unless you help, it'll be the death of him. Well, there it is! What more should I say? Do what you like—whether he lives or dies, it's up to you. But if you let him die, I'll die—take my word for it, niece, I'll not tell a lie—even if I had to slit my throat with this knife!' [325]

With that the tears burst from his eyes, and he said:

'If you make us both die innocently like this, then you've landed a fine catch of fish! How are you better off if we both die? Alas, he who is my lord so dear—that loyal man, that noble, excellent knight, who wants nothing but a friendly look from you!—I see him dying on his feet and hurrying with all his might to get himself killed, if his fortune permits. It's a pity God gave you such beauty! If it turns out you're so cruel as not to bother caring any more about the death of him (who, as you see, is so noble and true) than of some trick-ster or wretch—if you're such a person, your beauty can't go far enough to make amends for such a cruel act. It's a good idea to think carefully before the need arises. A curse on the beautiful gem* that lacks the power to heal! A curse too on that herb that fails to cure! A curse on that beauty that is pitiless! A curse on that person who tramples everyone under foot! And you, who are all beauty from top to toe, if there is no pity in you as well,* then it's a shame you're alive, upon my word! [350]

'And believe me—this is no trick! For sooner than be his pimp, I'd rather you and I and he were hanged high enough for everyone to see us! I'm your uncle—it'd be my shame as well as yours, if I agreed he should destroy your honour with my help. Now please understand, because I'm not asking you to bind yourself to him through any promise, but only that you'll be more friendly towards him than you've been up to now and more encouraging, so that at least his life is saved. This is the sum total of all we intend. God help me, I never meant anything else! Look, this request is only reasonable, to be sure, and, by God, there's no reason to be afraid. For the sake of argument, let's suppose the worst case that you fear: that people may be surprised to see him come and go. In reply to that I'd counter straightaway like this: that everyone, unless a born idiot, will judge it to be affection between friends. What! Who'd imagine—if he saw someone go into a temple—that he was eating the idols? Think too how prudently and well he conducts himself, so that he doesn't forget anything, and wins praise and gratitude wherever he goes. And besides, he'll be coming here so seldom, what would it matter if the whole town saw? Such love between friends prevails all over this city, so always cloak your actions under cover of that, and, God save me, as I've said, your best course of action is to do so. But anyway, dear niece, so as to put an end to his unhappiness, do let that reserved manner of yours be a bit sweeter, so that you're not to blame for his death.' [385]

Criseyde, while listening to him, thought:

'I'll probe him a bit on what he means, for sure,' and she said: 'Now, uncle, what would you suggest? What do you advise me to do about this?'

'That's well said,' said he. 'Certainly, it's best for you to love him in return for his love of you, as love for love is a reasonable reward. Think too how, with every hour, advancing age lays waste in each of you some portion of your beauty.* And so, before old age completely devours you, go and love—for when you're old, no one'll want you! Let this proverb be a motto to you: "Aware too late, said Beauty, when it's passed", and getting old humbles haughty airs in the end. When it seems to him a woman is acting proudly, the king's jester is in the habit of calling out loudly: "May you—and all proud people—live so long that crows' feet have grown underneath your eyes, and then let someone send you a mirror to peer into, where you can see your face first thing in the morning!" I wouldn't wish any greater sorrow on you, niece.' [406]

With that he stopped speaking and hung his head, and she immediately burst out crying, and said:

'Alas! I'm so unhappy! I wish I were dead, for good faith has completely disappeared from this world. Alas, what would strangers do to me, when he whom I took to be my best friend advises me to love and should be forbidding it to me? Alas, I would certainly have trusted that if I—through my bad luck—had fallen in love with either Troilus or Achilles, Hector or any other man alive, you wouldn't have had any mercy on me, or restraint, but would have always been reproaching me. This false world, alas, who can trust it? What! Is this all the happiness and all that I was to celebrate? Is this your advice? Is this my happy situation? Is this the true fulfilment of your promise? Was this whole highly coloured story* told—alas!—just for this purpose? O my lady Pallas,* please look after me in this frightening situation, because I'm so bewildered, I could die!' With that she began to sigh very bitterly. [428]

'Ah! Is this the best you can do?' said Pandarus. 'By God, I shan't come here any more this week, as God's my witness, since I'm so mistrusted! I can see you care little about us, or whether we die! Oh, how wretchedly unhappy I am! If only he could survive . . . it doesn't matter about me! O cruel god, O pitiless Mars, O three Furies of hell*—I call upon you! Let me never leave this house if I meant anything wrong or dishonourable! But since I see my lord must die, and I with him, here I make my confession and say that you wickedly cause both our deaths! But (since you'll be pleased when I'm dead), I swear by Neptune, who's god of the sea, that from now on I'll never eat bread again till I see my own heart's blood— for I'll certainly die as soon as Troilus!' [446]

And he jumped up and started to go, till she pulled him back by the hem of his clothes. Criseyde was nearly dying for fear—she was the most timid person that might be—and both heard and saw that the knight was sadly in earnest . . . and also saw no offence in his request . . . and considering the further harm that might ensue . . . she began to feel sorry, then became incredibly frightened, and thought to herself like this:

'Unfortunate things happen thick and fast all the time because of love, and especially in such kinds of situation as this, where men themselves can be cruel and wicked. And if this man should kill himself here—alas!—right in front of me, it will be no laughing matter. What people would think about it, I can't say. I need to play a very sly game.'

And with a sorrowful sigh she said three times over:

'Ah, Lord! What miserable luck has come my way! For my position is in jeopardy, and my uncle's life hangs in the balance too. But

nevertheless, with God's guidance, I'll act in such a way that I'll pre-
serve my honour and his life as well—' and she stopped crying. 'One
must choose the lesser of two evils. I'd still rather behave in a friendly
yet honourable way towards Troilus than lose my uncle's life. You
say you're not asking anything else of me?' [473]

'Certainly not,' he said, 'my own dear niece!'

'All right then,' she said, 'I'll do my utmost: I'll constrain my
heart against my inclinations. I won't play him along with false hopes,
and nor can I love a man against my will, but otherwise I'll try—
always safeguarding my honour—to be pleasant to him from day to
day. I'd never once have said no to that, except that I kept imagin-
ing things that frightened me. But if the cause stops, the illness always
stops. And here I make a solemn declaration, if you go any further
in this business, that certainly, not even to save your lives, even though
both the two of you die, and though the whole world in one day turn
against me, will he ever have any other pity from me.'

'I agree,' said Pandarus, 'upon my word! But can I trust,' he said,
'that, for your part, you'll keep faithfully to what you've promised
me here?'

'Yes, without a doubt,' said she, 'my dear uncle.'

'And that I shan't have any cause to complain in this matter,' said
he, 'or lecture you more often?'

'Why, no, indeed! What need is there to talk about it any more?'

Then they fell into other cheerful conversation until at last:

'O good uncle,' she then said, 'for the love of him who created us
both, tell me how you first knew about his unhappiness. Does no
one know about it except you?'

'No,' he said.

'Can he talk well about love?' she said. 'I beg you: do tell me, so
I'm all the better prepared!' [504]

Then Pandarus began to smile a little and said:

'Upon my word, I'll tell you! The other day,* not very long ago,
beside a well in the palace garden,* he and I spent quite half the
day talking about a plan, how we might repulse the Greeks. Soon
after that, we began to run about and hurl our spears back and forth,
till at last he said he wanted to sleep and lay down then on the grass,
and I roamed about, some distance away, till I overheard, as I was
walking by myself, how he began to groan very sorrowfully. Then
I crept up very quietly behind him and certainly, to tell the truth,

as I can now recall to mind, he complained to Love just like this,
saying:

"Lord, have pity on my suffering, although I have been rebellious
in my thoughts. Now I confess* my fault, Lord, and I repent! O
god—who at your disposal ordain everyone's end by just provid-
ence*—graciously accept my humble confession, and send me such
penance as pleases you, but out of your kindness, may you be my
shield against despair,* which may separate my spirit from you! For
truly, Lord, she who stood there in black has wounded me so deeply
with a look from her eyes that it has penetrated to the bottom of my
heart,* through which I know that I must indeed die. This is the
worst of it: I daren't reveal my thoughts. And all the hotter are the
glowing coals because people cover them with pale, dead ashes."*

'With that he hung his head down at once and began to mutter,*
truly I don't know what. I went quietly away and acted as if I'd known
nothing about it, and came back immediately and stood beside him
and said:

"Wake up! You're sleeping far too long! It doesn't seem like love's
making you pine with longing,* when you sleep so that there's no
waking you! Who ever saw such a dull fellow before?"

"All right, my friend," said he, "you lovers go ahead and make
your heads ache for love, and let me live as best I can." [550]

'But although he was pale and wan because of his unhappiness,
he still put on as cheerful an expression then as though he should
have led the latest dance. This went on until recently, the other day,
it so happened that I came wandering all alone into his bedroom and
found him lying on his bed. I never heard a man groan so bitterly,
but I didn't hear what he was complaining about, because as I came
in he quite suddenly stopped his lamenting. At this I became rather
suspicious, and I came nearer and found he was weeping bitterly.
And—God save me for sure—I never felt more pity for anything,
for, whether with schemes or with advice, I could barely save him
from death, so that I still feel my heart weep for him. And, God
knows, never since I was born was I so busy lecturing anyone, nor
ever so deeply sworn to secrecy, before he would tell me who might
be the doctor to cure his illness. Now don't ask me to repeat to you
all he said, all his sad words—unless you want to see me swoon!
Only to save his life, and for no other reason, and in no way to harm
you—am I driven like this. And for the love of God who made us,

show him such encouragement that he and I can go on living! Now I've bluntly confessed to you what's in my heart, and since you know my intentions are innocent, give all this some thought, because I mean nothing wrong. And I'm praying to God for you to have really good luck, who have netted such a man without using a net!* And if you're as wise as you're beautiful to see, then the ruby's well set in the ring!* Two people would never be so well met, when you are his, the whole of you,* as he is yours. . . . Almighty God, let us see that hour!'

'No! I didn't say anything about that, ha, ha!' said she. 'God help me, you're ruining everything!'

'Oh, forgive me, dear niece,' he said at once, 'whatever I said, I only meant well, by Mars, the god that is helmeted in steel! Now don't be angry, my own blood, my dear niece.'

'Well, all right,' said she, 'all's forgiven now!'

With this he took his leave and went home and Lord, he was glad and in high good humour! [597]

Criseyde got up; she delayed no longer but went directly into her own room and sat herself down, still as a stone, to turn over and over every word he had said, as it came back to her mind, and grew somewhat astonished in her thoughts precisely because of the novel situation; but when she had considered it fully, then she found absolutely nothing dangerous in it of which she ought to be afraid. For it is possible for a man to love a woman so much that his heart can be shattered, and she not love in return unless she wants to.

Just as she sat and thought like this,* a clamour went up at a skirmish outside, and people shouted in the street:

'Look! Troilus has just now put a crowd of Greeks to flight!'

At that all her household began to shout:

'Ah, let's look! Throw the gates wide open! For he must ride to the palace through this street, because there's no other way from the Gate of Dardanus,* where the chain is down.' [618]

With that he and all his people came along right away, riding in two companies at a slow pace, just as if it were his lucky day, to tell the truth, because of which, people say, what will occur of necessity cannot be prevented. Troilus sat on his bay horse, fully and richly armed, except for his head; and his horse, on which he rode very slowly at a walk, was wounded and bleeding. Without a doubt, to look upon Mars—who is god of battle—was in no way such a knightly sight as to look upon him! He looked so like a man of arms and a knight, full of high prowess, for he had both the body and the strength for it . . . as well as the daring. To see him accoutred in his armour, so eager, so young, and looking so vigorous* . . . it was heaven to look at him!* Hacked to pieces in twenty places was his helmet, which hung by a band behind at his back; shattered in pieces by swords and maces was his shield, in which could be found many an arrow that had pierced the horn, sinew, and hide; and all the time the people were crying out:

'Here comes our joy and—next to his brother—the mainstay of Troy!'

At this he turned a little red, out of modesty, when he heard the people acclaiming him, so that it was rare sport to watch how modestly he looked down. Criseyde absorbed everything about his manner, and let it sink so softly into her heart that she said to herself:

'Who gave me a drink?'*

For she went all red at her own thought,* remembering to herself, just like this:

'Look, this is the man who my uncle swears must die, unless I have mercy and pity on him!'

And with that thought, for very shame, she pulled in her head, and very quickly at that, while he and all the people passed by, and she began to consider and turn over and over in her thoughts his excellent prowess, and his rank, and his renown as well, his intelligence, his build, and also his nobility; but what found most favour with her was because his distress was all for her, and she thought it was a pity to kill such a man if his intentions were honourable. [665]

Now some envious person might chatter like this:

'This was a sudden love! How could it be that she loved Troilus so easily, just at first sight, indeed, by God?'

Now whoever says so, may he never prosper! For there is no doubt that everything must have a beginning before all is done. I am not saying that she gave him her love so suddenly, only that she began to be inclined to like him at first, and I have told you why; and after that, his manhood and his suffering made love mine away inside her, which is why he obtained her love in the course of time and through devoted service in love, and in no sudden fashion. In addition, blessed Venus, auspiciously positioned, was then seated in her seventh house* of the heavens, made propitious by aspects of other heavenly bodies and favourably inclined to help poor Troilus in his misery. And to tell the truth, she was not altogether an enemy to Troilus in the disposition of planets at the time of his birth. God knows that he succeeded all the sooner! [686]

Now let us stop speaking about Troilus for a while, who rides on his way, and let us quickly turn back to Criseyde, who hung her head very low where she sat alone, considering what she would decide upon in the end, if it so happened that her uncle would not stop exerting pressure on her on behalf of Troilus. And Lord! How she debated in her thoughts over this matter, of which I have told you; what it would be best to do, and what to avoid—that she often turned over in many ways. Now her heart was warm, now it was cold; and I shall write something of what she thought, as my author was pleased to set it down.* She thought indeed that she knew Troilus' person by sight, and also his nobility, and she said to herself in this way:

'Although it wouldn't do to grant him love, it would still (because of his excellent qualities) be an honour for me in my position to be on good terms with such a lord, with delight and pleasure in an honourable way—and it would be for his well-being as well. I'm also well aware that he's my king's son, and since he takes such pleasure in seeing me, if I were to avoid seeing him altogether, he might perhaps bear a grudge against me, through which I could be in a worse situation. Now would I be wise to make myself an enemy needlessly, where I could find favour? I know there should be moderation in all things; for although drunkenness may be banned, I don't suppose this requires everyone to go without a drink forever!* Also, since I know his unhappiness is on account of me, I oughtn't to look down on him because of that, since it so happens that he means well. I've known his good qualities from a long time back; he's no fool, and he's certainly no boaster,* people say—he's too intelligent to do something so very wrong. And as I'll never make so much of him that he can make any justifiable boast about it, he'll never tie me down with any such clause. [728]

'Now—just for the sake of argument—let's suppose the very worst that could happen: people might guess that he loves me. Where's the dishonour for me in that? Can I prevent him doing this? Why, no, indeed! I also know, and hear and see all the time, that men love women entirely without their permission, and when it pleases them no longer, let them leave off. I think too of how he could have the most attractive woman in all this noble city for his love, provided that she maintain her honour. He is altogether the most excellent man, excepting Hector, who is the best; and yet his life now lies completely in my power. But such is love, and also my destiny! Nor is it a surprise that I am loved; for I'm well aware myself, God help me—although I wouldn't want anyone to know of this thought—that, for anyone who has eyes to see, I'm undoubtedly the most beautiful, and the finest, in the whole city of Troy, so people do say. What wonder is it if he's pleased with me? I'm my own woman, well content—I thank God for it—as regards my position in life, quite young, and find myself without ties in pleasant pasture, untroubled by jealousy or such disputes. No husband is going to say "checkmate"* to me! For either they're full of jealousy, or domineering, or love novelty. What shall I do? What point is there in living like this? Can't I love, if I want to? What! By God, I'm not a nun! And though I settle my affections on this knight, who is the most deserving of men, and always keep my honour and my good name safe, it can't by rights bring any disgrace upon me.' [763]

But just as when the sun is shining brightly in March, which often changes its countenance, and the wind puts a cloud to flight which overspreads the sun for a while, a thought like a cloud passed through her soul and overshadowed all her bright thoughts, so that she almost collapsed for fear. That thought was this:

'Alas! Since I'm free, should I now love and put my security in jeopardy and my freedom in thrall? Alas, how did I dare think of such folly? Can't I perfectly well observe in other people their anxious happiness, their constraints, and their suffering? There's no woman in love, who doesn't have reason to lament it. For in itself love is the most stormy life that was ever yet begun; there's always some mistrust or silly strife in love—some cloud covers that sun! When we're unhappy, we wretched women can do nothing about it but weep and sit and think. This is our misery: to drink up the cup of our own woes.* Also, spiteful tongues are so ready to speak ill of us; and men are so unfaithful that, as soon as their desire is finished, love finishes, and off they go to love someone new. But harm that's done is done, there's no use regretting it. For though these men tear themselves apart for love at first, too keen a beginning often leads to break-up in the end.* How often have people known the treachery that's been done to women! I can't see the purpose of such love, or what becomes of it when it's gone. There's no one who knows what becomes of it, so I believe. Look, there's nothing left of it for anyone to trip over! What was nothing before turns back into nothing.* How busy, if I love, must I also be to please those who gossip about love and dream up things, and cajole them so that they speak no ill of me! For though there's no reason for it, it still seems to them that everything people do to please their friends is for some harmful purpose; and who can stop every wicked tongue or the sound of bells while they're being rung?'

Then her thoughts brightened up, and she said:

'Like it or not, nothing ventured, nothing gained!'*

And with another thought her heart trembles; then hope sleeps, and afterwards fear awakes; now hot, now cold;* but so, between the two, she got up and went to have a break. [812]

Down the stairs she then went at once into the garden* with her three nieces—Flexippe, Tharbe, Antigone,* and herself—and took many a turn up and down there to amuse themselves, such that it was a joy to see; and others of her women, a great throng of them, attended her all around the garden. This garden* was extensive, and all the paths were railed off, and well shaded with flowery green boughs, furnished with benches newly topped with turf; all the paths were sanded, where she walked arm in arm, until at last fair Antigone began to sing a Trojan song, so that it was heaven to hear her clear voice:

Antigone's Song*

'O Love,' she sang, 'to whom I have been and shall be a humble subject, true in my intent, as best I can, to you, Lord, I give my heart's desire in tribute, entirely and forever more; for your grace never yet sent anyone as blessed a reason as I have to lead my life in all joy and security, without a doubt. You, blessed god, have bestowed me so well in love, indeed, that no one alive could imagine how it might be better! For, Lord, without jealousy or strife I love one who is the most diligent there ever was in serving tirelessly and sincerely, and the least sullied with any wrong. He is the fount of worthiness, foundation of fidelity, mirror of excellence, an Apollo* of wisdom, rock of security, root of virtue, originator and source of pleasure, slayer of all my sorrow—indeed, I love him best,

as he does me! Now, blessings on him, wheresoever he be! Whom
should I thank but you, god of Love, for all this happiness I bask
in? Thanks be to you, Lord, that I am in love! This is the right way
of life that I am leading, to banish every kind of vice and sin. This
inclines me so towards virtue that day by day my will improves. And
whosoever says that to love is a vice or servitude, although he may
feel distress in it, he is either envious or very foolish, or is unable
to love because of his own wickedness. For I suppose that the kind
of people who slander love know nothing of it. They talk, but Love's
bow was never bent for them,* and they never tried it for them-
selves! How is the sun any the worse, in its proper nature, though
a man, because of the weakness of his eyes, cannot bear to look at
it on account of the brightness? Or love the worse, though wretches
complain about it? No well-being that cannot endure some sorrow
has any worth. And so, let him who has a head of glass beware of
the flying stones thrown in battle!* But I, with all my heart and all
my strength, as I have said, will love until my last day my dear heart
and all my own knight, in whom my heart has grown so firmly, as
his in me, that it will last forever. Although I was afraid at first to
begin to love him, I well know now that there is no danger in it!'
[875]

And with that very word she ended her song, and thereupon:
'Now, niece,' said Criseyde, 'who composed this song now with
such admirable sentiments?'

'Madam,' Antigone at once replied and said, 'certainly the most
excellent maiden of great rank in the whole city of Troy, and leads
her life in greatest honour and joy.'

'Truly, so it would seem by her song,' Criseyde then said, and at
that she sighed and said: 'Lord! Is there such happiness among these
lovers, that they can express it so beautifully?'

'Yes, indeed,' said young Antigone the fair, 'for not all the peo-
ple who have been or are now alive could properly describe the bliss
of love. You don't imagine that every wretched person knows the
perfect bliss of love? Why, no, indeed! They think it's all love if one
of them feels hot. Not at all! Not at all! They don't know anything
about it! People must ask saints if it's at all lovely in heaven—why?
because they can tell—and ask devils if it's foul in hell.'

Criseyde did not reply to that point but said:

'It'll be night very soon, I think . . .'

But every word that she heard her say, she imprinted firmly in her heart, and all the time love frightened her less than it once did, and sank into her heart, so that she became somewhat inclined to change her mind. [903]

The honour of the day and the eye of the heavens, the enemy of night—all this I call the sun!*—travelled quickly westward and went down, as he who had run his day's course, and white objects grew dim and dun-coloured in the half-light, and the stars came out, so that she and all her people went indoors together. When she wished to retire, and those who ought to withdraw had withdrawn, she said that she wanted to sleep. Her women soon escorted her to her bed. When all was hushed, she lay quietly and thought over this whole thing—there is no need to go over the mode and manner of everything again, for you are wise!

A nightingale* upon a green cedar tree beneath the bedroom wall where she was lying sang very loudly in the bright moonlight—perhaps, in its bird's way, a song of love, that refreshed and delighted her at heart. To that she listened willingly for a long time, until a dead sleep took hold of her at last. And as soon as she slept, she dreamed* that an eagle, with feathers as white as bone, fixed his long claws under her breast and suddenly tore out her heart, and put his own heart into her breast—at which she was neither frightened nor felt any pain—and on his way he flew, leaving heart for heart. [931]

Now let her sleep, and let us continue our story about Troilus, who rode to the palace from the skirmish of which I told, and sat in his room and waited while two or three of his messengers looked hard for Pandarus, until at last they found him and brought him back. Pandarus came bounding in at once and said:

'Who's taken a good beating today then with swords and sling stones but Troilus, who's caught a fever?' And he began to joke and said: 'Lord, how you're sweating! But get up, and let's have supper and then go to bed.'

'Let's do whatever you want,' Troilus replied.

With all the haste that they decently could, they hurried from supper to bed, and everyone went out of the door and hastened on his way wherever he wished. But Troilus, who thought his heart was bleeding for misery until he heard some news, said:

'Do I weep or sing, my friend?'

'Lie still, and let me sleep!' said Pandarus. 'And keep your shirt on*—your needs are provided for! And please yourself if you want to sing or dance or jump for joy! Briefly, you can take my word for it, sir,* my niece will do well by you and love you best, by God and on my oath, unless a lack of perseverance make it turn out otherwise, because of your sloth. For from one day to another I've got a long way with your business, until earlier today, this morning, I gained her affection as a friend for you, and to that she's pledged her word.— At any rate, one foot's lamed of the sorrow that's been dogging you!'* [964]

Why should I keep discoursing about it any longer? He told him everything you have heard already. But just as flowers, closed up by the cold of night-time, drooping low on their stalks, straighten themselves up again in the bright sun* and open out in their natural way in a row, just so Troilus threw up his eyes and said:

'O beloved Venus, praise be to your power and your grace!'

And to Pandarus he held up both his hands and said:

'Lord, all that I have is yours! You've restored my health and broken my chains! Whoever gave me a thousand Troys, one after the other, couldn't make me so happy, God save me! Look, my heart's swelling so for joy, it'll burst! But Lord, what shall I do? How shall I live? When shall I see my dear heart next? How is this long time going to be spent until you're with her again on my behalf? You may reply "Wait, wait", but, to tell the truth, a man who's hanging by the neck waits in great distress on account of the pain!' [987]

'Take it easy now, for the love of Mars,' said Pandarus, 'because there's a time for everything.* Wait just so long as until night is over, for as surely as you're lying here beside me, I swear before God, I'll be there first thing. And so, please (to some extent!) do as I say, or give this task to someone else. For God knows, indeed, I've always been ready to serve you up to now, and until this very night I've not held back but, as far as I'm able, done everything you wanted and shall do with all my strength. Do as I say now, and you'll do well; and if you won't, blame yourself for all your cares. Your bad luck isn't my fault. I know you're a thousand times smarter than I am, but if I were you, God help me, I'd absolutely write her a letter right now, in my own hand, in which I'd tell her how I was suffering, and beg her to have pity. Now help yourself, and don't neglect it out of laziness! I'll take it to her myself; and as soon as

you know I'm there with her, get up on a warhorse right away—
yes, for sure, absolutely in your best gear—and ride past the place*
as though there were nothing in it, and (if I can manage it) you'll
find us sitting at some window, looking into the street. And if you
like, then you can greet us, and direct your look at me. But—for the
life of you!—take care, and at all costs avoid hanging about. God
preserve us from any disasters! Ride on your way and keep yourself
under control. And we'll talk enough about you when you've gone,
I imagine, to make your ears glow!* [1022]

'Regarding your letter—you're smart enough. I know you won't
write it with haughty airs, showing off, or being argumentative; and
nor should you write it like some secretary, or artfully.* Blot it with
your tears* a bit, too! And if you write some fine and very tender
word, even if it's good, don't repeat it too often! For if the best
harpist alive, with all his five fingers, were always to harp on one
string* or always play one tune on the finest-sounding and most glori-
ous harp there ever was, it would make everyone bored to hear his
music and fed up with his strummings, even if his nails were ever
so sharply pointed! Oh, and don't jumble together things that clash,
such as using technical terms from medicine in the language of love.
Always stick to a form suitable for your subject-matter, and see to
it that it's consistent. For if a painter were to paint a pike with ass's
feet and give it the head of an ape, it wouldn't be at all fitting, unless
it were just a joke.'* [1043]

This advice was very appealing to Troilus, but like any anxious
lover he said:

'Alas, my dear brother, Pandarus, I'm ashamed to write, indeed,
in case through my innocence I said something out of place, or she
wouldn't receive it, out of resentment. Then I'd be a dead man!
Nothing could prevent it.'

'Do what I say, if you will,' Pandarus replied to that, 'and let me
take the letter. For by that Lord who created east and west, I hope
to bring an answer to it right away in her own hand. And if you
don't want to, forget it, and may anyone who helps you to succeed
against your will regret it for the rest of his life!'

'By God, I agree!' Troilus said. 'Since it's your wish, I'll get up
and write. And I do devoutly pray to blessed God to assist the under-
taking, and the letter I shall write! And you, Minerva* the fair, give
me the understanding to compose my letter!' [1063]

And he sat himself down and wrote exactly in this way.* First, he called her his true lady, the life of his heart, his delight, the healer of his sorrow, his bliss, and also all these other terms that in such cases these lovers all seek out; and in very humble fashion, as in his speech, he commended himself to her favour—to recount everything about how he did so would require a great deal of space! And after this, he most humbly begged her not to be angry although he, in his foolishness, was so bold as to write to her, and said that love caused it, or else he must die, and begged pitifully for mercy; and after that he said—and lied quite openly—he was of little worth and could do even less; and that she should excuse his lack of understanding, and he was so afraid of her too; and he repeatedly blamed his unworthiness; and after that, he then told of his unhappiness—but that was endless, without ceasing!—and said he would always stay true; then he read it over, and folded up the letter. And he bathed the ruby in his signet ring in his salt tears, and imprinted it deftly and quickly on the wax. Then he kissed the letter that he was sealing up a thousand times before he would stop, and said:

'Letter, a blissful destiny is ordained for you—my lady shall see you!'

Pandarus took the letter early the next morning, and hurried to his niece's palace,* and he swore blind that it was past nine o'clock, and began to joke and said:

'Although it's hurting badly, my heart's certainly so full of life I can never sleep on a May morning! I have a jolly woe, a cheerful sorrow!'*

When Criseyde heard her uncle—with anxious heart, and eager to hear the reason for his coming—she answered like this:

'Now, on your honour, my dear uncle,' said she, 'what kind of winds now guide you here? Tell us about your "jolly woe" and your suffering! How far have you got in love's dance?'*

'By God,' said he, 'I'm always hopping along behind!'

And she laughed—it seemed to her that her heart would burst.

'Take care,' Pandarus said, 'that you always find reason to laugh at me. But listen, if you will. A visitor's come into town right now, a Greek spy, and has news to tell, and so I've come to tell you the latest. Let's go into the garden, and you shall hear, totally confidentially, a long account of this.' [1115]

With that they went arm in arm together down into the garden from the chamber; and when he was far enough that no one could hear the sound of what he said, he spoke to her like this, and plucked out the letter:

'Look, he who is utterly and freely yours commends himself humbly to your favour, and sends you this letter here via me. Think it over carefully when you have the opportunity, and find some kindly way of answering, or—God help me!—to speak very frankly, he can't live long in such pain.'

Very apprehensively she then stood still, and did not take it, but all her humble manner began to change and she said:

'For the love of God, don't bring me any letter or anything in writing that relates to such a matter! And also, dear uncle, I beg you, do have more regard to my position than to his pleasure! What more should I say? Just think for a moment whether this is reasonable, and don't hesitate to tell the truth out of partiality or laziness. Would it be suitable for me in my position, by God and on your oath, to accept it or to take pity on him, and bring harm and reproach on myself? Carry it back again, for the sake of Him in whom you believe!' [1141]

Pandarus stared at her and said:

'Now this is the greatest marvel I ever saw! Stop this foolish behaviour! Strike me dead with a thunderbolt* if, for the whole city over there, I'd bring or give you a letter that could harm you! Why do you want to take it that way? But very nearly all of you behave like this! You care least about what becomes of him who longs to serve you most, and whether he lives or dies. If ever I may deserve anything of you,' he said, 'don't refuse it—!' and caught hold of her firmly and thrust the letter down into her bosom, saying to her:

'Now throw it away at once then, so that people will see, and stare at the two of us!'

'I can wait,' said she, 'till they've gone,' and smiled, and said to him: 'Uncle, come up with whatever answer you like, I beg you, for truly, I won't write any letter.'

'You won't? Then I'll write it,' said he, 'provided you dictate!'

At that she laughed and said:

'Let's have dinner.'

And he began to joke a lot at his own expense and said:

'Niece, I suffer so much because of love that I fast every other day—' and shot out his best jokes, and made her laugh so at his foolery that she thought she would die for laughing. And when she came into the hall:

'Now, uncle,' said she, 'we'll have dinner right away.' [1171]

And she called some of her women to her, and went straight into her own room, but one of her concerns—amongst other things, undoubtedly—was to read this letter very privately. Having considered every line word by word, and having found no fault, she thought he knew how to do such things properly, and put it away and went in to have dinner. But Pandarus was standing lost in thought and, before he was aware, she caught him by his hood and said:

'You were caught before you knew it!'

'I admit it,' said he. 'Do what you will!'

Then they washed and sat themselves down and ate. And after midday Pandarus very slyly took himself to the window nearest the street and said:

'Niece, who's done up the house opposite like that?'

'Which house?' said she, and came to look, and knew all about it, and told him whose it was; and they began to chat about trivial things, both sitting by the window. When Pandarus saw his moment, and saw that her people were all out of the way:

'Now, my dear niece, out with it, I say!' said he. 'How do you like that letter—you know which one I mean? Does he know about things like that? For, upon my word, I don't know!'

At that she then went a very rosy colour, and began to hum, and said:

'Mmm . . . So I believe!'

'For God's sake, pay him back handsomely for it then!' said he. 'In return I'll sew up the letter* myself.'

And he held his hands up and went down on his knees:

'Now, dear niece, however little it may be, give me the task of sewing and folding it!'

'Well, yes, I could write,' she then said; 'and yet I don't know what I should say to him.'

'No, niece,' said Pandarus, 'don't say that! At least say thank you to him for his goodwill, and don't cause him to die! For love of me, my dear niece, don't refuse my request now!'

'By God,' said she, 'God grant everything turn out all right! God help me, this is the first letter I ever wrote*—yes, either the whole or any part of one!' [1214]

And she went alone into a small private room, the better to collect her thoughts, sat herself down, unfettered her heart only a little from out of Disdain's prison,* and began to write a letter. (It is my intention to describe the gist of it briefly,* in so far as I am able to understand). She thanked him for all his good intentions towards her, but she would not play him along with false promises, nor make herself a slave to love; but, to please him, she would gladly comfort him as his sister. She shut it, and went in to Pandarus, where he sat looking into the street, and she sat down beside him upon a gold-embroidered cushion on a stone seat made of jasper,* and said:

'May the great God surely help me, I never did anything with more difficulty than write this, which you forced me to,' and gave it to him. He thanked her and said:

'God knows, something started reluctantly very often turns out well in the end.* And, my niece, Criseyde, he ought to be glad— by God and the sun up above!—that you're won over to him with difficulty now. For that's why people say: "Slight impressions are always ready to fade very quickly."* But you've acted the tyrant almost too long, and it was hard to make any impression on your heart. Now stop it, so that you don't stay undecided about things any longer, even if you want to keep up the appearance of being aloof, but hurry to make him happy! For believe me, resistance kept up too long very often makes unhappiness turn into resentment . . .' [1246]

And, just as they were discussing this subject, see! right at the end of the street Troilus came riding very slowly, together with his party of ten men, and turned towards where they were sitting, which was on his way towards the palace; and Pandarus noticed him and said:

'Niece, look who's coming riding this way! Oh, don't run away inside—he can see us, I think—in case he thinks you're avoiding him!'

'No, no!' said she, and turned as red as a rose.

With that, Troilus saluted her humbly, with a timid expression, and his colour often changed; and he looked up meekly, and nodded at Pandarus, and passed on by. God knows if he sat on his horse properly or was pleasing in appearance that very day! God knows whether he looked like a manly knight! Why should I delay, or describe his gear? To put it briefly, Criseyde, who saw all these things, was so pleased with the combination of his person, his clothes, his look, his expression, his kindly manner, and his nobility, that never since she was born did she have such pity for his distress; and although thus far she has been resistant, I hope to God that now she has a thorn she will not pull out* this coming week! God send more such thorns to extract! [1274]

Pandarus, who stood close by her, felt the iron was hot, and he began to strike, and said:

'Niece, I earnestly beg you, tell me the answer to something I'm going to ask you: would it be right for a woman to be to blame for his death, he being innocent, just because she was lacking in compassion?'

'No, upon my word!' said she.

'God help me,' said he, 'you're telling me the truth! You feel yourself that I'm not lying. Look, there he goes!'

'Yes,' said she, 'so he does!'

'Well,' said Pandarus, 'as I've told you three times already: give up your silly modesty and your foolishness, and speak to him to set his heart at ease. Don't let silly scruples cause you both pain!'

But in that matter there was still more than one last heave to be made! All things considered, it was not to be.—And why?—Because of talk.* And it would also be too soon to allow him so great a liberty. For her intention, plainly (as she said), was to love him without it being known, if she could, and reward him with nothing but with sight. But Pandarus thought:

'It won't be like that if I can do anything about it—this silly opinion won't last for all of two years!'* [1298]

Why should I make a long discourse of this? For the moment he had to agree with that decision; and when it was evening, and all was well, he got up and took his leave. He hurried on his way homewards, and for sheer joy he felt his heart was dancing; and he found Troilus alone in bed, lying, as these lovers do, in a trance between hope and black despair. But just as he came in Pandarus sang, as if to say 'I'm bringing something!' and said:

'Who's buried so soon in his bed like this?'

'It is I, friend,' said he.

'Who? Troilus? No, so help me the moon,' said Pandarus, 'you must get up and look at a charm that was just now sent to you, which can heal you of your fever, if you make an effort to look at it immediately.'

'Yes, with God's help,' said Troilus, and Pandarus gave him the letter, saying:

'God has indeed helped us! Have a light here, and look at all this black ink!'

Troilus' heart often felt happy and often trembled while he read it, according to whether the words gave him hope or fear. But in the end he took everything that she wrote to him for the best, for he noticed something in which it seemed to him his heart might find grounds for hope, even if she wrote guardedly. In this way he clung to the more worthwhile part, so that, what with hopefulness and Pandarus' promise, he at least put most of his unhappiness to one side. [1330]

But, as we ourselves can constantly see, the more wood or coal there is, the greater the fire,* and just as, if hope should increase, of whatever it be, desire very often increases at the same time as well, or, just as an oak tree comes from a little shoot, so this letter that she sent him served to increase the desire that was burning him. That is why, I repeat, day and night Troilus began to feel more desire than he did before, because of hope, and made an effort to press on, with Pandarus' advice, and write to her about his intense unhappiness. From day to day he did not let things cool down, so that he wrote or said something through Pandarus, and also performed his other observances that are appropriate to a lover in this situation. And according to the luck of the dice,* so was he either happy or said 'Alas!' and always paced himself according to progress;* and depending on such answers as he received, his days were either miserable or happy. But he continually had recourse to Pandarus, and lamented to him pitifully all the time, and begged him for advice and assistance. And Pandarus, who saw his insane agony, very nearly died for compassion, to tell the truth, and cast around diligently and with all his heart for a way to put an end to his misery, and that very quickly, and said:

'Lord and friend and dear brother, God knows, your distress makes me unhappy! But, upon my word, if you'll stop all these miserable looks, I swear before God I'll fix things yet so that, before two days are over, you'll come to a certain place where you can beg her for her favour yourself. And certainly—I don't know if you know it, but those who are expert in love do say—it's one of the most advantageous things for a man to have an opportunity to plead his cause, and a safe place in which to reveal his unhappiness. For it must strike some pity in a good heart, to hear and see the guiltless in distress.

Perhaps you're thinking: "Although it may be so that Nature would cause her to begin to have a kind of pity upon my unhappiness, Disdain says: 'No, you'll never overcome me!' The spirit in her heart so rules her inwardly that, although she may bend, she still stands firmly rooted. What use is this to help me?" [1379]

'Think, on the contrary, that when the sturdy oak*—which men are chopping at repeatedly for the purpose—has received the lucky stroke that makes it fall, the great momentum makes it come down all at once, as these rocks or millstones do; for something that is weighty runs a swifter course when it comes down than light things do. A reed that bends with every gust will straighten up very easily if the wind should drop; but an oak tree will not do so when it is felled. I don't need to instruct you for long by multiplying examples. People will rejoice at a great undertaking well accomplished—there can be no doubt—even if that much longer has been taken over it. [1393]

'But Troilus, do tell me, if you would, something I'm now going to ask you: in deepest confidence, which of your brothers do you love best?'

'My brother Deiphebus,* certainly,' said he.

'Now,' said Pandarus, 'within twenty-four hours he'll help you, without knowing it himself. Now leave me alone to do what I can,' said he; and he then went to Deiphebus, who had always been his lord and great friend. Apart from Troilus, no man meant more to him. To relate it briefly, and without any more words, Pandarus said:

'I beg you to be a friend to a cause that concerns me.'

'Yes, certainly,' said Deiphebus, 'as God is my witness, you know I'd do more for you than for anyone, unless it were for the man I most love, my brother Troilus. But tell me what it's about, for since the day I was born I neither was nor ever think to be against anything that might displease you.'

Pandarus thanked him and said to him:

'You see, sir, I have a lady in this town, who is my niece and is called Criseyde, to whom some men want to do wrong, and wrongfully to seize her possessions; and that's why, without saying any more, I am begging you for your patronage and friendship.' [1421]

'Oh,' Deiphebus answered him, 'isn't this person—whom you're speaking of to me like this as if she were a stranger—my friend Criseyde?'

'Yes,' he said.

'Then,' said Deiphebus, 'there's certainly no need to say any more, for you can rely on it that I'll be her champion with spur and spear! I wouldn't care though all her enemies heard it! But tell me—you know the whole of this business—what would be most helpful?'

'Now, let's see,' said Pandarus. 'If you, my dear lord, would for the present do me the honour of asking her to visit you tomorrow, you see, to set out her complaints—her enemies would tremble to hear of it! And if I dared beg more of you just now, and asked you to put yourself to so much trouble as to have some of your brothers here with you, who could be of help to her cause, then I know very well she could never lack for assistance, what with your urging, what with her other friends' guidance.' [1442]

Deiphebus, who was naturally disposed to assent to everything honourable and generous, replied:

'It shall be done, and I can think of something that will help even more in this affair. What would you say if I sent for Helen to discuss this? I believe it would be for the best, for she can lead Paris as she pleases. There's no need to beg my lord and brother Hector to be a friend, for I've heard him at one time or another speak so highly of Criseyde that he could say no better—she enjoys such favour with him. It isn't necessary to ask his help. He'll be just as we'd have him be. Speak to Troilus yourself too on my behalf, and ask him to dine with us.'

'Sir, all this shall be done,' said Pandarus, and took his leave, and never stopped, but came straight as a line to his niece's house, and found her getting up from dinner, and sat himself down and spoke just like this, saying:

'O true God, how I've run! Look, my niece, can't you see how I'm sweating! Whether you're any more grateful to me, I don't know. Haven't you heard how that treacherous Poliphetes* is just about to go to law again and bring new charges against you?'

'Oh, no!' she said, and her whole colour changed. 'Why is he at it again, to cause me trouble and do me wrong? What shall I do, alas? Not that I'd care about him at all in himself, if it weren't for Antenor and Aeneas,* who are his friends in this kind of situation. But, for the love of God, my dear uncle, it doesn't matter about that. Let him have everything. I have enough for us, without that.'

'No,' said Pandarus, 'it's not going to be like that at all. For I've just been with Deiphebus, with Hector, and many other of their lordships, and quickly made each of them his enemy, so that, whenever he begins, I swear he'll never win, whatever he does.' [1484]

As they deliberated upon the best course, Deiphebus, out of his characteristic courtesy, came to ask her personally to join him at dinner next day, a request she would not refuse, but graciously agreed to. He thanked her, and went on his way. When this was done, Pandarus got up at once and, to narrate it briefly, went on his way to Troilus, found him sitting as still as a stone, and told him this whole thing from beginning to end, and how he was hoodwinking Deiphebus, and said:

'Now tomorrow's the time, if you can, to play your part well and the whole prize will be won. Now speak, now beg, now lament pitifully—don't hold back out of silly modesty, or fear, or lack of effort! Sometimes a man must talk about his own pain. Believe me about this—and she'll have pity on you. You'll be saved by your faith, in truth!* But I'm well aware you're afraid now, and I bet I can guess what it is. You're thinking: "How am I to do all this? For people are bound to notice from my looks that I'm suffering for love of her. I'd still rather die unknown, in misery." Don't think like that, for you're being very foolish, because I've just thought of a sort of trick* which can be a cover for your whole manner. You are to go the night before and promptly to Deiphebus' house, as if to relax and so to help shake off your illness—because you don't appear well, to tell the truth. Soon after that, lie down on your bed and say you can't bear to stay up any longer, and lie right there and wait for what happens. Say that your fever usually comes over you at the same time of day and that it lasts until the next morning. And let's see how well you can fake it, for sick is he who is in sorrow, by God! Go now—goodbye! And, with Venus present as guarantor, I hope, if you keep firmly to this plan, she will confirm her favour to you there in full!' [1526]

'I certainly don't need any advice from you on pretending to be ill,' said Troilus, 'because without a doubt I'm so genuinely ill, I'm very nearly dying with the pain!'

'You'll lament all the better,' said Pandarus, 'and have less need to sham, for people think a man they see sweating is hot. Look, you lie low in your hide, and I'll drive the deer towards your bow.'

With that he quietly took his leave, and Troilus went quickly to the palace. He was never so happy before in his whole life; he agreed completely with Pandarus' advice, and at night he went to Deiphebus' house. What need is there to tell you all about the welcome that Deiphebus gave his brother, or his attack of fever or his sickly manner, how people began to load him with bedclothes when he was put to bed, and how people tried to cheer him up? But in vain; all the time he kept up the act that you have already heard Pandarus devise. But it is certain that before Troilus took to his bed, that night before Criseyde came, Deiphebus had asked him to be a friend and supporter of hers. God knows that he agreed immediately to be her true friend with all his might! But there was as much need to ask him that as to bid a mad man to run mad! [1554]

The morning came, and the mealtime approached, when the lovely Queen Helen intended, at ten o'clock,* to be with Deiphebus, to whom she would not fail to keep her word; but, to tell the truth, she willingly came to dinner in an informal way, as his sister. But God and Pandarus knew what all this meant! Criseyde came too, quite innocent of this, with Antigone and her sister Tarbe as well. But, for the love of God, it is best that we avoid being prolix* now, and, without more talk, let us quickly go right to the point, as to why all these people assembled in this place; and let us pass over how they greeted each other.

Deiphebus certainly treated them with great honour, and fed them well with everything that might give pleasure. But all the time his constant refrain was:

'Alas, my good brother, Troilus, who's not well, is still confined to bed—' and with that he sighed; and after that he took pains to make them as happy as he could, and he was very welcoming. [1575]

Helen, too, lamented his illness so sincerely that it was pitiful to hear, and everyone began on account of his fever to turn into a doctor right away, and said:

'People cure folk in this way—'

'I'll teach you this charm—'

But one person sat there, although she did not choose to teach, who was thinking:

'I could be his best doctor yet.'

After lamenting, they began to praise him, as people do even now when someone has begun to praise a man, and raise him up with praise a thousand times still higher than the sun:

'He is . . . he can do . . . what few lords can . . .'

And Pandarus did not forget to corroborate their praise and what they wanted to aver. Criseyde heard all this well enough and took note of every word; and so, while looking solemn, at heart she was laughing. For who would not be proud of herself, to have power of life and death over such a knight? But I pass over everything, in case you delay too long, since all I ever relate is for one purpose. [1596]

The time came to get up from dinner, and everyone got up as they should do, and chatted for a while about this and that. But Pandarus interrupted all that talk at once and said to Deiphebus:

'If you're agreeable, would you start to speak here about the needs of Criseyde, as I asked you?'

Helen, who was holding her by the hand, was the first to speak, and said:

'Let's begin at once,' and she looked at Criseyde in a kindly way and said: 'May Jove let him who does you harm never prosper and soon take his life, and give me sorrow but he shall regret it, if I can do anything about it, and if all people are loyal!'

'Would you describe your niece's case,' said Deiphebus to Pandarus, 'because you can do it best?'

'My lords and ladies,' he said, 'it's like this—why should I hold you up any longer?'

Clear as a bell, he rang out to them so heinous a case against her enemy, called Poliphetes, that it would have made people spit. Each of them responded to this worse than the other, and they began to curse Poliphetes in this way:

'That sort of person ought to be hanged, even if he were my own brother! And so he shall, for there's nothing else for it!'

Why should I tarry over this tale? All at once, they simply promised to assist her in every way they ever could. Helen then spoke and said:

'Pandarus, does my lord, my brother—I mean Hector—know about this matter at all? Or does Troilus know of it?'

'Yes,' he said, 'but would you listen to me a moment? If you agree, it seems to me—since Troilus is here—that it would be a good thing if she told him all about this herself before she went. For he'll take her troubles all the more to heart, you see, because she's a lady; and by your leave, I'll just pop in and let you know, and quickly at that, for sure, if he's sleeping, or wants to hear anything about this.' [1636]

And in he darted and whispered in his ear:

'May God receive your soul—I've brought your bier!'*

Troilus then began to smile at this, and Pandarus, without more ado, went out at once to Helen and Deiphebus and said to them:

'Provided there's no hanging about and not too many people, he's very willing that you should bring in my lady, Criseyde, who is here; and he'll listen for as long as he can stand it. But you well know that the room is only small, and a few people can easily make it warm. Now just think about whether it would be better if she waited till another time, because I'm not going to get the blame for bringing in such a crush as might harm him or make him uncomfortable— for my right arm, I wouldn't! Now think about it, those of you who know what's best! As for me, I say the best thing, as far as I can see, is that no one went in but you two, unless it were myself, because I can run through her case in an instant better than she can. And after this, she can briefly ask him once to be a friend to her cause, and take her leave. This can't disturb his rest very much. And also, because she's not one of his family, he'll feel less at ease, which he needn't do on your account. I know he also wants to tell you something else that's nothing to do with her, which is secret and for the good of the city.' [1664]

And they, who knew nothing of his motives, went in to Troilus without more ado. In her most kindly and gentle way Helen greeted him, and with womanly charm joked and said:

'You must certainly be up soon, by all means! Now, my handsome brother, get well soon, I beg you!'

And she slipped her arm round his shoulder, and gave her whole mind to comforting him; she cheered him up as she best knew how. So after this she said:

'My dear brother Deiphebus and I, we beg you, for the love of God—and so does Pandarus too—to be a good friend and patron with all your heart to Criseyde, who is certainly having wrong done to her, as Pandarus here well knows, who can set out her case much better than I can.'

Pandarus once more filed smooth his tongue, and immediately went over her whole case again. A little while after everything had been said, Troilus soon declared:

'As soon as I can get up, I will very gladly, with all my might— I swear to God—be one of the supporters of her cause.'

'Bless you!' said Queen Helen.

'Is it your wish,' said Pandarus, 'that she take her leave before she goes?'

'O God forbid otherwise,' he then said, 'if she would be so kind as to do so.' And with those words Troilus said: 'You two, Deiphebus and my dearest sister, I have to speak to you about a matter, to have the benefit of your advice.'

And by his bed's head he found, as chance would have it, a copy of a document and a letter that Hector had sent him, to ask his advice about whether such and such a man deserved to die. I do not know who it was, but he grimly asked them to study it at once. Deiphebus began to unfold the letter in great earnest—as did Queen Helen—and strolling outside, down a staircase, into a leafy arbour, they studied it intently. They read this same thing between them and, for fully the space of an hour, they read and pored over it. [1708]

Now let them read, and let us turn back immediately to Pandarus, who very quickly spied out that all was well, and went out hastily into the big room and said:

'God save all this company! Come, my niece! My lady, Queen Helen, is waiting for you, and both my lords as well. Get up! Take with you your niece Antigone, or whoever you please, it doesn't matter. Certainly, the less crowd the better. Come along with me, and mind you thank all three of them humbly, and when you can politely see the right moment, take your leave of them, in case we deprive him of his rest for too long.'

Altogether innocent of Pandarus' intentions, Criseyde then said: 'Let's go, dear uncle.'

And she went to go in, arm in arm with him, having carefully considered her words and her manner. And Pandarus said very earnestly:

'For the love of God, I beg you all to stay right here and amuse yourselves quietly! Think which people are inside here, and what a state one of them is in—God make him get well!' and on the way in, like this: 'Gently does it, niece, I implore you, and I strictly forbid you—for the sake of him who sent us all souls, and by the power of two crowns*—do not kill this man, who has this pain because of you! Shame on the devil! Think what sort of a person he is, and what a state he is in! Come on now! Think how time spent in such delaying is only wasted. You'll both say that, when you two are one! In the second place, no one as yet suspects anything about you two.

Come on now, if you can! While people are taken in, you see, that whole time is pure gain. In vacillation, and prolonged entreaty, and delays, people are suspicious if a straw moves; and though you would like to have pleasant times after this, you dare not for the present. And why? Because such and such women spoke such and such a word; and this man or that looked like this! Oh, wasted time, alas, I daren't have anything to do with you! So come on then, and bring him back to health!'

But now, all you lovers who are here, was not Troilus in a predicament,* who lay and could hear their whispering, and thought:

'O Lord, my destiny is approaching right now!—to die once and for all, or to find comfort straightaway!'

And this was the first time he was to ask her for her love—O God Almighty, what is he to say? [1757]

Here ends the second book.

BOOK THREE

*Here begins the proem of the third book.**

O blessed light, whose brilliant beams adorn all the lovely third sphere of heaven! O beloved of the sun! O dear daughter of Jove!* Delight of love! O excellent and gracious one, always ready to make your home in noble hearts!* O true cause of well-being and of happiness, praised be your power and your goodness! In heaven and hell, in earth and salt sea, your power is felt, if I discern correctly, as man, bird, beast, fish, plant, and green tree feel your eternal influence at certain seasons. God loves, and will deny nothing to love, and in this world no living creature is of any worth or may endure without love.

You first moved Jove* to those happy desires through which all things live and have their being; and you made him amorous towards mortals, and, as you pleased, you continually gave him success or misfortune in love, and sent him down in a thousand forms for love on earth, and whoever you wished, he took. You appease fierce Mars* of his wrath and, as you please, you make hearts noble. At any rate, those whom you wish to kindle with your fire—they fear disgrace and reject vice.* You cause them to be courteous, lively, and considerate; and in all respects, according to how a person is inclined, the happiness that he has is sent by your power. [28]

You maintain realm and house in unity. You are also the true cause of friendship. You know all that hidden quality of things, which people are so curious about when they cannot understand how it may happen that *she* loves him, or why *he* loves her, any more than why this fish and not that one swims into the fish-trap at a weir! You have established a law for people universally—and this I know from those who are lovers—that whoever contends with you has the worst of it!

Now, radiant lady, out of your kindness and in honour of those who serve you—whose scribe I am—teach me how to describe some of that joy which is experienced in serving you. Pour feeling into my naked heart, and cause me to express something of your sweetness. Calliope,* let your voice be present now, for now is need for it! Do you not see my distress? How I must straightaway relate the happiness of Troilus, to the glory of Venus?—To which happiness, may God bring whoever needs it! [49]

Here ends the proem of the third book.

Here begins the third book.

Meanwhile Troilus lay going over what he had prepared, like this:

'Upon my word,' he thought, 'I'll speak like this, and like so . . . I'll lament like this to my dear lady . . . That word's good . . . and this is going to be my expression . . . No way will I forget this . . .'

May God let him perform as he imagines! And Lord, how his heart began to pound—hearing her come—and how he sighed, breathing quickly! And Pandarus, who was leading her along by the hem of her clothes, came close, and peeped in round the bedcurtains, and said:

'God cure all sick folk! See who's come here to visit you! Look, here she is who's to blame for your death!'

At that it seemed as though he almost wept.

'Aah . . . ! Aaagh . . . !' cried Troilus so pitifully, 'O almighty God, you know whether I'm in a sad way! . . . Who's there? . . . I can't see exactly.'

'Sir,' said Criseyde, 'it's Pandarus and I.'

'You, sweet heart? Alas, I can't get out of bed to kneel down and honour you in some way—' and he raised himself up, and just then she gently laid both her hands upon him:

'Oh, for the love of God, don't do this for me,' said she. 'Ah, what does this mean? Sir, I've come to you for two reasons: first, to thank you, and also I want to beg you for your continued support and protection.'

Hearing his lady beseech him for his protection, Troilus went into a state neither dead nor alive, and out of embarrassment could not say a word in reply, even if his head should have been struck off. But Lord, how red he suddenly became, and Sir, his prepared speech, to entreat her with—that he thought he knew—had run clean through his mind! [84]

Criseyde observed all this well enough, for she was understanding, and loved him none the less, even though he was not presumptuous, nor too self-assured, nor too bold in using flattering words.* But, if I can keep up my rhymes, I shall tell you (as old books teach)* what he said when he to some extent got over his embarrassment. In altered voice (precisely because of his sheer dread), which voice also trembled . . . with his manner becomingly abashed as well . . . his complexion now flushed, now pale . . . with lowered gaze and humbly submissive expression . . . see! the very first word that escaped him to Criseyde, his dear lady, was twice:

'Mercy, mercy, sweet heart!'

And he stopped for a while, and when he could bring anything out his next word was:

'God knows that, in so far as I have had any understanding at all, I have been entirely yours, God save me, and shall be until I, miserable wretch, am buried! And though I neither dare nor know how to make my lament to you, I certainly don't suffer any the less pain. This much for the present, O most womanly of women, I am able to express and, if this displease you, I shall soon avenge it upon my own life, I think, and bring relief to your heart, if your anger can be appeased by my death. But since you have heard me say something, now I don't care how soon I die.' [112]

To have seen his manly sorrow then might have made a heart of stone to feel pity;* and Pandarus wept as if he would turn to water,* and prodded his niece repeatedly, and said:

'It's true hearts that feel sorrow! For the love of God, make an end of this business, or kill both of us before you go!'

'Ah, what?' said she, 'upon my word, by God, I don't know what you want me to say.'

'Ah, what?' said he, 'that you have pity on him, for the love of God, and don't let him die!'

'Now then,' said she, 'I'd like to ask him to tell me the object of his intentions. I've never yet quite known what he did mean.'

'What do I mean, O sweet, dear heart?' said Troilus. 'O excellent, pure, noble one, that with the beams of your bright eyes you would sometimes look at me in a friendly way, and then agree that—without a trace of wrongdoing in any way—I may be the one who is always to do you faithful service, as to my own lady and chief source of help, with all my intelligence and all my diligence; and that I should have—exactly as you please, and subject to your rule—such comfort as is appropriate to however I have offended, such as death, if I disobey your prohibition; and that you grant me so great an honour as to command me to do anything at any hour; and that I should be your loyal, humble, and true servant, discreet and patient in my sufferings, and to be always freshly and newly desirous to be of service, and to be always equally diligent, and well receive your every wish quite entirely with good will, however painful to me it may be—you see, this is what I mean, my own sweet heart!' [147]

'Well,' said Pandarus, 'there's a hard request—and reasonable—for a lady to refuse! Now, my niece, by the feast of Jupiter, god of nativities,* if I were a god you would die very quickly, when you hear very well that this man desires nothing but your honour, and see him nearly die, and are so reluctant to let him serve you.'

With that she turned her look towards him very gently and modestly, considering to herself, and, without a word, she did not hurry too fast, but then said to him quietly:

'Without prejudice to my honour, and in such form as he has just set forth, I'm truly willing to receive him fully into my service, imploring him, for the love of God and in honour of faithfulness and nobility that, as I mean well, he would also mean well towards me, and always safeguard my honour with judgement and diligence; and indeed, if I can make him happy from now on, I'll not hold back. Now please get completely well again! Don't go on with your lamenting any longer! But nevertheless, I give you this warning,' said she, 'although you may be a king's son, indeed, you shall have no more sovereignty over me in love than is right in that case. Nor will I refrain, if you go wrong, from getting angry with you; and, while you serve me, I'll hold you just as dear as you deserve. And briefly, dear heart and my very own knight, be happy and enjoy life again, and I'll truly, with all my strength, turn all your bitter sufferings into sweetness. If I am the woman who can make you happy, you shall have happiness to compensate for every sorrow,' and took him in her arms and began to kiss him. [182]

Pandarus fell on his knees and threw up his eyes to heaven, and held his hands up high:*

'Immortal god,' said he, 'who cannot die—I mean Cupid—you may glory in this! And Venus, you may make music! It seems to me that, because of this marvel, I can hear every bell in the town ring of its own accord!* But stop! No more of this subject for the present, because they'll be coming back up here straightaway, when they've read that letter. Listen! I can hear them. But I urge you Criseyde, and you too, Troilus, when you're able to walk, to be at my house when I tell you, for I'll make all the arrangements for you to come, and there let your hearts find some relief, right enough! And let's see which of you will take first place* in speaking well of love'—with that he laughed—'because there you'll have an opportunity to talk!'

'How long must I wait before this happens?' said Troilus.

'When you can get up,' said Pandarus, 'this whole thing will be exactly as I describe to you.'

With that, Helen and Deiphebus too were coming up, just at the end of the stairs. And Lord, how Troilus then began to groan, so as to deceive his brother and sister! [207]

'It's time we left,' said Pandarus. 'My niece, take your leave of all these three people, and let them talk, and come away with me.'

She took her leave of them in a very becoming way, as she well knew how, and they certainly paid their respects to her unreservedly, and, when she had gone, spoke wonderfully well of her, in praise of her excellent qualities. It was a joy to hear them commend her composure, her understanding, and her bearing.

Now let her proceed to her own place, and let us turn back to Troilus, who very quickly glanced over the letter that Deiphebus had seen in the garden; and he would gladly have got rid of Helen and Deiphebus, so said that he wished to sleep and rest after talking. Helen kissed him and quickly took her leave, Deiphebus also, and everyone went home; and, as fast as he could go, Pandarus then made a bee line back to Troilus. And in a jolly mood he lay on a mattress on the floor beside Troilus for the whole of that happy night in order to chat; and they were glad that they were together. [231]

When everyone had left* except the two of them, and all the doors were shut tight—to tell it briefly, without more words—Pandarus got up without any delay, and sat down on his bedside, and began to speak to Troilus in a sober manner, as I shall relate to you:

'My most beloved lord and dear brother, God knows, and you know, that it upset me so badly when I saw you languishing so this year* for love—and your unhappiness over that was increasing all the time—that I, with all my know-how and all my might, have been busy ever since to bring you to happiness from that distress. Now I've brought matters to such a state of affairs as you know, so that through me you're likely to be successful. I don't say it as a boast—and do you know why? I'm ashamed to say it! For you I've begun to play a game which I'll never do again for any one else, even if he

were my brother a thousand times over. That's to say, for you I've
become—half in jest, and half in earnest—the sort of go-between
who makes women come to men . . . Even if I say nothing, you know
very well what I mean . . . For you, I've made my innocent niece
trust so completely in your nobility of character, that everything will
be exactly as you wish. [259]

'But I take God, who knows everything, to witness that I never
did this out of any desire for gain, but only to cut short that dis-
tress from which, as it seemed to me, you were nearly dying. But,
good brother, do now as you ought to do, for the love of God, and
keep her out of any disgrace, since you are prudent, and always safe-
guard her good name. For you well know that among the people her
name as yet is—as one might say—held sacred. For I'd dare take an
oath that the man is still unborn, who ever knew she did anything
wrong. But it makes me very unhappy that I, who am the cause of
all this, may think that she is my dear niece, and I at once both her
uncle and her betrayer!* If it were known that through my con-
trivance I had put this inclination to do your pleasure and be wholly
yours into my niece's head—why! the whole world would cry out
against it, and say that in this I committed the worst treachery that
was ever begun, and that she was utterly ruined, and you had gained
nothing at all. And so, before I'll go a step further, I beg you again,
even if you should die for it, that secrecy accompany us in this affair—
that's to say, that you never give us away. And don't be angry though
I often ask you to keep secret such an important affair, for you well
know that my request is reasonable. [287]

'Think what unhappiness has occurred before now because of the
making of boasts, as people read; and what misfortune there still is
in this world from day to day, precisely because of that wicked act.
For that reason, wise scholars now dead have always expressed them-
selves in proverbs to us young folk* that: "The first virtue is to hold
one's tongue."* If it weren't that I now wish to cut short any long-
winded speech, I could cite to you almost a thousand old stories of
women ruined through falsehood and fools' boasting. You know enough
proverbs yourself, and you know enough against that vice, to be a
tell-tale, even if men spoke the truth as often as they talk idly. Often
before now, alas, one tongue has caused many a radiant lady to have
said "Alas the day that I was born!" and renewed many a young girl's
sorrow. For the most part, if it were put to the test, everything that

men boast about is untrue. By nature no boaster is to be believed. A boaster and a liar are the same thing. For example: suppose that a woman grants me her love, and says that she'll have no one else, and I'm sworn to keep it secret, and afterwards I go and tell it to two or three people—to be sure, I'm at least a boaster, and a liar, because I'm breaking my promise. Now just think then whether they aren't to blame, such sort of people—what shall I call them? what?—who boast about women, and by name, who never yet promised them anything, nor knew them any more than my old hat? It's no wonder—as God may send me health—though women are afraid to have any dealings with us men! I'm not saying this out of any distrust of you or of any man of sense, but because of silly fools,* and because of the harm arising in the world nowadays, often as much from folly as from malice. For I well know that no woman is afraid of that fault in people of sense, if she has thought it over; because the wise take warning from fools' misfortune.* [329]

'But now to the point, dear, dear brother: keep in mind everything that I've said, and keep things to yourself, and now be in good spirits, because on the day you'll find me true. I'll set up the proceedings in such a way—as God is my witness—that you'll be satisfied, because it'll be exactly as you'd have it. For I know you mean well, by God, and for that reason I dare to assert this so fully. You know too what your lady granted you, and a day is set for exchanging contracts!* Goodnight now—I can't stay awake any longer. And since you're now in bliss, pray for me that God soon send me either death or happiness!' [343]

Who could tell half the joy or jubilation that the soul of Troilus then felt, hearing the essence of Pandarus' promise? His old unhappiness, that made his heart grow faint, then wasted and melted away for joy, and all his store of bitter sighs fled away at once—he felt them no longer. Just as woods and hedgerows, that have been dead and dry in winter, clothe themselves in green again when it is May, when everyone who is full of the joys of life most likes to have fun—just in the selfsame way, to tell the truth, his heart suddenly became full of joy, so that there was never a happier man in Troy. And he raised his look to Pandarus in a very grave but friendly way, and said:

'My friend, you'll remember—as you know very well—how near to dying from unhappiness you found me in April last,* and how you did all you could to discover from me the cause of my distress.

You know how long I held back from telling it to you, who are the man I most trust; and—as I well know—there was no danger in revealing it to you. But tell me, if you would: since I was so reluctant that you should know of it, how would I dare tell others about this matter—I who am trembling now, when no one can hear us? [371]

'But nevertheless, by that God who may govern all this world as he pleases, I swear to you—and, if I lie, may Achilles cleave my heart* with his spear, even though my life were eternal, as I am mortal, if I early or late would disclose it, or would dare to, or would be able to, for all the wealth that God created under the sun—that I would rather die and come to an end, as it seems to me, in the stocks in prison, in wretchedness, in filth, and among vermin, captive to cruel King Agamemnon! And I will swear this to you upon all the gods in all the temples of this town tomorrow morning, if you would care to hear it. And I know very well that you have done so much for me that I can't ever deserve it, even if I could now die for you a thousand times in a day. I can't say any more, except that— wherever you go—I will serve you just as your slave forever more, until the end of my life! [392]

'But here I beg you with all my heart that you never suppose such insanity in me as I'll now describe. You talk as if I might think that what you're doing for me out of friendship was pimping. I'm not mad, even if I'm ignorant! It's not so—I well know that, by God! But he who goes on such an errand for gold or riches—call him what you like; and what you're doing, call it nobility, compassion, friendliness, and trust. Differentiate things* like that, for it's very widely known how a distinction needs to be made between similar things, as I've learned. And so that you know I in no way think this service is anything to be ashamed of or laughed at, there's my lovely sister Polyxena, Cassandra, Helen, or any of the company—however beautiful or shapely she is, tell me which one of them you want to have for your own, and then leave the rest to me! But since you've done me this service, to save my life and not in any hope of reward, then see through this great enterprise to the end, for the love of God, because my greatest need is now! For I'll undoubtedly always obey all your commands in every respect. Goodnight now, and let's both sleep.' [420]

Thus each considered himself so well satisfied with the other that the whole world could not have improved upon it; and next day, when they were up and dressed, each attended to his own affairs. But though Troilus burned like fire with sharp desire of hope and pleasure, he did not forget his fine self-control, but manfully restrained in himself every hasty action and every uncontrolled look, so that—to tell the truth—not a living soul would have known from his words or from his manner what was in his mind regarding this matter. He was as distant from everyone as the clouds, so well could he dissemble. And this was the life he led during the whole time that I am telling you about: by day, with all his might, he was in the lofty service of Mars—that is to say, in arms as a knight; and for the greater part of the long night, he lay and thought how he might best serve his lady, in order to deserve her gratitude. I will not swear that, although he lay very comfortably, he was not somewhat troubled in his thoughts, or that he did not turn often on his pillows, and wish to be in possession of what he lacked. But in such cases, for all I know, people do not find pleasure all the time, and no more did he then; I can imagine that to be a possibility! [448]

But, to come to the point, it is certain that during this time, as is written in the story,* he saw his lady sometimes, and she also spoke with him when she dared or pleased; and in the judgement of both of them, as was best, they decided very prudently, as far as they dared, how they would proceed in this affair. But everything was spoken so briefly, and always in such watchfulness and in such fear, in case anyone should be suspicious or conjecture about the two of them, or overhear anything, that this whole world was less precious to them than Cupid's sending them the grace to carry their conversation to a conclusion. But in the little that they did speak or do, his wise spirit always paid such heed to everything, that it seemed to her he knew what she thought without a word being spoken, so that there was no need to ask him to do anything, or to forbid anything; and so she thought that love, even if it came late, had opened the gate of all happiness to her. [469]

And to pass briefly over this sequence of events: he so well employed his words and efforts that he found so much favour with his lady that, before she would stop, she thanked God twenty thousand times that she ever met with Troilus. He could so conduct himself in such love-service that the whole world could not imagine anything better. For she found him so circumspect in everything, so discreet, and so obedient to her wishes, that she felt indeed he was a wall of steel to her, and a shield against everything disagreeable, such that she was no longer afraid (so prudent was he) to be subject to his excellent guidance—I mean, as far as ought to be expected in such a case. And Pandarus was always invariably prompt and diligent to quicken the fire; all his desire was set on helping his friend. He always pressed on; he was sent to and fro; he carried letters when Troilus was absent, such that no man ever conducted himself better than he did in his friend's time of need, without a doubt. [490]

But now perhaps someone would expect me to rehearse Troilus' every word, or message, or look, or expression to his dear lady during all this time—I think it would be a very long thing to listen to! —or to describe in detail all the words and every look of whatever person that was in such a plight. In truth, I have not heard of it being done before now in any story—and nor has anyone here, I believe. And even if I wanted to, I certainly could not, for there was some letter between them that would, as my author says,* take up nearly half this book, of which he did not wish to write. How then am I to compose a line of it? [504]

But to the main point! For Criseyde and Troilus, being (as I have described) in harmony and in quietness during this sweet time, save only that they could not often meet or have leisure to finish their conversations, things then happened* exactly as I shall tell you: for Pandarus, who continually applied himself precisely to the end that I shall speak of here (namely, to bring his lovely niece and Troilus together some night at his house, where at leisure all this high affair concerning their love might be fully concluded) had certainly found the right time for it. For with great deliberation he had planned and carried out everything that might be of help in this matter, and had left nothing undone because of trouble or expense. If they wished to come, they should lack for nothing; and as for being discovered there in any way—that, he well knew, was an impossibility. Without a doubt, it was downwind from every tell-tale magpie* and every spoilsport. Now all is well, for the whole world is blind in this matter. This timber frame* is all ready to set up; the only thing we are lacking is to know a definite time at which she is to come. [532]

And Troilus (who knew everything about all this preparation, and was on tenterhooks in readiness) had also made his arrangements in this matter and devised his pretext and his plans accordingly—if he were missed by day or night whilst he was about this love-service

—that he had gone to perform a sacrifice, and must keep vigil alone at such and such a temple, in order to receive an answer from Apollo, and be first to see the sacred laurel tremble before Apollo spoke from the tree, to tell him when the Greeks should next retreat.—And therefore let no man hinder him, God forbid, but pray to Apollo to help in this hour of need! [546]

Little more remains to be done now, but Pandarus got up and, to put it briefly, very soon after the changing of the moon, when the world is lightless* for a night or two, and the sky looked like rain, he went to his niece first thing in the morning—you have already heard the object of his intention. When he arrived he at once began to play about, as he was accustomed to do, and to tell jokes against himself; and in the end he swore by one thing and another and said to her that she should not evade him or make him run around after her any longer; but she must certainly, by her leave, come and dine with him at his house that evening. At which she laughed and quickly excused herself and said:

'It's raining, look! How can I go?'

'Enough of this!' said he. 'Don't stand around like this, musing what to do. You've got to come! You'll be there in no time!'

So in the end they came to an agreement about this, or else, he softly swore to her in her ear, he would never visit her again. Soon after this she began to whisper to him, and asked him if Troilus would be there? No, he swore to her, for he was out of town, and said:

'Supposing he were, niece, you wouldn't need to be any more afraid; for I'd rather die a thousand times than that people should notice him there.' [574]

My author does not care to state in full* what she thought—as to whether he was telling the truth about it or not—when he said that Troilus had gone out of town; only that she agreed to go with him without delay, since he requested that of her and, as his niece, obeyed as she ought to do. Nevertheless, she still begged him—although there was nothing to fear in going with him—to beware of silly people's talk, who dream up things which never were, and consider carefully whom he brought there; and said to him:

'Uncle, since I must trust you,* make sure everything is all right, and now do as you please.'

Yes (he swore to her), by stocks and stones,* and by the gods that dwell in heaven, or else he would rather, soul and bones, be as deep in hell with King Pluto as Tantalus!*—What more should I say? When everything was all right, he got up and took his leave, and she came to supper in the evening, with a certain number of her own men, and with her lovely niece Antigone, and nine or ten other of her women. [598]

But who was happy now, who, do you think, but Troilus, who stood and could see everything through a little window, closeted as he was in a small room,* where he had been cooped up in hiding since midnight, unbeknown to everyone except Pandarus? But to the point! When she arrived, Pandarus at once took her in his arms in the happiest and friendliest way, and when it was time they sat down afterwards very comfortably to supper, one and all. God knows, there was no delicacy lacking! And after supper they got up, well content, and at heart full of life and gaiety; and he was a lucky man who could best contrive to please her, or who made her laugh: he sang; she played; he told the tale of Wade.* But at last, as everything comes to an end, she took her leave and must be going home. [616]

But O Fortune, executrix of the fates!* O influences of the high heavens! True it is that, under God, you are our shepherds, though the causes are concealed from us creatures. This is my meaning here: for she was about to hurry homewards, but the gods' will was carried out quite without her consent, because of which she must remain. The crescent moon with her pale horns, Saturn, and Jupiter* were in conjunction in the sign of Cancer, so that such a downpour fell from the heavens that every sort of woman that was there had a real fear of that smoky rain—at which Pandarus laughed, and then said:

'Now's a fine time for a lady to be leaving! But dear niece, if I ever pleased you in any way, then I beg you now,' he said, 'to give me the great pleasure of staying here overnight with me, because this is your own house, by God! For upon my word—and I'm not joking—it would shame me if you left right now.'

Criseyde, who had as much good sense as half the world together, took heed of his request; and since it was pouring and everything was flooded, she thought:

'I might as well remain here, and agree to it gladly in a friendly manner, and be thanked for it, as grumble and then stay. For as to going home, that's just not going to happen.'

'I will stay,' said she, 'my dear, dear uncle. Since it's your wish, it's only reasonable that I should. I'm very happy to stay here with you. I was only joking when I said I'd go.'

'Thank you, niece, to be sure,' he then said. 'Whether you were joking or not, to tell the truth, I'm happy now, since you want to stay.' [651]

So all is well, and then the whole party started up again right away, with renewed pleasure. But if he could decently have done so, Pandarus would gladly have hurried her to bed, and said:

'Lord, this is a huge downpour! This is weather to sleep through —and my advice is that we begin on that soon! And niece, do you know where I'll have you sleep, so that we shan't be far apart and so that, I dare say, you won't hear any noise of rain or thunder either? By God, in my little room* right over there. And in that outer room I alone will be guardian of all your women. And in this middle chamber that you see, your women will sleep comfortably and well; and you yourself will be where I said. And if you sleep well tonight, come often, and don't trouble about what the weather is doing.—The wine, at once!*—And whenever you're ready, let's go to bed. I think it's for the best.' [672]

There is no more to say; but soon after this, when nightcaps had been drunk and curtains drawn, everyone who had no further business there went out of the room. And all the while it rained so violently and blew so amazingly loudly as well, that people could hardly hear each other speak. Then her uncle Pandarus, exactly as he ought to do, with such women as were closest to her, very gladly escorted her to her bedside, and took his leave, bowing very low, and said:

'All your women will be sleeping outside this chamber door here, directly opposite, so that you can call whichever one of them you want.'

So when she had gone to bed in the inner room, and all her women were in bed as arranged, where I have said, there was no more skipping or tramping about, but if anyone was stirring anywhere he was ordered to go to bed, curse him! and let those who were in bed get to sleep. [693]

But when he saw that everything was fine, Pandarus—who knew the old game* completely, every detail of it—thought he would begin his work. He softly undid the door to Troilus' little room, silently sat down beside him without more delay, and briefly (to come straight to the point) he told him everything about this from beginning to end, and said:

'Get ready at once, for you're about to enter heavenly bliss!'

'Now, blessed Venus, send me grace!' said Troilus, 'for I never had such need for it before now, nor half the fear!'

'Don't be a bit afraid,' said Pandarus, 'because it'll be exactly as you'd like it. As I hope to thrive, I'll make things go well tonight, or make a complete mess* of everything.'

'Inspire me tonight, blessed Venus,' said Troilus, 'as surely as I serve you and ever shall do, better and better, until I die! O joyful Venus, if at the time of my birth* I was subject to evil influences from the planets Mars and Saturn, or if your influence were then rendered powerless by the sun, or otherwise hindered, pray to your father, of his grace, to deflect any harmful influences, so that I may be happy again, for love of him you loved in the woods—I mean Adonis,* who was slain by the boar! O help now Jove,* too, for the love of fair Europa,* whom you carried off in the form of a bull! O Mars, you with your bloody cloak, for the love of Cyprian Venus, don't you hinder me! O Phoebus, think of how Daphne* shut herself under the bark and out of fear turned into a laurel tree—yet, for love of her, O help me now at this time of need! Now Mercury, help too, for love of Herse (over which Pallas was angry with Aglauros)!* And Diana,* too, I implore you not to be displeased with this enterprise! O fatal sisters,* who spun me my destiny before any clothes were made for me, now help with this piece of work that has begun!'

'You miserable mouse's heart!' said Pandarus. 'Are you scared she'll bite you? Why! Throw this fur-lined cloak over your shirt and follow me, because I'll take the blame. Wait, let me go a little in front.'
[740]

And so saying, he began to undo a trapdoor, and led Troilus in by the hem of his clothes.* The high wind was roaring so loudly that no one could hear any other noise, and those who were in bed outside the door all slept very soundly. And with a very serious expression Pandarus at once went over without delay to the door where they lay, and quietly shut it. And as he was coming back again stealthily, his niece woke up and asked:

'Who's there?'

'My dear niece,' he said, 'it is I! Don't be surprised, and don't be frightened!'

And he came up close and whispered in her ear:

'Not a word, for the love of God, I beg you! Don't let anyone get up and hear us talking!'

'Why, bless us! Which way did you come in?' said she. 'And how, without any of them knowing?'

'Here at this secret trapdoor,' he said.

'Let me call someone!' Criseyde then said.

'Ah, God forbid you should do anything so crazy!' said Pandarus. 'They might imagine something they never thought before . . . It's not a good idea to wake sleeping dogs, nor to give anyone a cause for conjecture. I guarantee your women are all asleep—so that, for all they know, men could be undermining the house—and they'll sleep until the sun shines. And when I've finished what I have to say I'll leave just as undetected as I came. [770]

'Now, my niece, you must understand,' said he, 'as all you women suppose, that for a woman to play a man along in love with false hopes, and call him her "dear one" and "dear heart", and be two-timing him—I mean, be loving another all the while—she deceives him and shames herself. Now why am I telling you all this? You know yourself, as well as anyone, how your love is completely granted to Troilus, the worthiest knight in this world, and your loyalty is pledged to him, such that, unless it were his fault, you would never betray him for as long as you live. Now the situation is this. Since I left you, to speak bluntly, Troilus has come in all this rain via a secret route, by a gutter,* into my room, unbeknown to everyone except myself, indeed, as I hope to be happy, and by that loyalty I owe to Priam of Troy! And he's come in such torment and distress that, if he's not quite mad by now, he must quickly sink into madness, without God's help! And the reason why is this: he says he's been told by a friend of his how you're said to love someone called Orestes*—and for sorrow over that, this night will be his last!' [798]

As she listened to this whole astonishing story, Criseyde felt a sudden chill around her heart, and with a sigh she sorrowfully replied:

'Alas, I would have thought that—whoever told tales—my dear heart wouldn't so easily think me unfaithful! Alas, mistaken imaginings, what harm they do—for now I've lived too long! Orestes, alas?

And betray Troilus? I don't know him, so help me God!' said she. 'Alas, what wicked spirit* told him such a thing? Now certainly, uncle, if I see him tomorrow, I'll excuse myself as completely of this matter as a woman ever did, if he likes,' and with these words she sighed very bitterly. [812]

'O God,'* said she, 'how worldly happiness, which scholars call "false felicity", is intermingled with much bitterness! God knows,' she said, 'the condition of vain prosperity is very painful: for either joys don't come together, or else no one has them here continuously. O fragile good fortune of man's unstable joy! Whatever person you're with, or however you play things, either he knows that you, joy, are changeable, or he doesn't know it—it must be one of the two. Now if he doesn't know it, how can he say that he has true joy and happiness, who is always in the darkness of ignorance? And if he knows that joy is transient, as every joy in worldly things must pass away, then every time he remembers that, the fear of loss affects him so that he can't be in perfect happiness; and if he doesn't care a bit* about losing his joy, then it seems that joy is worth very little. And so I will conclude on this subject that truly, as far as I can discern, there is no true happiness here in this world. But O jealousy, you wicked serpent, you misbelieving and envious madness, why have you made Troilus distrustful of me, who never yet did him any wrong that I know of?' [840]

'That's how things stand,' Pandarus said.

'Why, uncle?' said she. 'Who told him this? Alas! Why is my sweet heart acting like this?'

'You know, to be sure, dear niece,' said he, 'what it is. I hope everything that's gone wrong will turn out all right, for you can put an end to all this, if you want—and do just that, because I think it's the best thing.'

'I'll do so tomorrow, for sure,' said she, 'and so that it will be more than enough, as God is my witness!'

'Tomorrow?! Alas, that'd be a fine thing!' said he. 'No, no, things can't stay like this, dear niece, because wise scholars write to this effect, that "Danger is introduced by delay". No, such delays aren't worth a bean.* There's a time for everything,* niece, I venture to say. For when a room is on fire, or a hall, there's more need to save it promptly than to argue, and ask everyone how that candle fell into the straw! Ah, bless us, because while all that's going on, the bird has flown,* and the damage is done! And my niece—don't take this badly—if you let him remain in this misery all night, God help me, you never loved him! I dare to say that, now there's just the two of us. But I know very well that you won't do so. You're too sensible to do anything so insane as to put his life at risk all night.' [868]

'I never loved him? By God, I think you never loved anything so much!' said she.

'Now, upon my word,' said he, 'we'll see about that! Since you make this example of me: if I'd keep him in sorrow all night, for all the treasure in the town of Troy, I pray God I may never be happy! Now look: if you, who are his love, will put his life at risk all night for no reason, then, by that God above, this delay stems not only from folly but from malice, if I'm not going to tell any lies! What! To be blunt, if you let him remain in distress, you're acting neither kindly nor well.'

'Will you do one thing,' Criseyde then said, 'and with that you'll put an end to all his distress? Take this blue ring* and give it to him, for there's nothing that might please him better—except I myself—nor soothe his feelings more. And tell my dear heart that his sorrow is causeless—he'll see that tomorrow.' [889]

'A ring?!' said he. 'Fiddlesticks!* Yes, niece, that ring would need a stone that could make dead men alive again*—and I don't believe you have such a ring. Good sense has gone clean out of your head. I feel that now,' said he, 'and that's a pity. O lost time, you may well curse slothfulness!* Don't you know very well that a high and noble nature neither grieves, nor stops grieving, for any little thing? If a fool were in a jealous temper, I wouldn't care a jot about his sorrows, but bestow a few white lies upon him another day, when I happened to see him. But this matter is of an altogether different kind. This man is so noble and so tenderhearted that he will make up for his sorrows with his own death. For believe me, however much he may be suffering, he won't say any jealous words* to you. And so, niece, before his heart breaks, do speak to him yourself about this matter, for you can steer his feelings with a single word. Now I've told you what danger he's in, and his coming here is unknown to everyone; nor can there be any harm or wrong in it, by God— I'll be with you myself all night. You know too how he is your own knight, and that by rights you should trust him, and I'm ready to fetch him when you like.' [917]

This incident was so touching to hear, and so like the truth too, on the face of it . . . and Troilus, her knight, so dear to her . . . his secret coming, and the secure place . . . that, all things considered, it is no wonder that she then granted him a favour, since she did everything for the best.

'How sorry I am for him, God rest my soul!' Criseyde replied. 'And uncle, indeed, I'd gladly act for the best, if I had the grace to do so. But, whether you stay here or go and fetch him, till God lets me see things more clearly I am on the horns of a dilemma,* and absolutely at my wits' end!'

'Yes, niece, will you listen to me?' said Pandarus. 'In geometry a "dilemma" is called "banishment of wretches". It seems hard, because wretches won't learn, through sheer laziness or other wilful faults, and this is said of those who aren't worth two beans.* But you are wise, and what we are concerned with is neither difficult, nor reasonable to resist.'

'Then, uncle,' said she, 'do as you please about this. But first, before he comes in, I'll get up. And for the love of God, since I'm placing my whole trust in the two of you, and you are both wise, act now in so discreet a way that I may have honour and he pleasure—for I am entirely guided by you here.'

'That's well said,' said he, 'my dear niece. Bless that wise and noble heart! But don't get up! You can receive him right here—there's no need for you to move on account of him. And may each of you ease the other's painful sadness, for the love of God! And Venus, I praise you! For I hope we'll all be happy soon!' [952]

Very soon Troilus was kneeling down most solemnly just by her bed's head, greeting his lady in his best fashion. But Lord, how red* she suddenly became! All at once—even if she were to have been beheaded—she could not get a word out properly, because of his coming in suddenly. But Pandarus, whose feelings in everything were so acute, at once began to play about and said:

'Niece, look how this lord can kneel! Now, upon your word, look at this noble man,' and with that word he ran for a cushion and said: 'Kneel now, for as long as you want—may God soon set your hearts at rest!'

I cannot say—because she did not ask him to get up—if sorrow put it out of her mind, or if she took it in the way of something due to her, as part of his proper observance towards her as a lover. But

I do find that she did him this favour: that she kissed him, although she sighed deeply, and without more ado asked him to sit down.

'This is a good start!' said Pandarus. 'Now, good, dear niece, have him sit on the side of your bed, right inside the bedcurtains there, so that each of you can hear the other better.' And with those words he withdrew towards the fire, and took a light, and assumed the appearance of looking at an old romance. [980]

Criseyde felt herself to be Troilus' true lady and on sure ground—although she thought her servant and her knight rightfully should not have suspected any faithlessness in her. Yet nevertheless, considering his distress, and that love is the reason for such folly, she spoke to him like this about his jealousy:

'You see, my heart, because the excellence of love would have it so, against which no one can (nor should, either) properly put up any resistance . . . and also because I felt and saw your great loyalty and service every day . . . and that your heart was completely mine, to tell the truth—this drove me to have pity on your suffering. And, my dear heart and my own knight, I thank you as much as I know how—even if I can't as much as were right—for the goodness that I've always found in you up to now. And I—to the limit of my ability and my strength, however painful to me it may be—have been and always shall be completely true to you, and wholly yours with all my heart, and doubtless that will be proved when tried and tested. [1002]

'But, my heart, I'll certainly say what all this is about, provided that you don't take offence, though I complain about you to your face, because by doing so I mean to put an end, finally and completely, to the suffering that keeps us both sad at heart, and to put right all that's wrong. My very own one, I don't know why or how that wicked viper, jealousy, has crept into you like this without cause, alas, and I'd gladly get rid of the harm it does. How sad that the whole or even a sliver of jealousy should have its refuge in so fine a place—may Jove soon root it out of your heart! [1015]

'But O Jove,* O author of nature, is this an honour to your godhead, that innocent people suffer injury, and he who is guilty goes scot-free? O, if it were legitimate to bring a complaint against you, who permit undeserved jealousy, I would complain of you and cry out against you about that! And my whole unhappiness is this: that people are now accustomed to say, just like this, "Yes, jealousy is love!'"* and would excuse a whole bushel of venom because one grain of love is dropped into it! But the great God who sits above knows if it is more like love, or hate, or anger, and it ought to be named according to that. But it's certain that one kind of jealousy is more excusable than another, indeed, as when there is a reason, and some such delusion of this kind is so well and dutifully suppressed that it scarcely does or says anything amiss but nobly drinks up all its cup of distress*—and that I excuse, for the nobleness of it. And some jealousy is so full of fury and spite that it overwhelms all attempts at restraint. But, my heart, you're not in that state—I thank God for that—and so I'll call this suffering of yours nothing but an illusion, caused by abundance of love and anxious care, that makes your heart suffer all this distress. I'm very sorry, but not angry. But as my duty, and to put your mind at rest—for the love of God—it's for the best to let it be put to the test, wherever and however you please, whether through trial by ordeal, or by oath, or by the drawing of lots.* And if I'm guilty, put me to death! Alas, what more can I do or say?' With that a few bright, fresh tears fell from her eyes, and she said: 'Now God, you know that Criseyde was never yet untrue to Troilus in thought or deed!' [1054]

With that she laid her head down in the bed, and covered it with the sheet, and sighed bitterly, and held her peace—not one more word did she speak. But now may God help to put an end to all this sorrow! And so I hope he will, for he best can! For after a very misty morning I have often seen follow a pleasant summer's day, and after winter follows verdant May. People see all the time, and also read in stories, how after fierce assaults come victories.* [1064]

When Troilus heard her words, don't worry, he had no wish to sleep! For to hear or see his lady Criseyde weep seemed to him not merely like the blows of a rod; but indeed, for every tear that escaped her, he felt creep around his heart the cramp of death, which clutched at his heart. And in his mind he began to curse the time that he came there, and the hour he was born, for now bad had turned into worse, and he imagined all that work he had done before was wasted. He thought he was all but lost.

'O Pandarus,' he thought, 'alas, your wiles are no use at all—what an awful moment this is!'

And thereupon he hung his head, and fell to his knees, and sighed sorrowfully. What could he say? He felt he was as good as dead, for she who alone could lighten his sorrows was angry. But nevertheless, when he could speak, he then said:

'God knows that, if the truth be known, I'm not to blame for all this!'

At that, sorrow shut his heart so tightly that not a tear fell from his eyes, and each of the spirits* contracted into itself and stopped functioning, as if they were stunned or overcome. He lost all feeling of his sorrow, or his fear, or anything else, and very suddenly fell down in a faint.* It was no small sorrow to see this, but all was hushed, and Pandarus was up in a trice:

'O niece, keep quiet, or we're ruined!' said he. 'Don't be afraid!'

But certainly, in the end, one way or another, he threw Troilus into bed, and said:

'O you wretch! Call this being a man?'—and he tore off everything down to his shirt, and said:

'Niece, unless you help us now, alas, your own Troilus is done for!'

'I certainly would, very gladly, if only I knew how!' said she. 'How I wish I'd never been born!'

'Yes, niece, but will you pull out the thorn* that's been sticking in his heart?' said Pandarus. 'Say "All's forgiven!" and all this fuss will be over!'

'Yes,' said she, 'I'd rather have that than all the goods under the sun!'

And with that she swore into Troilus' ear:

'My dear heart, I'm certainly not angry, I give you my word!'—and many another oath. 'Now speak to me, for it is I, Criseyde!' [1112]

But all in vain; he still did not come to. Then they began to rub his wrists and the palms of his hands and to wet his temples; and, to release him from this bitter constraint, she often kissed him. To put it briefly, she did all she could to revive him. At last he began to draw breath, and soon after that he came round from his swoon, and his consciousness and his reason were restored to him. But he felt abashed—incredibly deeply so, in fact—and with a sigh, when he came round, he said:

'O mercy, God, what's all this?'

'Why are you behaving so strangely?' Criseyde then said. 'Is this any way for a man to behave? For shame, Troilus, why are you acting like this?'

And with that she laid her arm over him, and forgave him every-thing, and often kissed him. He thanked her, and spoke to her, and said what was to the purpose for his peace of mind; and she replied to that as she pleased, and cheered him up with her pleasing words, and often comforted his sorrows.

'As far as I can see,' said Pandarus, 'neither this light nor I are serving any useful purpose here. Light isn't good for sick folk's eyes! But, for the love of God, since you've been brought to such a good situation as this, don't let any gloomy thoughts be hanging over the two of you now!'—and carried the candle away to the fireplace. [1141]

Soon after this, when she had made Troilus take such oaths as she cared to devise (although there was no need for it), there did not then seem to her any reason to be frightened, nor any reason either to ask him to get up from there. Yet a lesser thing than oaths can be enough in many cases, for I imagine everyone who loves well intends only what is noble. But, in effect, she wanted to know at once what man he was jealous of—and also where and why—since there was no reason for it; and she also pressed him earnestly to tell her the signs that had prompted his jealousy, or else, to be sure, she accused him that this was done out of malice, to test her. Without more ado, to put it briefly, he must obey his lady's command, and—to limit the damage—he had to pretend. He said to her, when she was at such and such a festival, she might at least have looked at him—I don't know what, all worthless nonsense, like someone who has to fish about for a reason! [1162]

'My sweet,' she replied, 'even if it were so, what harm was there in that, since I mean nothing wrong? For, by that God who redeemed* both of us, my intentions in everything are innocent. Such arguments aren't worth a bean! Are you going to act like some child-ish, jealous person? Then you deserve to be spanked!'

Troilus then began to sigh sorrowfully—it seemed to him his heart was dying within him, in case she were angry—and said:

'Alas, my sweet heart, Criseyde, have mercy on my sick man's sorrows! And if there's anything wrong in the words that I said, I won't transgress any more. Do what you please. I'm completely dependent on your favour.'

'Upon guilt, mercy!' she replied. 'That's to say, that I forgive all of this. And always remember this night, and take care that you don't go wrong again!'

'No, indeed, my dear heart!' said he.

'And now,' said she, 'forgive me that I've caused you pain, my own sweet heart.'

Seized with rapture at that, Troilus put everything in God's hands, as one who meant nothing but good, and, suddenly resolved, he took her tightly to him in his arms. And Pandarus, full of good-will, lay down to sleep,* and said:

'If you're wise, don't swoon now, in case more folk get up!'

What can the hapless lark say, when the sparrowhawk has it in its talons?* I can say no more! But no matter to whom this tale be sweet or bitter,* even though I delay for a year, I must sometime, follow-ing my author, tell of the happiness of these same two, just as I have told of their misery. Criseyde, who felt herself taken like this—as scholars write in their old books—started to tremble just like an aspen leaf,* when she felt him enfold her in his arms. But Troilus, quite recovered from his chill cares, then gave thanks to the seven bright gods.* Thus various pains bring people to paradise! Troilus began to clasp her in his arms and said:

'O my sweet, for the life of me, you're caught now—there's no one now but the two of us! Now submit . . . there's no other way!'

To that Criseyde at once replied like this:

'If I hadn't, my dear, sweet heart, submitted before this, I cer-tainly wouldn't be here now!'

O, it is truly said that, to be healed of a fever or other great sick-ness, people must drink a very bitter drink,* as can often be seen; and, in order to have happiness, people often swallow pain and great distress—I mean it in this case, which has found its whole cure through pain. And now sweetness seems sweeter, because bitterness was experienced before;* for now they float out of sorrow into bliss, such as they had never felt in their lives. Now this is better than that both of them should be lost! For the love of God, let every woman take heed to act like this if the need arises! [1225]

Criseyde, quite free from all fear and trouble, as she who had just cause to trust him, made such a fuss of Troilus that it was a joy to see, when she knew of his faithfulness and pure intent; and just as the sweet honeysuckle* with many a tendril encircles and wreathes around a tree, so they entwined themselves in each other's arms. And like the suddenly startled nightingale that stops just as she is begin-ning to sing, when she hears any shepherd talk or anyone stirring in

the hedgerows, and afterwards makes her voice ring out confidently
—just so Criseyde, when her fear was over, opened her heart and told
him what was in her thoughts. And just like he who sees his death
decreed and must die, as far as he can see, when suddenly, rescue
enables him to escape, and from death he is brought to safety—for
all the world Troilus was in such present happiness, and he had his
sweet lady. God let us never meet with worse luck! [1246]

Her slender arms . . . her straight and soft back . . . her long sides,
shapely, smooth and white . . . he began to stroke them . . . and over
and again he called down blessings on her snow-white throat and
her small, round breasts. So in this heaven he delighted, and at the
same time he kissed her a thousand times, so that he hardly knew
what to do for happiness . . .

Then he declared in this way:

'O Love! O Charity! May your mother too, the sweet Cytherea,*
be praised next after yourself—I mean Venus, the benevolent planet!
—and after that I salute you, Hymen,* for never was a man
beholden to you gods as I am, whom you have brought in out of the
cold of misery. Gracious Love—you sacred binding force of things
—whoever seeks for grace and does not care to honour you, see! his
desire will be trying to fly without wings. For if you did not wish,
out of kindness, to help those who serve best and always labour most,
all would still be lost—that I dare well say indeed—unless your grace
surpassed what we deserve.* And because you have helped me (who
am the least deserving among those counted as recipients of your
grace) when I was likely to die, and have bestowed me in so high a
place* that there is no happiness more boundless—I can say no more;
but praise and reverence be to your goodness and your excellence!'
[1274]

And with that he at once kissed Criseyde, at which she certainly
felt no distress, and so he said:

'Now would to God I knew, my sweet heart, how I might please
you! What man,' said he, 'was ever so content as I, on whom the
fairest and the best I ever saw deigns to settle her heart's affections?
Here may be seen that mercy surpasses justice*—I feel that in my
own experience, who am unworthy of so sweet a person. But out of
your kindness, my love, please think that, though I may be unworthy,
still I really must improve in some respects, from the benefit of being
in your noble service. And for love of God, my dear lady, since God

has created me to serve you—by which I mean: he wishes you to be at the helm, to cause me to live, if you please, or die—then teach me how I may deserve your thanks, so that through my ignorance I do nothing to displease you. For certainly—you lovely, most womanly of women—I dare say this: that you will find me loyal and diligent all my life; nor indeed will I go against what you have forbidden; and if I do, while together or apart, for the love of God, let me be killed at that very instant, if that's what, as a woman, you would wish.' [1302]

'Indeed,' said she, 'my own heart's desire, the foundation of all my happiness and altogether my darling—thank you, for my whole reliance is on that! But let's drop this subject, because enough has been said here, and in a word, and with no second thoughts: Welcome my knight, my peace, my fulfilment!'*

To express the very least of their delight or joys would be beyond my understanding. But you who have been at such a feast of happiness, you judge whether they wanted to enjoy themselves! I can say no more, but thus these same two that night—between anxiety and assurance—experienced the great excellence of love.*

O blissful night, sought by them for so long, how joyous you were for them both! Why had I not bought such a night at the price of my own soul? Yes, or the least joy that was there! Away with you, wretched reserve and timidity! And let them remain in this heaven's bliss, that is so exalted that I cannot describe all of it! But the truth is—though I cannot tell all, as my author can, in his excellence—nevertheless, I swear before God, that I have given and shall give the substance of his meaning in everything. And if, out of respect for Love, I have added in any word for the best—do exactly as you please with that. For I utter my words, here and everywhere, under correction of you who have feeling in the art of love, and submit it completely to your judgement to increase or diminish the language I have used, and I beg you to do that. But now back to the point of what I was saying earlier. [1337]

These same two, that we left in each other's arms, were so reluctant to separate that each thought the other would be torn away, or else—and this, you see, was their greatest fear—that this whole thing was only fond dreams; for which reason each of them very often said:

'O my sweet, am I embracing you like this, or else am I dreaming it?'

And Lord, how intently he gazed at her! His look never wavered from her face, and he said:

'O dear heart, can it be true that you're here in this place?'

'Yes, my heart, I thank God for his grace!' Criseyde then said, and with that she kissed him, so that he did not know where his spirit was, for happiness!

Troilus very often kissed both her eyes and said:

'O bright eyes, it was you who caused me such misery, you modest nets with which my dear lady caught me! Although there is mercy written in your looks, God knows, the text is truly very hard to find! How could you bind me without a cord?'

With that he took her tightly in his arms and sighed a good thousand times—not such sorrowful sighs as people heave when unhappy, or else when folk are ill, but gentle sighs, such as are pleasing and that showed his inner feelings. He could not stop such sighing. Soon after this they spoke of various things that were relevant to this experience, and made a playful exchange of their rings,* but, as to any inscriptions on the rings,* I cannot say. But I do know that Criseyde gave him a brooch*—of gold and lapis lazuli, in which was set a heart-shaped ruby—and pinned it on his shirt. [1372]

Lord! Do you imagine a covetous or wretched person, who criticizes love and scorns it, was ever granted such delight from those pennies that he can hoard and scrape together, as there is in love in a single detail in some circumstances? No, doubtless, God save me, for no miser can have such perfect joy! They will say 'yes', but Lord, how they lie, those anxious wretches, full of misery and fear! They call love madness or folly, but I shall tell you what will happen to them: they shall forgo the silver, and gold* too, and live in misery—may God give them misfortune, and advance every lover in his faithfulness! Would to God those wretches who despise the service of love had ears as long as Midas had, who was full of covetousness, and had also drunk as hot and strong a draught as Crassus* did for his wrongful desires, to teach such wretches that they are in the wrong and not lovers, although they consider lovers foolish! [1393]

When these same two that I am telling you about felt quite reassured at heart, they then began to speak and amuse themselves, and also go over how and when and where they first knew each other, and every past misery and dread. But all such gloom—I thank God for it—was turned into happiness! And continually, whenever they happened to speak of any unhappiness of such past times, all that talk would break off with kissing, and they would at once fall into some new happiness, and did all in their power, since they were together, to recover their bliss and be at ease, and counterbalance past unhappiness with joy. It is unreasonable for me to mention sleep, because it does not accord with my subject-matter. God knows, they cared very little about sleeping! But so that this night, that was so precious to them, should not pass them by in any way in vain, it was spent in joy and eagerness for everything tending to nobility. [1414]

But when the cock—that communal astrologer*—began to beat his breast and then crow, and the morning star Venus,* messenger of day, began to rise and cast forth her beams, and eastwards (to whoever knew how to recognize it) *Fortuna major* was rising—then Criseyde, with heavy heart, spoke at once to Troilus like this:

'Life of my heart, my trust, and my whole delight! How unhappy I am that I was ever born, alas, that day must separate us!* For it's time to get up and leave here, or else I'm ruined for ever more! O night, alas, won't you hover over us as long as when Alcmena* lay with Jove? O black night, that was created by God, as people read in books, to hide this world at certain times under your dark cloak, so that beneath it people could remain at rest, well may beasts complain* and people chide you that, when day is to break us with toil, you flee away like this, and do not grant us rest. You perform your office too briefly, you hasty night! May God, creator of nature, bind you so tightly and always to our hemisphere, because of your haste and unnatural offence, that you never again revolve beneath the ground! For now, because you so hurry out of Troy, I have thus quickly lost my happiness!' [1442]

With those words it then seemed to Troilus that, for piteous distress, he felt bloody tears distil from his heart, as he who had never yet experienced such sadness to grow out of such great happiness. Then he clasped his dear lady Criseyde in his arms, and spoke in this fashion:

'O cruel day, betrayer of the happiness that night and love have stolen and closely concealed, accursed be your coming into Troy, for one of your bright eyes looks through every chink! Envious day, why do you want to spy like this? What have you lost? What are you looking for in this place? May God in his grace quench your light!

Alas, how have lovers offended you, pitiless day? May yours be the pain of hell! For you have killed, and will kill, many a lover. Your staring in will let them remain nowhere. Why do you offer your light here for sale? Go and sell it to those who engrave small seals!* We don't want you! We don't need to have any daylight!' [1463]

And he also began to chide the sun, Titan,* and said:

'O fool! Well may people despise you, who have the dawn by your side all night, and let her get up so soon from beside you in order to distress lovers like this. What! Stay in bed, you, and your mistress the dawn as well! I pray God send you both sorrow!'

With that he sighed very deeply, and in this way he said:

'My true lady, the fount and root of my happiness or sorrow, O my own excellent Criseyde! Must I get up, alas? Must I really? Now I feel my heart must break in two, for how should I go on living for an hour, since all the life I have is with you? What shall I do? For certainly, I don't see how or when, alas, the time will come when I can be with you like this again. And God knows what my life may be like, since I'm in the grip of such desire right now that I'll die at once unless I can come back. How should I stay away from you for long, alas? But nevertheless, my own fairest lady, if I could be certain that I, your humble servant and your knight, were fixed as firmly in your heart as you are in mine—which, truly, I'd rather have than two worlds such as this one*—then I could endure all my pain the better.' [1491]

To that Criseyde replied right away, and with a sigh she said:

'O dear heart, the game has certainly gone so far now that sooner shall Phoebus fall from his sphere, and every eagle consort with a dove, and every rock spring out of its place,* than Troilus will leave Criseyde's heart. You are so deeply engraved in my heart that, even if I wanted to turn you out of my thoughts, God save me, I couldn't —even though I were to die by torture! And for the love of God who has created us, don't let any other delusion creep into your brain and be the death of me! And I would implore you to have me as firmly in mind as I have you; and if I were sure of finding that, God could not increase my happiness one jot. But, without any more talk now, be true to me, my dear, or else it were a pity, for I am yours, by God and upon my oath! So be happy, and live your life feeling sure of me! I never spoke like this before now, nor shall I to any others. And if it would make you happy to come back soon after you

leave, I would be as glad as you that it were so, God rest my soul!'
And she took him in her arms and often kissed him. [1519]

Against his will, since it had to be, Troilus got up, and dressed quickly, and took his noble lady in his arms a hundred times, and hurried on his way; and with a voice as if his heart was bleeding he said:

'Farewell, dear, sweet heart! May God grant that we meet soon, safe and sound!'

To which she answered not one word for sorrow, so intensely did his departure afflict her. And Troilus went to his palace as distressed as she was, to tell the truth. He was wrung so hard by the pain of sharp desire to be where he had been in ecstasy once again, that he could never forget it. Soon returned to his royal palace, he crept quietly into his bed to sleep late, as he was accustomed to doing. But it was all in vain: he might well lie there and close his eyes, but he could not fall asleep, thinking how she for whom desire burned him was worth a thousand times more than he had supposed. And he began to turn over in his thoughts all her words and every look, and to imprint firmly in his mind the least detail that gave him pleasure, and truly, with those memories, desire burned him anew, and his longing grew greater than before, and yet he paid no heed.

In exactly the same way, Criseyde was also storing away in her heart the memory of Troilus' excellence, his vigour, his wise deeds, his nobility, and how she met him, thanking Love that he had bestowed her so well, longing to have her dear heart again in a situation where she could make him happy. [1554]

In the morning* Pandarus came to his niece and greeted her pleasantly, saying:

'All night long it's rained so hard, alas, my sweet niece, that I'm afraid you've had little opportunity to sleep and dream. . . . All night,' said he, 'the rain has so kept me awake that some of us, I think, have a headache.' And he came closer and said: 'How do things stand now, this merry morning? How are you getting on, niece?'

'Never any the better for you, fox that you are!' Criseyde replied. 'God give your heart care! God help me, you caused this whole affair, I believe,' said she, 'for all your white lies. O, whoever only sees you knows you very little!'

With that she covered her face with the sheet and went all red for shame. And Pandarus peeped underneath and said:

'Niece, if I'm going to die, take this sword here, and chop off my head!' With that he thrust his arm very suddenly under her neck, and in the end he kissed her.

I pass over everything which it is not important to say. What! God forgave his death,* and she also forgave, and began to joke with her uncle, for there was no reason not to. But to go straight to the essentials of this matter: when it was time, she went home to her house, and Pandarus had accomplished all he intended. [1582]

Now let us turn back to Troilus again, who lay restlessly in bed for a very long time, and secretly sent for Pandarus to come to him as quickly as he could. He came straightaway—he never once refused—and he greeted Troilus gravely and sat down on the side of his bed. With all the affection of love between friends that heart may imagine, Troilus fell down on his knees to Pandarus, and before he would get up from there he thanked him as best he could a hundred times, and blessed the time that he was born, to rescue him from unhappiness.

'O best of all friends that ever was, to tell the truth!' he said. 'From out of Phlegethon,* the fiery river of hell, you have brought my soul to rest in heaven, so that even though I might sell my life a thousand times a day in your service, it would not be remotely enough to pay you back! I'd be willing to bet that the sun, which overlooks the whole world, never yet saw, in my lifetime, someone so entirely beautiful and excellent as she is, whose I am completely, and shall be till I die. And that I am hers like this, I dare to say— for that, thanks be to the high excellence of Love, and also to your kind diligence! This is no small thing you've given me, and I'll owe my life to you forever because of it. And why? Because through your help I'm alive, and otherwise I'd have been dead now for many a day!' [1614]

And with those words he lay down in his bed, and Pandarus listened to him gravely until he had had his say, and then he replied, like this:

'My dear friend, if I've done anything for you in any situation, God knows, I'm as pleased and happy as a man can be about it, God help me! But don't be annoyed now at what I'm going to say. Beware of this particular misfortune: that you're not yourself responsible for making your current happiness come to grief. For of all fortune's keen adversities the worst kind of misfortune* is this: for a man to have been in good times and to remember them when they're past. You're smart enough, so don't make any mistakes. Though you're sitting pretty now, don't be too rash, because if you are, it'll certainly do you harm. You're content—now keep yourself that way. For keeping is as great a skill as winning*—as sure as every fire's red! Always keep your talk and your desire well reined in, because happiness in this world only holds on by a thread. The fact that it falls apart so often all the time certainly proves as much, and so it's necessary to treat it gently.'

'I swear before God, my dear friend,' Troilus said, 'I hope I'll behave so that nothing will be lost through any fault of mine, and nor will I act so rashly as to upset her. There's no need to keep bringing this matter up, Pandarus, for if you knew what was in my heart, God knows, you'd worry very little about this.' [1645]

Then he began to tell him of his happy night, and of what his heart was first afraid, and how, and said:

'Friend, as I am a true knight, and by that loyalty I owe to God and you, I swear I never had it half so hot as now—and the more that desire gnaws at me all the time to love her best, the more I'm delighted! I don't know for sure myself what it is, but I now feel a new quality—yes, quite unlike anything I felt before this.'

Pandarus replied like this, saying:

'Someone who's once been in the bliss of heaven feels otherwise— I'd be prepared to bet—than he did when he first heard tell of it.'

To put it in a nutshell, Troilus never had enough of speaking about this matter, of praising to Pandarus the goodness of his own dear lady, and of thanking and making much of Pandarus. This topic was always just like new each time it was begun again, until night parted them. [1666]

Soon after this, as Fortune would have it, the blissful sweet time came when Troilus was forewarned that he was to meet his lady where he had before—at which he felt his heart was swimming in joy, and began to praise all the gods devoutly. And let's see now if he can be happy! And all the proper form and manner of her coming, and of his too, were observed as they were before, which need not be described. But simply to go straight to the essentials: in joy and security Pandarus brought the two of them to bed together when they both wished, and so they were in quietness and at rest. You need not ask me, since they have met, if they were happy! For if all was well before, now it was a thousand times better—there is no need to enquire about this! Gone was every sorrow and every fear, and they both indeed had, so they believed, as much happiness as heart can contain. This is no small thing to say. It surpasses all intelligence to express it. For each of them was obedient to the other's desire. It is not enough in this case to term it that perfect felicity* which these wise scholars so commend. This happiness cannot be written about with ink! This surpasses all that heart can conceive! [1694]

But cruel day—alas the time!—began to approach, as they knew by the signs, at which they seemed to feel the wound of death. They were so unhappy that their colour changed, and they started to revile day once more, calling it 'traitor', 'envious', and worse, and they bitterly cursed the light of day.

'Alas,' Troilus said, 'I now realize that Pyrois,* and those other three swift steeds that draw the sun's chariot, have taken some short cut to spite me, which makes day come so soon. I shall never again do sacrifice to them, because the sun hurries so to rise.'

Of necessity, day must soon separate them, and when their talk was done, and their endearments, they parted immediately, as they were used to doing, and arranged a time to meet together again. And on many nights they proceeded in this way; and thus, for a time, Fortune led along in happiness Criseyde and this son of the king of Troy. [1715]

Completely fulfilled, Troilus began to pass his whole life in blissful happiness and in song. He spent, jousted, held feasts; he gave generously and often, and wore many different clothes; and without doubt he always kept around him, as became him by nature, a whole world of the liveliest and best people that he could find, so that there was such fame and report of him throughout the world for honour and generosity that it resounded up to heaven's gate. And, as to his love, he was in such happiness that in his heart he judged, I guess, that there was no lover in this world so well content as he was—so much did love please him. The excellence or beauty which nature had placed in any other lady could not untie so much as one knot of all Criseyde's whole net from around his heart. He was so closely enmeshed and fastened that to undo it on any side was not to be, whatever might happen. And he would very often take Pandarus by the hand and lead him into the garden, and he would talk to him at

such length and in such a celebration of Criseyde, and of her woman-
liness, and of her beauty, that without doubt it was heaven to hear
his words. And then he would sing like this:

*Troilus' Song**

'Love, that rules the earth and sea; Love, that has its commands in
heaven on high; Love, that holds peoples united in beneficial alli-
ance as it is pleased to direct them; Love, that knits together law of
companionship* and causes couples to live together in virtue—bind
together this accord that I have talked of and talk of still! [1750]

'That the world, with constant fidelity, so varies its harmonious
seasons; that elements so inclined to discord maintain a perpetually
enduring bond; that Phoebus brings forth his rosy day, and that the
moon has dominion over the nights; that the sea, ever eager to flood,
restrains its waters within a fixed limit so that they do not increase
so violently as to drown the earth and everything for evermore—
Love does all this, ever praised be its powers! And if Love ever let
go its bridle, all that now loves would fly apart, and everything would
be lost that Love now holds together!

'Would to God, creator of nature, that Love through its power
be pleased to encircle all hearts with its bond, and bind them fast,
so that no one might know the way out from its control. As for cold
hearts, those I wish that it would wring to make them love and always
be pleased to have pity on sorrowing hearts and sustain those that
are faithful!' [1771]

In every necessity in the city's war he was always the first one to
be armed, and certainly, unless books are mistaken, the most feared
of anyone, except Hector. And this increase in audacity and strength
came to him from love—which so changed his spirit within him
—in order to win his lady's gratitude. In times of truce he would
ride out hawking, or else hunt boar, bear, or lion—he let the small
animals alone. And when he came riding into town, very often his
lady—as fresh as a falcon just come from its pen—was very ready
to greet him graciously from her window. His talk was mostly about
love and virtue, and he scorned all mean conduct. And undoubtedly,
there was no need to beg him to honour those who were deserving,
and relieve those who were in distress. And he was glad when he
knew or heard if anyone who was a lover was getting on well. For,

to tell the truth, he considered everyone as lost unless he were in Love's high service—I mean people who ought rightfully to be in it. And moreover, he knew so well how to shape all his behaviour feelingly and in such striking fashion that every lover thought that whatever he said or did was well done. And although he came of royal blood, he had no wish to harass anyone because of pride. He was well disposed to everyone, for which he won himself gratitude everywhere. So Love willed—praised be its grace!—that Troilus began to shun pride, envy, anger, avarice, and every other vice. [1806]

You bright-shining lady, daughter of Dione,* and also your blind and winged son,* Lord Cupid, you nine sisters* too, that choose to dwell by Helicon* on Mount Parnassus—since you now wish to depart, I can only say 'May you be praised forever without end, who have deigned to guide me thus far!' Through you I have fully expressed in my song the essence and the joy of Troilus' service, although there was some unhappiness mixed in, as my author was pleased to describe. My third book I now end in this way, and Troilus is with Criseyde, his own sweet heart, in delight and in peace. [1820]

Here ends the third book.

BOOK FOUR

But alas, such happiness lasts all too short a while, thanks to Fortune,* who seems truest when she wishes to deceive, and knows how to sing her song to fools so that she catches and blinds them—she betrays everyone! And when a person is thrown from her wheel, then she laughs and grimaces at him. She began to turn her bright face away from Troilus, and took no heed of him, but cast him clean out of his lady's favour, and she set up Diomede on her wheel, at which my heart bleeds even now. Alas, the pen with which I am writing now shakes with fear at what I must write! For how Criseyde forsook Troilus—or, at least, how she was unkind—must henceforth be the subject of my book, as is written by those through whom the story is remembered. Alas, that they should ever find reason to speak ill of her! And if they lie about her, indeed, they should themselves be shamed! O you Furies,* Night's three daughters, who lament forever in unending pain, Megaera, Alecto, and also Tisiphone—and you too, cruel Mars, father to Quirinus*—help me finish this same fourth book, so that Troilus' loss of both life and love* at once be fully set forth here! [28]

Here ends the proem of the fourth book.

Here begins the fourth book.

While the Greeks were besieging Troy with a great army, as I have said before, and when Phoebus was shining in the first part of the sign of Leo,* it so happened that Hector, together with many a bold nobleman, decided one day to fight with the Greeks, as he was accustomed to do, so as to do them what harm he could.

I do not know how long or short was the interval between this decision and the day they meant to go forth, but one day Hector and many an excellent man went out well and resplendently armed, with spears in their hands and strong bows bent for action; and without any longer delay they soon encountered their enemies face to face on the field of battle. All day long, with sharply whetted spears, with arrows, javelins, swords, deadly maces, they fought and brought horse and man to the ground, and dashed out brains with their axes. But in the last assault, to tell the truth, the people of Troy conducted themselves so badly that they had the worst of it and fled homewards at nightfall. On which day Antenor was captured—in spite of Polydamas or Mnestheus, Antiphus, Sarpedon, Polymnestor, Polites, or the Trojan lord Riphaeus* too, and such other lesser folk as Phebuseo—so that because of that reverse the people of Troy feared to lose a great part of their happiness that day. [56]

At the request of the Greeks,* Priam granted a period of truce, and they then began to negotiate to exchange their prisoners great and small, and to pay large sums for those prisoners for whom they had no one to exchange. This thing was known immediately in every street, in the besieging army, in the city, and everywhere, and it soon came to Calchas' ear. When Calchas knew that this negotiation would be held, he pressed forward with other old lords among the Greeks in the council, and sat himself down where he was used to do; and with a changed face requested them, for the love of God, to do him the courtesy to cease their noise and give him a hearing. Then he spoke as follows:

'My lords, I was a Trojan, as is doubtless known, and, if you remember, I am Calchas, who was the first of all to give comfort to you when you needed it, and told you how you would succeed. For without doubt, through you Troy will in a while be burnt and razed to the ground. You've heard me describe to you before now in what kind of way you are to destroy this city and achieve all your desire. You know this, my lords, as I believe. Because the Greeks were so dear to me, I came myself in person to instruct you how it was best to act in this matter. Having no regard to my capital or my income, in comparison with what was to your advantage, I left behind all my property and came over to you, thinking to please you in this, my lords. Yet all that loss causes me no distress. As I hope to be happy, I am willing for your sake to lose everything I have in Troy, except for a daughter that I left at home asleep, alas, when I fled from Troy. O stern and cruel father that I was! How could I have been so hardhearted in that? How I regret that I didn't bring her, even in her nightshirt! For sorrow over this I won't live another day, unless you lords have pity on my unhappiness. Because I saw no moment before now to release her, I have held my peace. But, now or never, undoubtedly, I can have her very soon, if you please. O let there be some help and favour for me from amongst all this press of people! Have pity on this wretched old man in distress, since I have all this unhappiness because of you! You now have enough Trojans captured and chained in prison and, if you agree, my child can be ransomed with one of them. Now for the love of God, and of your goodness, give me one of so many, alas! What need could there be to refuse this request, since you shall have both town and people very soon? On peril of my life, I shall not lie: Apollo has told me this faithfully. I have also discovered it by astrology, through casting of lots, and through augury as well, truly, and dare well say the time is close at hand when fire and flame shall spread through the whole city, and so Troy shall turn to lifeless ashes. For certainly, both Apollo and Neptune,* who constructed the walls of the city, are still so angry with the people of Troy that they will bring it to ruin out of hostility towards King Laomedon; because he would not pay them their wages, the town of Troy shall be set on fire.' [126]

As this old greybeard told his tale, humble in his speech and in his looks too, the salt tears ran down copiously from his eyes over both cheeks. He begged them for help for so long that, to cure him of his grievous sorrows, they granted him Antenor without more ado. Who was happy enough then but Calchas? He soon entrusted his requirements in this matter to those who were to go to the negotiations, and repeatedly asked them to bring home King Thoas* and Criseyde, in exchange for Antenor. When Priam sent his safe conduct, the ambassadors went straight to Troy. Once the reason for their coming had been announced, the aged King Priam promptly had his parliament* summoned together, of which I shall tell you the essentials. The ambassadors were finally answered: the exchange of prisoners and this whole business were agreeable to them, and so they proceeded. [147]

Troilus was present there when Criseyde was requested in exchange for Antenor, at which his face very quickly began to change, for he very nearly died at those words. But nevertheless, he did not say a word against it, in case people noticed his emotion. He endured his sorrows like a man and, full of anguish and terrible dread, waited to see what the lords would say about it. And if they should agree to her exchange—which God forbid!—then he thought of two things: first, how to safeguard her honour, and how he might best oppose her exchange. He considered very intently how the whole situation might stand. [161]

Love made him all eager to have her remain, and rather die than that she should go, but on the other hand Reason said to him: 'Don't do so without her agreement, in case she were to be antagonized by your action, and say that through your interference the love between you both is made public, where it was previously unknown.' He therefore considered it for the best that although the lords agreed that she was to go, he would let them grant what they pleased, and first tell his lady what they intended. And when she had told him her wishes, he would swiftly act accordingly, even though the whole world were against it. [175]

Hector, who heard how the Greeks wanted to have Criseyde in exchange for Antenor, opposed it and replied gravely:

'Sirs, she is not a prisoner,' he said. 'I don't know who entrusted you with this commission, but for my part you can tell them in reply that it's not our custom here to sell women.'

An outcry then immediately arose from the people, as fierce as the blaze of straw* set on fire. For bad luck would have it that they should desire their own ruin at that time.

'Hector!' they said, 'What spirit can be inspiring you to shield this woman like this, and make us lose Lord Antenor, who is such a wise lord, and a bold one too? You're choosing the wrong course of action now. We have need of people, as anyone can see, and he is also the very greatest of this city. O Hector, forget such fantasies! O King Priam,' said they, 'we say this: that we all vote to surrender Criseyde.' And they begged that Antenor be released. [196]

O Lord Juvenal, your maxim* is true: that people so little know what is to be desired that they discover disaster in what they crave, for a cloud of error hinders them from discerning what is best. Here is an example forthwith: these people now desire the release of Antenor,* who brought them to disaster; for he was afterwards a traitor to the city of Troy. Alas, they released him too soon! O, see, foolish world, so much for your judgement! Criseyde, who never did them any harm, shall now no longer bask in her happiness. But Antenor, he shall come home to the city, and she must leave—thus said all and sundry. And so it was decided by parliament to surrender Criseyde for Antenor, and the vote was declared by the president of the parliament, although Hector very often urged against it.

And in the end, whoever spoke against it, it was in vain; it must and should be, for the majority of the parliament wished it. [217]

When everyone had left parliament, Troilus sped* without another word to his bedroom, alone except for a man or two of his, whom he told to leave at once because he wanted to sleep, as he said, and soon flung himself down upon his bed. And just as in winter the leaves are removed one after the other until the tree is bare, and there is nothing left but bark and branch,* so Troilus lay, bereft of every happiness, bound fast inside the black bark* of sorrow, and in a state to go mad out of his mind, the exchange of Criseyde affected him so deeply. He stood up and shut every door and window too, and then this sorrowful man sat himself down upon the side of his bed, just like a lifeless statue, pale and wan; and the heaped-up misery in his breast began to burst out, and he in his madness to behave in this way, as I shall describe to you. [238]

Just as the wild bull, when pierced to the heart by a dart, begins to lunge now here, now there, and roars out in lamentation of his death,* just so Troilus began to fling himself around the room, all the time pounding his breast violently with his fists; he repeatedly crashed his head against the wall and battered his body against the ground, in order to destroy himself. His two eyes, in sympathy with his heart, streamed with tears like two swift springs; in his bitter sorrows his loud sobs deprived him of speech; he could scarcely say:

'O death, alas, why won't you make me die? Accursed be that day that Nature created me to be a living creature!' [252]

But afterwards, when all the fury and rage which wrung and oppressed his heart began to diminish somewhat through length of time, he lay down to rest on his bed. But then his tears started to burst out more, so that it was a wonder the body was able to endure half this sorrow that I am describing to you. Then he spoke as follows:

'O Fortune, how sad a time this is! How have I offended? What have I done wrong? How, for pity's sake, could you deceive me? Is there no grace, and am I to be destroyed just like this? Must Criseyde go away like this, because you wish it? Alas, how can you find it in your heart to be so cruel and unkind to me? Have I not honoured you all my life, as you well know, above all the gods? Why will you deprive me of happiness like this? O Troilus, what may people call you now, but most wretched of all wretches, fallen from a place of honour into misery,* in which I will lament for Criseyde, alas, until my breath fails me? Alas, Fortune, if my life in happiness was displeasing to your vile envy, why didn't you deprive my father, the king of Troy, of his life? Or cause my brothers to die? Or kill me, who lament and cry out so—I, an encumbrance to the world, who can serve no useful purpose, but am continually dying and yet can never completely die? If Criseyde were left to me, I wouldn't care wherever you wanted to steer me; and alas, you have taken her from me. But this is always your way, I see, to take away from a person that which is most dear to him, to demonstrate through that your unpredictable violence. So I am lost: no remedy can help me! O true lord! O Love! O god, alas, you who best know my heart and all my thoughts! What shall my sorrowful life do in this event, if I lose what I have bought so dearly? Since you have brought Criseyde and me fully into your grace and set your seal on both our hearts, how can you allow it to be repealed, alas? What shall I do? As long as I can endure alive, in torment and in cruel pain, I shall lament this misfortune or this calamity, all alone as I was born! Nor will I ever see it rain or shine but, like Oedipus,* I will end my sorrowful life in darkness and die in anguish! [301]

'O weary spirit, you who wander to and fro, why won't you fly out of the most sorrowful body that ever walked on earth? O soul, lurking in this misery, leave your nest, take wing out of my heart and let it break, and always follow your dear lady, Criseyde. Your rightful place is now no longer here. O sorrowful two eyes, since your whole delight was to see Criseyde's bright eyes, what will you do now, except be useless* because of my distress, and weep your sight away, since her light is quenched,* that used to give you light? From this time on I have been endowed in vain with two eyes, since your power has gone. O my Criseyde! O sovereign lady of that same sorrowful soul that cries like this, who shall now give comfort to my pain? Alas, no one! But when my heart dies, receive my spirit that hastens so to you, for that shall always serve you. It doesn't matter therefore, though the body die. O you lovers, who are placed high up in good luck on Fortune's wheel, God grant that you always find love of steel, and long may your life endure in happiness! But when you come by my tomb,* remember that your fellow lover rests there, for I loved too, though I was unworthy. O you corrupt and wicked old man—I mean Calchas!—alas, what's wrong with you, to want to become a Greek though you were born a Trojan? O Calchas, who will be the death of me, for me you were born in an accursed time! If only blessed Jove would grant, of his joy, that I had you where I wanted in Troy!' [336]

A thousand sighs, hotter than the glowing coals went one after another out of his breast, mingled with new laments, to nourish his misery, and so his sorrowful tears never ceased. And briefly, his griefs so tore him apart, and he became so dejected, that he felt neither joy nor suffering, but lay there in a trance.

Pandarus, who had heard at the parliament what every lord and citizen said, and how it had been completely agreed with one accord to hand over Criseyde for Antenor, went very nearly mad out of his mind, so that, for sorrow, he did not know what he was intending, but he went in a rush to Troilus. A certain knight who at that time was guarding the chamber door undid it for him at once, and Pandarus, who was weeping most tenderly, went softly into the darkened room towards the bed, so confused that he did not know what to say. His mind was nearly gone, for sheer misery. With his manner and look completely distraught for sorrow at all this, and with his arms folded,* he stood before this sorrowful Troilus and gazed at his pitiful face. But Lord, how often his heart went cold, seeing his friend in misery, whose unhappiness was—it seemed to him—killing his heart with distress. [364]

This unhappy man, Troilus, who was aware that his friend Pandarus had come to see him, began to melt like snow in the sunshine; at which this sorrowful Pandarus, out of compassion, started to weep as tenderly as he; these same two were speechless, so that neither could say one word for sorrow. But at last this unhappy Troilus, nearly dead with pain, burst out in loud cries, and in a sorrowful voice, amongst his sobs and his bitter sighs, said:

'You see, Pandarus, I'm a dead man—there's nothing more to be said! Haven't you heard at parliament,' he said, 'how my Criseyde is given up for Antenor?'

Very deathly pale in appearance, Pandarus replied very piteously and said:

'Yes! If only what I've heard and know all about were as certainly false as it's true! O mercy, God, who would have believed it? Who would have imagined that Fortune would have overturned our happiness in so short a time? As far as I can see, nobody ever saw a stranger downfall through chance or destiny than this. But who can avoid or foresee everything? That's how the world is! So I come to this conclusion: don't anyone ever believe that what comes from Fortune is their personal property—everyone holds her gifts in common.* [392]

'But tell me this: why are you now so crazy as to grieve the way you do? Why are you lying here like this, since you've had what you desired so fully that, by rights, it ought to be enough for you? But I, who in my own service of love never experienced a friendly expression or glance—let me weep and wail like this till I die! And besides all this, as you well know yourself, this town and all around is full of ladies; and in my opinion, I'll find one or two in some crowd, twelve times as beautiful as she ever was—yes, don't you doubt it! So cheer up, my own dear brother! If she's lost, we'll get another instead. What! God forbid that all pleasure should always be in one thing and in no other! If one can sing, another can dance well; if this woman is demure, that one is happy and light-hearted; this one is beautiful, and that one has a good understanding of things. All are valued* for their particular virtue—both the falcon for hunting herons, and the falcon for hunting waterfowl. And also, as Zanzis* wrote (who was very wise): "The new love often drives out the old";* and a new situation requires new consideration.* Remember too, that you're under an obligation to save your life. By nature such fire must grow cold in the course of time, for since it's only chance pleasure, some chance event will put it out of your mind. Some new love, work, or other sorrow, or else seldom seeing a person, makes old affections quite pass away, as sure as day comes after night. And, for your part, your sharp and bitter pains will be shortened in one of these ways: her absence will drive her out of your heart!' [427]

He said all this on purpose, to help his friend, in case he died of sorrow. For undoubtedly, he did not care what nonsense he said in order to lessen his misery. But Troilus, who was nearly dying for sorrow, took little notice of anything he said—it went in one ear and out of the other.* But at last he replied and said:

'Friend, this medicine, or to be healed like this, would be very suitable if I were a fiend—to betray a person who is loyal to me! I pray God, let this advice never succeed, but make me die here immediately before I do as you would teach me to do! She whom I serve, indeed, to whom my heart is rightfully devoted, shall have me wholly

(margin notes) I repeat to try to see the good side

actually proverb drawn from Ovid

hers till I die, whatever you say. For Pandarus, since I've promised her loyalty, I'll not be unfaithful for anyone, but I'll always live and die as her man and never serve another creature. And when you say you'll find another as beautiful as her—don't even try! Don't compare her with any creature formed here by nature! O dear Pandarus, in conclusion, I can't be of your opinion regarding all this. And so, be quiet, I beg you! You're killing me with what you're saying! You tell me I should love someone else, starting all over again afresh, and let Criseyde go! It doesn't lie in my power, dear brother, and even if I could, I wouldn't do so. But Pandarus, can you play a game of rackets with love, to and fro, now this, now that—first the nettle stings, and then the dock-leaf soothes?* Now bad luck to her who may care about your love-sickness! You act towards me—you, Pandarus—like someone who, when a person is woebegone, comes up to him briskly and says, just like this: "Don't think about pain, and you won't feel any."* You must first turn me into a stone, and take all my feelings away from me, before you make my sorrow stop so easily! This sorrow may undermine me for so long that death may well remove the life from my breast, but Criseyde's arrow will never leave my soul, and when I am dead I will go and dwell in misery with Proserpina,* and there I will lament my woe eternally, and how we two are separated. [476]

'You've put forward an argument that it should be less painful to lose Criseyde because she was mine and we lived in contentment and happiness. Why do you talk such nonsense, who once said to me* that "it is worse for him whose good fortune is overturned than if he had known nothing of it previously"? But tell me now, since it seems so easy to you to change like this in love back and forth, why haven't you done all you could to change her who causes you all your unhappiness? Why won't you let her pass from your heart? Why won't you love another sweet lady, who may set your heart at rest? If you, who as yet have always had bad luck in love, can't drive it out of your heart, how should I—who lived in as much delight and pleasure with her as anyone alive—forget that, and so quickly? O where have you been cooped up so long, who can argue finely and formally? [497]

'No, God knows, your advice is worthless, and so, whatever may happen, and without any more talk, I shall die! O death, ender of all sorrows, come now, since I call for you so often! For, to tell the truth, happy is the death that, often summoned, comes and puts an end to pain.* While I lived in peace, I well know, I would have paid a ransom before you killed me. But now your coming is so sweet to me that I desire nothing in this world so much. O death, since I am on fire with this sorrow, either drown me at once in tears, or quench this heat of mine with your cold stroke. Since you kill so many in various ways, against their will, unasked for, day and night, do me this service at my request! Now rid the world of me—you'd be doing the right thing—who am the most sorrowful person that ever was, for it's time for me to die, since I can serve no useful purpose at all in this world!' [518]

Troilus melted into tears, like liquor distilling swiftly from an alembic;* and Pandarus held his tongue and looked at the ground. But nevertheless, he finally thought like this:

'What! By God, rather than my friend die, I'll still say something more to him!' And he said: 'Friend, since you're so distressed, and since you like to find fault with my arguments, why won't you help set matters right yourself, and—by acting like a man—prevent all this grief? Go and carry her off by force! Can't you do it? Shame on you! And either let her leave town, or keep her here, and stop your foolish behaviour! Are you in Troy, and don't have the daring to take a woman who loves you and would herself be in agreement with you? Now isn't this silly and futile? Get up at once, and stop this weeping, and show you're a man! Either I'll be dead inside the hour, or she'll remain ours!' [539]

To this Troilus replied very quietly and said:

'By God, my dear, dear brother, I've very often thought of all this myself, and of more than you suggest here. But I'll certainly tell you why I haven't done this, and when you've listened to me, you can say what you think afterwards. You know that first, since our city has this whole war because of the abduction of women* by force, I couldn't be allowed to break the law as things now stand, nor do so great a wrong. Everyone would blame me too if I opposed my father's decree like that, since she's being exchanged for the good of the city. I've also thought, provided she agreed, of asking for her from my father,* out of his kindness. Then I think this would only be to betray her, since I know very well I can't gain her like this. For since my father has ratified her exchange in so high a place as parliament, he won't repeal his decree for me. Most of all, I dread upsetting her feelings by the use of violence if I adopt such a strategy. For if I were to intervene publicly in the arrangements, it must be slander to her reputation. And I'd rather die than disgrace her—God forbid that I shouldn't hold her honour dearer than saving my life! And so I'm done for, as far as I can see! For certainly, since I'm her knight, I must value her honour more highly than myself in every situation, as a lover ought by rights to do. And so I'm pulled both ways between desire and reason: desire advises me to prevent her going, and reason won't have it, and so at heart I'm afraid!' [574]

Weeping as if he could never stop, he went on:

'Alas, wretched creature that I am! What am I to do? For I certainly feel my love continually increasing, though there is always less and less hope, Pandarus! The causes of my sorrow are increasing too, so alas, why won't my heart break? For there's very little rest to be had in love!'

'My friend,' replied Pandarus, 'as far as I'm concerned, you can do as you please. But if I had it as hot as you do, and had your high rank, she should go with me, though all this town cried out in unison against it. I wouldn't care a jot* for all that commotion! For after people have shouted a lot, they'll quieten down to a whisper. And also, a wonder only ever lasts nine nights in town! Don't always enquire so deeply into arguments, nor too scrupulously,* but help yourself first. It's better that someone other than yourself should cry, and specially since the two of you are as one! Get up! For, by my head, I swear she shan't go! Better to be found a little at fault than die here like a gnat, without a wound! It isn't a rape,* in my view, nor anything wrong, to detain her whom you love most of all. Mightn't she perhaps think you a fool to let her go to the Greek army like this? Think too, as you well know yourself, how Fortune helps the bold man* in his enterprise, and abandons wretches because of their cowardice. And though your lady might be a little annoyed, you'll be able to make your peace yourself afterwards! But as for me, I certainly can't believe that she'd take it amiss at this point. Why then should your heart be quaking with fear? Think too how your brother Paris has a love, and why shouldn't you have another? [609]

'And Troilus, I dare swear one thing to you: if Criseyde, your beloved, loves you now as much as you love her, God help me, she won't be upset if you come right up with a remedy in this trouble. If she's willing to leave you, then she's unfaithful—so love her all

proverb

the less for it! So take heart, and remember you're a knight! Laws are broken all the time through love.* Show a bit of your spirit and your strength! Take pity on yourself, despite any fear you feel. Don't let this miserable depression gnaw at your heart but, like a man, stake the world on a throw of the dice,* and if you die a martyr*— go to heaven! I'll stand by you myself in this action, though I and all my kin shall in one hour lie dead in a street like dogs, pierced through with many a gaping and bleeding wound! In every situation you'll find me a friend. And if you want to die here like a wretch— goodbye, and to hell with anyone who cares about it!' [630]

At these words Troilus began to come to life and said:

'Thanks, friend, I agree! But briefly—even though I should die otherwise—you certainly can't needle me so much, nor can any pain so torture me, that I would in any way plan to carry her off, unless she wishes it herself.'

'Why,' said Pandarus, 'that's what I've been meaning all this time!* But tell me then, you who are sorrowing like this: have you sounded her out on what she wants?'

'No,' he replied.

'What are you so dismayed about then, when you don't know whether she'll be upset if you carry her off, since you haven't been there—unless Jove whispered it in your ear? So get up at once, as if nothing were the matter, and wash your face, and go to the king, before he wonders where you've gone. You must deceive him and other people by acting wisely, or he may perhaps send for you before you're aware. In brief, dear, dear brother, cheer up, and let me get to work on this matter. For I'll arrange it so that—tonight, some-time, somehow—you'll certainly come and speak secretly with your lady, and by her words and her manner you'll very soon see and hear all she intends, and what's the best thing in this situation. And now goodbye, for I'll leave it at that!' [658]

Swift Rumour, which reports false things equally with the true, had flown on swift wings* throughout Troy from one person to another, always retelling this story, how Calchas' daughter with her radiant looks had, without any more to be said, been granted at par-liament in exchange for Antenor. As soon as she had heard this story, Criseyde—who did not now care at all about her father, nor whether he lived or died—earnestly begged Jupiter to visit misfortune on those who had brought about this treaty. But, in brief, she did not dare, out of fear, ask anyone about it, in case these stories were true. She had so wonderfully firmly set her heart and her whole mind on Troilus, that this whole world itself could not loosen the ties of her love, nor cast Troilus out of her heart: she will be his, while her life may last! She burned so in both love and fear, that she did not know what was best to do. [679]

But, as can be seen in town and all around, women make a habit of visiting their friends, and so a crowd of women came to Criseyde out of well-meaning happiness, thinking to please her. And with their tales, not worth much at all, these women who lived in the city sat themselves down and spoke as I shall relate:

'I'm truly happy for you, because you'll be seeing your father,' said one first.

'I'm not, indeed, because she's been with us all too little,' said another.

'I certainly hope that she'll bring us peace on all sides, so may almighty God guide her when she goes!' said the third then. [693]

Those words and those woman-like things Criseyde heard just as though she was not there. For God knows, her heart was on something else! Although her body sat amongst them there, her attention was always elsewhere. Her spirit was seeking intently for Troilus; without saying a word, she was thinking about him all the while. These women, thinking to please her like this, made conversation about nothing. Such idle talk could not bring any comfort to her, who all this meanwhile was burning with a different passion than they imagined, so that she felt her heart almost dying out of grief and weariness of that company. Then she could no longer hold back her tears—they welled up so—that signalled the bitter pain in which her spirit was, and must remain, remembering to herself from what heaven into what hell she had fallen, since she was losing the sight of Troilus, and she sighed sorrowfully. Those same fools sitting around her supposed that she wept and sighed bitterly because she was to leave that group of people and never enjoy their company again. When those who had known her for a long time saw her weep like this, they thought it was out of kindness, and each of them wept too for her distress. They began to comfort her diligently for something, God knows, that she thought very little about, and thought to cheer her up with their tales, and they often begged her to be happy. But they gave her about as much relief with that as one gets from a headache* by being scratched on the heel! After all this foolish and idle talk they took their leave, and home they all went. [730]

Full of piteous sorrow, Criseyde went up out of the hall into her room, and she fell on to her bed as if she were dead, intending never to get up from there, and she behaved in this way, as I shall now describe to you. She tore her wavy hair, that was the colour of sunlight, repeatedly wringing her long and slender fingers too, and asked God to have pity on her, and to remedy her suffering with death. Her once radiant complexion, which now was pale, bore witness to her sorrow and her distress, and she spoke like this, sobbing in her lament:

'Alas,' said she, 'I, sorrowful wretch, luckless being, and born under an unfavourable constellation* of the planets, must leave this place, and so part from my knight! How I curse the very light of day in which I first saw him, who causes me, and I him, all this pain!'

With that, the tears fell from her eyes as swiftly as an April shower; she beat her white breast, and because of her misery she cried out for death a thousand times, since she must lose him who was accustomed to soothe her unhappiness, and because of this misfortune she considered herself a creature utterly lost. [756]

'What will he do?' she said. 'And what will I do too? How should I live if I part from him? O dear heart too, that I love so, who will put an end to the sorrow that you are in? O Calchas, father, this is all your doing! O my mother, Argia,* how I curse the day that you brought me into the world! To what purpose should I live on and sorrow like this? How should a fish last out of water? What is Criseyde worth, apart from Troilus? How should a plant or any living creature live without its natural nourishment? And so I often repeat a proverb here, that "when rootless, greenery must soon die". Since I daren't handle sword or spear, because of the cruelty of it, I shall act in this way: from that same day that I part from you (if the sorrow of that doesn't kill me), no meat or drink shall enter me till I unsheath my soul* from my breast, and in this way I'll put myself to death! And Troilus, all my clothes shall be black, as a sign— sweet heart—that I, who was accustomed to set your heart at rest, am as if withdrawn from this world. And, in your absence, till I meet with death, the observance of my "order"* will always be sorrow, lamentation, and abstinence. I bequeath my heart* (and also the sorrowful spirit inside it) to complain with your spirit eternally, for they shall never part. For though on earth we two may be separated, yet in the field of compassion, beyond pain, which is called the Elysian Field,* we shall be together, like Orpheus and his consort Eurydice. So, my heart, I shall soon be exchanged for Antenor, alas, as I believe! But what will you do in this sorrowful event? How will your sensitive heart bear this? Oh, my heart, forget this sorrow and affliction, and me as well, for, to tell the truth, provided you're all right, I don't care if I die!' [798]

How could it ever be read or sung,* the lamentation that she made in her distress? I do not know! But as far as I am concerned, if I were to describe her sadness, my little tongue would make her sorrow seem less than it was, and childishly spoil her lofty lament, and so I pass over it.

You have heard tell how it was agreed to be for the best that Pandarus should be sent from Troilus to Criseyde (and he was very happy to do him that service), so in a secret fashion he came to Criseyde, where she lay in torment and in frenzied grief, to tell her the whole of his message. He found her behaving very pitifully, for her breast and face were wet with her tears; and the great tresses of her sun-like hair were hanging dishevelled all about her ears, which gave him a true sign of the martyrdom of death that her heart desired. [819]

When she saw him, she at once hid her tear-stained face in her arms for shame,* at which Pandarus felt so overwhelmed with sadness that he could scarcely remain in the house. His heart went out to the suffering that surrounded him on all sides, for if Criseyde had lamented bitterly before, she then began to lament a thousand times more. And she spoke like this in her bitter lamentation:

'Pandarus was, in the first place, the primary cause* of more than a few joys to me, Criseyde, which have now been transmuted into cruel unhappiness! Shall I say welcome to you or not, who first of all brought me into the service of love—alas!—that ends in such a fashion? Does love end in misery? Yes, or people are lying, and so ends all worldly happiness, as it seems to me. Sorrow always takes possession of the end of bliss.* And whoever doesn't believe that it's so, let him look at me, sorrowful wretch, who hate myself and continually curse my birth—always in suffering, I am moving from a bad state to a worse. Whoever looks at me sees all grief in one—pain, torment, lamentation, misery, distress! No hurt is absent from my sorrowful body, such as anguish, suffering, cruel bitterness, trouble, smarting pain, fear, fury, and also sickness. I truly believe tears rain down from heaven for pity of my cruel and bitter pain!' [847]

'And you, my sister, so full of distress,' said Pandarus, 'what do you think you're doing? Haven't you any regard for yourself? Why will you destroy yourself like this, alas? Stop all this grieving, and pay attention now to what I'm going to say. And listen faithfully to this message which your Troilus sent you via me.'

Criseyde then turned round, lamenting so much that it was like death itself to see it.

'Alas,' said she, 'what words can you bring? What will my dear heart say to me, whom I fear I'll never see again? Would he like to have some lamentation or tears before I go? I have enough, if he sends for any!' [861]

To look at, in the face, she was just like someone that people tie on a bier. Her face—once the image of paradise—was altogether changed into quite another sort. The gaiety, the laughter, that people were used to find in her, and all her happiness too, have deserted her; and so Criseyde now lies alone. A purple ring encircles each of her eyes, as a true sign of her pain, so that it was a dreadful thing to behold; at which Pandarus could not restrain the tears raining from his eyes. But nevertheless, as best he could, he delivered the message from Troilus to Criseyde:

'Look, niece, I believe you've heard how the king and other lords, acting for the best, have made an exchange of Antenor and you, which is the cause of this sorrow and distress. But no earthly man's tongue can say how this development afflicts Troilus—he is like someone preparing to die shortly. We have sorrowed so much because of this, he and I, that it nearly killed us both, but on my advice he has in the end given up weeping today to some degree, and it seems to me that he's eagerly longing to be with you all night, to think up a remedy in this matter, if there were any way to do it. This, briefly and simply, is the essence of my message, as far as I can understand, for you, who are in such a frenzy of torment, can't attend at present to any long preamble. And you can send him an answer about all this. For the love of God, my dear niece, do leave off this lamenting before Troilus is here!' [896]

'Great is my unhappiness,' said she, and sighed bitterly, like one who felt agonizingly sharp distress, 'but yet to me his sorrow is much worse, who love him better than he loves himself, I suppose! Alas, does he have such unhappiness because of me? Can he lament for me so piteously? His sorrow certainly doubles all my pain. God knows, it grieves me terribly to part,' said she, 'but it's harder still for me to see the sorrow that he's in, for I know very well that it'll be the death of me, and I'll die for certain,' she then said. 'But tell him to come before death, that threatens me like this, drives out the spirit beating in my heart.' [910]

Having said these words, she fell face down on her arms and began to weep piteously.

'Alas,' said Pandarus, 'why are you acting like this, since you well know it's nearly the time that he'll come? Get up quickly, so that he doesn't find you in tears like this, unless you want to have him mad out of his mind. For if he knew you were behaving like this, he'd kill himself. And if I expected to have this sort of behaviour, he shouldn't come here for all the wealth that Priam can spend. For I know too well the end he would at once be aiming at. And so I say again: leave off this sorrowing, or plainly, he will die. And find a way to shorten his sorrow and not increase it, dear, sweet niece! Touch him with the flat of the blade, not the cutting edge,* and calm his sorrow with some wise advice. How does it help to weep a streetful, or for you both to drown in salt tears? Time spent on a remedy is always better than time spent on complaining. This is what I mean: when I bring him here, since you're sensible and both of one mind, then plan how to prevent your going, or how you may come back again soon after you've gone.* Women are clever at quick thinking.* Let's see how your wits will now prove helpful, and what I can do to help shall not be wanting.' [938]

'Go,' said Criseyde, 'and truly, uncle, I'll do all I can to restrain myself from weeping in his sight. I'll do everything in my power to make him happy, and explore my heart in every vein: if a salve can be found for his wound, it will certainly not be wanting on my part.'

Pandarus went, and he looked for Troilus until he found him all alone in a temple, like one who no longer cared about his life. But he was lamenting and praying very feelingly to all the merciful gods to cause him soon to pass out of this world, for he well believed there was no other favour for him. And briefly, to tell the whole truth, he was so fallen into despair that day, that he utterly prepared himself to die. For all the time his argument went just like this: he said he was as good as lost, alas! [957]

Derived from translation of B

'For everything that happens, happens by necessity:* thus, it is my destiny to be lost. For certainly, I know this well,' he said, 'that foresight of divine providence has always seen that I would lose Criseyde, since God sees all things, without doubt, and through his decree disposes them truly according to their deserts, as they shall come to pass by predestination.

'But nevertheless, alas, whom shall I believe? For there are many great scholars who prove predestination* by arguments. And some men say that, of necessity, there is no such thing, but that free choice is given to every one of us. O, alas! Old scholars are so cunning that I don't know whose opinion I can accept. For some men say if God sees everything before—and God cannot be deceived, indeed!—then that which providence has foreseen to be must happen, though men had sworn to the contrary. Therefore I say that if from eternity He has foreknown our thoughts and our deeds as well, we have no free choice, as these scholars advise. For other thoughts, or other deeds too, could never be, but such as providence, which may never be deceived in any way, has infallibly perceived in advance. For if there could be various alternatives to wriggle our way out from God's providence, there would not be any foreknowledge of things to come, but rather, it would be an uncertain opinion, and not stable foresight. And that would certainly be an absurdity, that God should have no more perfect and clear knowledge than we men who have only doubtful conjecturings. But to imagine such an error in God would be disloyal and vile, and accursed wickedness.

'This is also an opinion of some who have the tops of their heads very smoothly shaven: they say precisely this, that a thing is not to come about because providence has foreseen that it shall happen; but they say that because it shall happen, therefore providence foreknows it infallibly. And in this way necessity is reversed and moves in the opposite direction. For it is not necessary that things that are foreseen certainly happen; but it is necessary, as they say, that things that do happen are certainly foreseen. I intend, as if I were taking pains over this, to enquire which thing is the cause of which thing: whether God's foreknowledge is the certain cause of the necessity of things that are to come, indeed; or if the necessity of things to come be certain cause of the providence. But I do not trouble myself now with showing the order these causes stand in. Yet I well know

that it is necessary that the happening of things foreknown certainly
must be, although it does not seem to follow from that that fore-
knowledge makes necessary the occurrence of the thing to come, how-
ever it turns out, for good or ill. [1022]

'For if a man sit over there on a seat, then certainly it must neces-
sarily be so, that your opinion be true, who think or conjecture that
he is sitting. Moreover, on the other hand now, you see, it is just the
same for the converse, as thus—now listen,* because I won't linger!
—I'm saying that if your opinion is true, because he is sitting, then
I say this: that he must be sitting, of necessity; and so necessity is
in both. For in him there is necessity of sitting, indeed, and in you,
necessity of truth. And so, in truth, there must be necessity in you
both. But you may say: the man does not sit for the reason that your
opinion that he is sitting is true; but rather, because the man was
sitting there already, therefore your opinion is true, indeed. And I
say: though the cause of the truth of this comes from his sitting, yet
there is interchange of necessity between both him and you! [1043]

'Thus, in this same way, without doubt, I may well conduct, as
it seems to me, my reasoning on God's providence and on the things
that are to come, by which reasoning it may well be seen that those
things that happen on earth all come by necessity. For although it
is certainly true that because a thing is to come, indeed, it is there-
fore foreseen—not that it comes because it is foreseen—yet never-
theless, it must necessarily be that a thing to come be foreseen, truly,
or else, things that are foreseen happen of necessity. And this is cer-
tainly enough to destroy our free choice completely. But now, this
is an absurdity, to say that occurrence of temporal things is cause of
God's eternal foreknowledge! Now truly, that is a false conclusion,
that things to come should be cause of his foreknowledge! What might
I suppose, if I had such a thought, but that God foresees a thing
that is to come because it is to come, and otherwise not? So might
I suppose that all things that have formerly happened and come to
pass have been cause of that sovereign providence that foreknows
everything infallibly. And in addition to all this, I say further on this
subject: that just as when I know there is a thing, indeed, that thing
must necessarily be so; just so, too, when I know a thing to be com-
ing, come it must. And thus, the happening of things that are known
before the event may not be evaded in any way!' [1078]

Then he continued thus:

'Almighty Jove enthroned, who know the truth of this whole thing, have pity on my sorrow. Either make me die soon, or deliver Criseyde and me from this distress!'

And while he was in all this heaviness of heart, disputing with himself on this subject, Pandarus came in, and said as you may hear:

'O mighty God enthroned!' said Pandarus. 'Ah! Who ever saw a wise man behave like this? Why, Troilus, what are you thinking of doing? Do you have such a desire to be your own enemy? What! By God, Criseyde hasn't gone yet! Why do you want to destroy yourself so with fear that your eyes look dead in your skull? Haven't you lived for many years before now without her and got on perfectly well? Are you born for her, and for no other? Has Nature created you solely to please her? Forget it! And think just like this in your misery: that just as winning throws happen at dice, just so pleasures in love come and go. [1099]

'Yet the biggest surprise of all to me is why you're sorrowing like this, since you don't know yet how things will turn out regarding her going, nor if she can herself prevent it. You haven't yet sounded her out on what she has in mind. A man may offer his neck all in good time—when he must lose his head—and grieve when it becomes necessary! So pay attention to what I'm going to say. I've spoken to her and been with her for a long time, as was agreed between the two of us. It always seems to me that in her heart's private thoughts she has something with which she can—if I guess correctly—put a stop to all this that you're afraid of. So my advice is that you go to her when it's night and make an end of this. And I hope blessed Juno,* through her great power, shall send her grace to us. My heart says: "She certainly shan't go." So set your heart at rest for a while, and keep to this plan, because it's for the best.' [1120]

'What you've said is very good, and that's just what I'll do,' replied Troilus and sighed bitterly. And he said further on the subject whatever he wanted.

And when it was time to go, he came secretly to her, himself and nobody else, as he was accustomed to do, and I shall soon tell you how they behaved. The truth is that, when they first met, the pain so wrung their hearts that neither of them could greet the other, but they embraced each other, and afterwards kissed. Even the one who was less sorrowful scarcely knew their whereabouts, nor could get a word out, as I said before, because of unhappiness and because of sobbing. Because of the pain, those sorrowful tears that they let fall were as bitter (quite beyond the nature of tears) as lign-aloes* or gall—the woeful Myrrha* did not weep forth such bitter tears through the bark, as I discover. There is not so hard a heart in this world that would not have pitied their keen sufferings!

But when their two weary and unhappy spirits* had returned to where they were supposed to dwell, and the pain began to weaken somewhat because of the length of time spent lamenting, and the spring of their tears started to ebb, and their hearts grow less swollen, Criseyde said these same words to Troilus, in a broken voice all hoarse and worn out from shrieking:

'O Jove, I am dying, and I beg for mercy! Help, Troilus—' And with that she laid her face on his chest and lost the power of speech —with those very words her unhappy spirit was poised at the point of passing away from its proper place. And so she lay there with a pallid and greenish complexion that once was fresh and loveliest to see. [1155]

Troilus gazed at her, calling out her name, and felt her cold limbs— she lay as if dead, without answering, and with her eyes rolled upward in her head. This sorrowful man can think of nothing else to do, but often kissed her cold mouth. Whether he was unhappy, God and he knew! He got up, and stretched her out at length. Whatever he did, he could find no sign of life in Criseyde, and so his refrain was very often 'alas!'. When he saw that she lay speechless, he said—with sorrowful voice and heart bereft of all happiness—that she was departed from this world. So after he had lamented over her for a long time, wrung his hands, and said what was to be said, and rained his salt tears down on her breast, he then began to wipe and dry away the tears, and prayed piteously for her soul, and said:

'O Lord, who are seated on your throne, have pity on me too, for I shall soon follow her!'

She was cold and without sensation, for all he knew, for he felt no breath, and this was a compelling argument to him that she had gone forth from out of this world. When he saw there was no other way, he arranged her limbs in such a way as is done for those who will be laid on a bier. And after this, with stern and cruel heart, he at once pulled his sword out of its scabbard to kill himself, however agonizing the pain, so that his soul might follow her soul wherever the judgement of Minos* would dispose of it, since Love and cruel Fortune would not have it that he should live any longer in this world. [1190]

'O cruel Jove, and you, adverse Fortune,' he then said, full of high disdain, 'this is the whole of it: that you have treacherously killed Criseyde, and since you can do no worse to me, I scorn your power and hostile actions! You will never conquer me this cowardly way. No death shall part me from my lady. For since you have killed her like this, I will abandon this world and follow her spirit high or low. No lover shall ever say that Troilus dared not die with his lady out of fear, for I will certainly keep her company. But since you will not allow us to live here, yet allow that our souls be together. And you, city, that I leave in sorrow, and you, Priam, and all my brothers, and you, my mother—farewell, for I am leaving you! Atropos,* make ready my bier! And you, Criseyde, O sweet, dear heart, receive my spirit now—' he was about to say, with his sword at his heart, all ready to die.

But, as God would have it, she thereupon revived from her swoon and began to sigh, and cried out:

'Troilus!'

'My lady, Criseyde! Are you still alive?' he answered, and let his sword slip down.

'Yes, my heart, thanks be to Venus* for that!' said she, and with that she sighed bitterly. And he began to comfort her as much as he could, and took her in his arms, and often kissed her, and did his utmost to cheer her; and so her spirit, which was all the time fluttering above, entered her sorrowful heart again. Then at last, as her eye glanced to one side, she straightaway noticed his naked sword as it lay there out of its scabbard, and cried out with fear, and asked him why he had drawn it out? And Troilus at once told her the reason, and how he would have killed himself with it, at which Criseyde began to gaze at him, and folded him tightly in her arms and said:

'O mercy, God! To think, what a dreadful deed! Alas, how nearly we both were dead! Then if I hadn't spoken, as luck would have it, you would have killed yourself right away?' said she.

'Yes, undoubtedly.'

'Alas,' she replied, 'for by that same Lord who made me, I wouldn't have remained alive for even a few minutes* after your death, even to have been crowned queen of all the land the sun shines brightly on. But with this selfsame sword that is here I would have killed myself,' she then said. 'But stop, because we've had quite enough of this, and let's get up and go straight to bed, and let's talk there of our unhappiness. For by the nightlight* that I see burning, I know very well that day is not far off.' [1246]

When they were in their bed, folded in each other's arms, it was not like those nights previously. For each gazed piteously at the other, like those who had lost all their happiness, always lamenting the day that they were born, till at last this sorrowful person, Criseyde, said to Troilus these very words:

'Look, my heart, you well know this,' said she, 'that if a person is continually bemoaning his unhappiness and doesn't seek a remedy, it's nothing but folly and an increase of suffering. And since we two have got together here to find a remedy for the unhappiness that we're in, it's high time to begin soon. I'm a woman—as you're very well aware!—and as I've made my mind up all of a sudden,* I'll tell you while it's fresh in my thoughts. It seems to me that neither you nor I, reasonably speaking, ought to be making half this to-do, for there are means enough to set right what's still amiss and put an end to this gloom. The truth is, for all I know, that the sorrow we're in is for no other reason than because we're to part. All things considered, there's nothing else wrong! But what then is the solution to this, but that we contrive to meet soon? This is the sum of the whole matter, my dear, sweet heart! Now, I'm in no sort of doubt that I shall certainly bring it about that I come back again soon after I leave. For I'll be here within a week or two, without a doubt. And in few words, I'll certainly show you heaps of ways how it can quite rightly be so. I won't make a long speech about it— for lost time can't be recovered—but I'll go straight to my conclusion, and for the best, as far as I can see. And for the love of God, forgive me if I say anything contrary to your peace of mind, because I truly am saying it for the best, always solemnly protesting that what I shall now say is only to show you my desire to find the best way to help us. So don't take it any other way, I beg you, but in fact, whatever you command me, I will do—of that there is no question. [1295]

'Now listen to this. You've well understood that my going is agreed by parliament to such an extent that in my opinion it can't be opposed for anything. And since no thinking about it will help prevent it, put it out of your mind, and let's contrive to find a better way. The truth is this: our separation will distress and disturb us cruelly, but he who serves love must sometimes have suffering if he wants to have happiness.* And since I'll be going no further out of Troy than I can ride back again in half a morning, it ought to make us less unhappy. I shan't be so cooped up—since you well know there is now a truce—that you won't hear full well how I am from day to day. And before that truce is over I'll be here again, and then you've gained both Antenor and me as well. Cheer up now, if you can, and think just like this: "Criseyde is gone now. What then, she'll come back soon!" And when, alas? By God, right away, you know, before ten days, I can safely say! And then at last we'll be so happy, because we'll stay together always, that this whole world couldn't express our happiness. [1323]

'In our present situation I see that—for the best, and to conceal our intentions—you often don't speak with me for a fortnight, nor I with you, nor do I even see you pass by. Then can't you wait ten days for the sake of my honour in such a situation as the present one? If not, you can certainly put up with very little! You know too how all my family is here, except for my father, and every other thing of mine too, and especially you, my dear heart, whom I wouldn't stop seeing for this whole wide world, or else may I never see Jove's face in heaven! Why do you think my father so desires to see me like this, except for fear in case people in this town despise me on account of him, because of his unfortunate deed? What does my father know about what life I'm leading? For if he knew how well I'm getting on in Troy, we wouldn't need to care about my leaving. [1344]

'You see that every day too, more and more, people are discussing peace, and it's supposed that Queen Helen will be returned, and the Greeks will make reparations to us, so although there were no other comfort than this—that peace is being proposed on all sides—you can wait with more peace of mind. For if there be peace, my dear heart, the nature of the peace must of necessity compel people to have dealings with one another, and also ride and walk readily to and fro all the time, as thick as bees fly from a hive,* and every person will have liberty to remain where he prefers, without anyone's permission. And if there can be no peace, I must still come back here—even though there were never any peace! For where should I go, or how should I remain there—curse it!—in constant fear, among

those armed men? And therefore—as God may surely guide my soul
—I can't see what you should be afraid of. [1365]

'Here's another way, if all this is not enough for you. My father
is old, as you're well aware, indeed. Old age is full of covetousness,
and I've just discovered the whole way in which I can catch him,
without a net!* And listen how, if you will. You see, Troilus, peo-
ple say "it's hard to have the wolf full and the sheep unharmed".*
That's to say, that one must very often spend part to save the remain-
der. For with gold one can always make an impression on the heart
of a man set on covetousness. I'll tell you what I mean. I'll take to
my father the property I have in this town, and say that it is sent in
trust and for safe keeping from a friend or two of his, which friends
eagerly beg him to send for more, and quickly, while this town is in
danger like this. And I'll tell him that it will be a huge amount, but,
in case people should notice, it can't be sent by anyone except by
me. I'll also show him, if peace should come about, what friends I
have on all sides at court, to cause Priam's anger to pass and cause
him to be in favour. [1393]

'So what with one thing and another, my sweet, I shall so enchant
him with my speeches that he will dream his soul is in heaven! For
Apollo, or his learned precepts, or divination, are worth next to noth-
ing at all.* Desire for gold shall so blind his soul that I will end the
matter as I please. And if in any way he wants to test whether I'm
lying by casting lots, I'll certainly try and frustrate him, and tug him
by the sleeve while he's making his divination, and make him believe
he hasn't rightly understood the gods. For gods speak in ambigui-
ties, and for one truth they tell twenty lies. Also "Fear first invented
gods,* I suppose"—I'll say that—and that his coward heart made
him misinterpret the gods' text when he fled in fright from Delphi.*
And unless I make him soon change his mind, and follow my advice
within a day or two, I'll pledge myself to you to die.'

And truly, I find it written* that all of this was said with good
intentions, that her heart was true and kind towards him, that she
spoke exactly as she meant, that she nearly died for unhappiness when
she went, and that she intended always to be true. Those who knew
of her actions write in this way. [1421]

All ears, and his heart all attention, Troilus heard all this discussed
to and fro, and it truly seemed to him that he was of the same mind;
yet his heart continually misgave him over letting her go. But in the

end he constrained his heart to trust her, and took it for the best.
As a result, the furious agony of his suffering was quenched with
hope, and with that, for sheer joy, love-making* began between them.
Just as the birds, when the sun is bright, delight in their song among
the green leaves, so the words they spoke together delighted them
and unclouded their hearts. But nevertheless, in spite of everything,
he could not get Criseyde's departure out of his mind, and so he
repeatedly begged her pitifully that he might find her true to her
promise, and said to her:

'If you're cruel, and don't come into Troy on the appointed day,
I'll certainly never have health, honour, or happiness. For as truly
as the sun rises in the morning—and may God as surely bring me,
unhappy wretch, out of this cruel sorrow to rest!—I'll kill myself if
you delay. But though there's little to care about in my death, still,
before you cause me to suffer so, stay here instead, my own sweet
heart. For truly, my own dear lady, these stratagems that I've so far
heard you propose are all of them very likely to fail. For people say:
"The bear thinks one thing, but his leader thinks quite another."
Your father is wise, and it's said, without a doubt: "One can outrun
the wise, but not outwit them." It's very hard to pretend to limp
undetected in front of a cripple, because he understands the art. When
it comes to trickery, your father has as many eyes as Argus.* For
although his property is taken from him, his old cunning still remains
so much with him that you won't deceive him for all your woman's
ways, nor pretend successfully, and that's my whole fear. [1463]

'I don't know if peace will ever come about. But, peace or no
peace, I know in any event that, since Calchas has once been on the
Greek side and so disgracefully lost his good name, he won't dare
come here again for shame. So to trust on that course of action, as
far as I can see, is just a fantasy. You'll also see that your father will
cajole you to get married and, as he well knows how to preach, he'll
so praise and commend some Greek that he'll carry you away with
his words, or compel you by force to do as he instructs. Then this
way Troilus, on whom you'll have no pity, will die without cause
and always faithful! And besides all this, your father will speak ill of
us all, and say this city is as good as lost, and that the siege will never
be raised, because the Greeks have all sworn it, until we're killed
and our walls torn down. And he'll frighten you with his words like
this, so that I'm always afraid that you'll remain there. You'll see

among the Greeks so many fine knights, full of zest and distinction, and each of them will do his best with heart, mind, and strength to please you, that you'll become bored with the lack of refinement of us simple Trojans, unless pity makes you feel remorse, or the strength of your loyalty. And to think this is so terrible for me that it will tear my soul out of my heart. Nor, without a doubt, can I have any hopeful expectation if you go, because your father's cunning will destroy us. As I've told you before, if you go, think of me as all but dead—there's nothing more to it! [1498]

'And so with humble, true, and piteous heart, I beg you a thousand times for mercy! Have pity on my sharp and bitter pains, and do as I shall say. Let's steal away, the two of us, and think that it's folly, when a person can choose, to exchange the substantial reality for some accidental attribute.* This is what I mean: that since we can certainly steal away before day and be together like this, what sense would it make to put it to the test—if you went to your father—whether you might come back again or not? I mean, it would be folly to risk what we can be sure of. To speak in an ordinary sense about "substance"—about money—we can both carry with us enough to live in honour and pleasure until the day we die; so we can avoid all this anxiety. (For every other way you can think of, indeed, at heart I can't agree with.) You certainly shouldn't fear any poverty, for I have family and friends elsewhere so that, even though we turned up in our bare shirts, we shouldn't lack for money or possessions, but be honoured while we stayed there. Let's go immediately, for to my mind this is the best thing, if you'll agree.' [1526]

With a sigh Criseyde replied exactly like this:

'Indeed, my dear, true heart, we may well steal away as you describe, and take such unrewarding new directions, but afterwards we'll regret it very much. God help me in my hour of greatest need, you endure all this anxiety without cause! For that day that I am false to you, my Troilus, my knight—whether because of love or fear of my father or someone else, or because of position, pleasure, or because of marriage—may Saturn's daughter, Juno, through her power, cause me to remain as mad as Athamas,* eternally in Styx, the pit of hell!* And I swear this to you on every celestial god, and on each goddess too, on every nymph and deity of the infernal regions, on satyrs and fauns,* greater and less, that are demigods of the wilderness. And may Atropos* break my life's thread in two if I be false! Now believe me if you will! And you, Simois,* that like a bright arrow run through Troy ever downwards to the sea, bear witness to this word that is spoken here: that, on the day I am untrue to Troilus, my own noble heart, you flow backwards to your source,* and I sink body and soul into hell! [1554]

'But when you talk of going away like this and abandoning all your friends, God forbid you should do so for any woman's sake, and especially since Troy now has such need of help! And consider one other thing, too: if this were known, my life and your honour would lie in the balance. God protect us from misfortune! And if peace should take effect sometime later—as anger continually gives way to goodwill—why, Lord, how miserable you would be, because you wouldn't dare come back again for shame! Before you so jeopardize your reputation, don't be too hasty in this rash behaviour, because a hasty man never lacks for sorrow. What do you think people all around here would say about it? It's very easy to predict. They would say, and swear to it certainly, that love didn't drive you to do this deed, but just sheer lust and cowardly fear. Your honour, which now shines so brightly, would certainly be completely lost this way, my dear heart. And also give some thought to my reputation, as yet unblemished, and how shamefully I should ruin it, and how it would be stained with infamy, if I went away with you in this manner. Even if I lived till the end of the world, I should never get my good name back again. So I would be ruined, and that would be a pity and a sin. Be reasonable then, and cool down. People say: "Patience conquers," by God! Also: "Whoever will have something he wants, must give up something he wants." Make a virtue of necessity* like this by patience, and think that he is always lord of Fortune who won't care anything about her, and she frightens no one but a wretch! And believe this, sweet heart: that before Phoebus' sister, bright Lucina, having left this sign of Aries, passes the sign of Leo,* I will be here, without a doubt. As help me Juno, queen of heaven,* I mean I will see you on the tenth day without fail, unless death strikes me down!' [1596]

'Provided that's true,' said Troilus, 'I'll endure it till the tenth day, since I see it has to be so. But for the love of God, if it's possible, let's steal away secretly, for my heart keeps telling me it will be the best thing to live in peace.'

'O mercy, God, what life is this?' said she. 'Alas, you're killing me for sheer vexation! I see very well now that you mistrust me—it's clearly shown by your words. For the love of Cynthia* the bright, don't mistrust me like this without cause, for pity's sake, since I've given my word to be true to you! And remember it's sometimes wiser to let one occasion pass in order to gain another. I'm not yet lost to you, by God! though we're apart for a day or two. Get rid of these fantasies of yours, and trust me, and give up your grieving too, or I give you my word: I won't live another day! For if you knew how badly it hurts me, you would stop this. For, O God, you know, the very spirit weeps in my heart to see you weep that I most love, and that I must go to the Greeks. Yes, if it weren't that I knew a way to come back, I would die right here! But I'm certainly not so foolish a person that I can't imagine a way to come back the day that I've promised. For who can hold on to a thing that yearns to be elsewhere? Not my father, for all his ingenious devices! If I succeed, my departure from Troy will make us all happy another day. So I beg you with all my heart—if you'd care to do anything that I ask you, and for that love I have for you too—that before I leave you here I may see you so cheered up and comforted that you set my heart at rest, which is on the point of breaking. Besides all this I beg you,' said she then, 'my own heart's true fulfilment, since I'm completely yours alone, that while I'm away no pleasure in anyone else put me from your thoughts, for I'm afraid all the time, because people say "love is something always full of anxiety".* For if you were unfaithful— as God forbid!—there's no woman alive in this world who would feel so betrayed or miserable as I, who think of all loyalty as being represented by you. If I thought otherwise, I'd undoubtedly just die, and—until you find reason to be—for the love of God, don't be unkind to me!' [1652]

To this Troilus replied, saying:

'Now may God, from whom no cause is hidden, give me happiness, as surely as I was never false to Criseyde since that day I first saw her, nor ever shall be till I die! You may well believe me, in short. I can't say any more than that; it'll be proved by experience.'

'Thank you, indeed, my treasure!' said she, 'and may blessed Venus never let me die before I'm in the happy position to reward well someone who deserves so well! And while I still have my right mind (which God preserve), I'll act in such a way—I've found you so faithful—that honour shall continually rebound on me. For rely on it* that neither your royal position, nor empty pleasure, nor merely your valour in war or martial tournament, nor pomp, splendour, nobility, or riches either, made me have pity on your distress, but moral virtue, grounded in fidelity—that was the reason I first had pity on you! Also, the noble heart and manliness that you had, and that, as it seemed to me, you disdained everything that tended towards the bad, such as crudeness and vulgar desires, and that your reason reined in the pleasure you took. . . . This was why I was yours in preference to any one else alive, and shall be as long as I live. And this can't be destroyed by length of years, or obliterated by changeable Fortune. But may Jupiter, who through his power can make the sorrowful happy, grant us the favour of meeting here before ten nights, so that your heart and mine may find contentment enough! And now farewell, for it is time for you to get up.' [1687]

And after they had long lamented, and had often kissed, and tightly clasped each other in their arms, the day began to break. Troilus dressed, gazing ruefully at his lady, like a man who felt the cold pains of death, and commended himself to her favour. I think there is no question whether he was sorrowful! For the mind of man cannot imagine, nor understanding consider, nor tongue tell,* the cruel pains of this sorrowful man, which surpassed every torment down in hell. For when he saw that she could not stay—which tore his soul out of his heart—without anything further he left the room. [1701]

Here ends the fourth book.

BOOK FIVE

Here begins the fifth book.

The fatal destiny was approaching* that Jove has the power to control and entrusts to you three sisters,* the angry Fates, to carry out; by which Criseyde must leave the city, and Troilus live on afterwards in suffering, until Lachesis no longer spins the thread of his life. Golden-tressed* Phoebus on high had three times* completely melted away the snows with his pure beams, and Zephyrus* had as often brought back again the tender green leaves, since Queen Hecuba's son* had first begun to love her for whom all his sorrow was that she was to depart in the morning.

At the hour of prime* Diomede was all prepared to conduct Criseyde to the Greek host, for sorrow at which she felt her heart bleed, not knowing what was best to do. And truly, as people read in books, never was a woman known to have such sorrow or to be so reluctant to leave a city. Troilus, at his wits' end, and like a man who has also lost all his happiness, was continually waiting for his lady, who was the beginning and end of all his joys or pleasure before this. But Troilus, farewell now to all your happiness, for you will never see her in Troy again! [28]

The truth is that while he waited he hid his unhappiness very manfully, so that it was hardly noticed from his manner. But he lingered to wait for her with certain people at the gate where she was to ride out, so wretchedly unhappy (although he would not complain), that he could scarcely sit on his horse for grief. He shook with anger—it gnawed his heart so—when Diomede mounted his horse, and he said to himself:

'Alas, why do I put up with such despicable misery? Why won't I set it to rights? Wouldn't it be better to die at once than endure suffering like this for ever more? Why don't I immediately give everyone enough to do before she leaves? Why don't I throw the whole of Troy into an uproar? Why don't I kill this Diomede too? Why don't I steal her away instead, with the help of a man or two? Why do I put up with this? Why don't I help to put things right for myself?'

But let me explain why he would not commit so fierce an act and why he chose to refrain from it. He always had at heart a kind of fear in case—in all the uproar of this action—Criseyde should have been killed. This was his whole concern. Otherwise, as I said previously, he would certainly have done it without any more words. [56]

When she was ready to ride, Criseyde heaved a sad sigh and murmured: 'Alas!' But she must leave, whatever may happen. There is no other remedy in this case, and she slowly rode out, full of sorrow. What wonder is it that she suffered grievously, when she was giving up her own sweet heart? By way of courtesy, Troilus rode, with a hawk on his hand and with a huge crowd of knights, and kept her company, passing far beyond the valley; he would certainly have ridden further very gladly and was sad to leave so soon, but turn he must. It had to be done. Just at that moment Antenor emerged from the Greek host, and everyone was glad about it and said he was welcome. And Troilus—although he was far from light-hearted—tried with all his might to restrain himself from weeping at least, and he kissed Antenor and made much of him. Then Troilus had to take his leave and gazed at Criseyde piteously; he rode nearer to plead his case and took her very gravely by the hand. And Lord, how tenderly she wept! And he very quietly and secretly said to her:

'Keep to your appointed day! Don't make me die!'

Then, with a pale face, he turned his horse round and spoke not a word to Diomede nor to any of his company. This the son of Tydeus* noticed—like one who knew more than the rudiments* of such an art—and he seized the reins of Criseyde's horse;* and Troilus returned home towards Troy. [91]

When Diomede, who was leading Criseyde's horse along by the bridle, saw that the people of Troy were gone, he thought:

'All my efforts won't be wasted, if I can help it, because I'll say something to her. At the worst it may help shorten our journey. I've also heard it said two dozen times: "He's a fool that will forget himself."'*

But nevertheless, he thought this well enough, too:

'I'm certainly wasting my time if I speak of love or am too pressing. For undoubtedly, if she's thinking about the one I suspect, he can't be displaced so soon. But I'll find a means, so that she won't know as yet what I'm intending.' [105]

CONTRAST

When it was opportune Diomede—who knew what was to his advantage—struck up a conversation* about this and that, and asked why she was so upset, and also begged her, if he could improve or add to her comfort in any way, that she should command it him, and he would do it, he said. He swore to her as a knight that, truly, there was nothing in which he might please her, that he would not strive with all his might to do, in order to gratify her; and he asked her to calm her sorrow and said:

'We Greeks can certainly take as much pleasure in honouring you as the people of Troy.' He also spoke thus:

'I know it seems strange to you—and no wonder, since it's new to you—to exchange the acquaintance of these Trojans for Greek people that you never knew before. But God forbid that you should not find as true a Greek among us all as any Trojan is, and as kind too! Because I swore to you just now to be your friend and as helpful as I could, and because I've also had more acquaintance with you than any other stranger has, then from this time forward, day and night, I beg you: command me to do everything that may please your heart, however severely I may suffer—treat me as your brother, and do not despise my friendship. And though your sorrows may be because of some important matters—I don't know why—but my heart would take great pleasure in making things better without further delay. If I can't put your troubles right, I'm very sorry for your unhappiness. For though you Trojans have been on bad terms with us Greeks for many a day, by God, we both still truly serve one god of Love, and for the love of God, my noble lady, whoever you hate, don't be angry with me, for truly, no one can serve you who would be half so reluctant to deserve your anger. And if we weren't so near the tent of Calchas (who can see both of us), I'd tell you all that's in my mind about this—but this must be kept under seal until another day. Give me your hand.* I am and shall always be—God help me, while my life may last—your own above every other creature! I never spoke like this before now to any woman, for (as I hope to be happy!) I never loved a woman before this in the way of a lover, nor ever will love any others. And for the love of God, don't be my enemy, even if I can't complain to you in the correct form because I still have to be taught. And don't be surprised, my own fair lady, though I speak to you of love so quickly, for I've heard before this of many a person who loved something he never saw in his life. Also, I'm not able to struggle against the God of Love, but I'll always obey him, and I beg you for mercy! There are such worthy knights in this place, and you are so beautiful, that every one of them will strive to be in your favour. But if such good fortune befell me that you would call me your servant, none of them would serve you so humbly or so truly as I shall till I die.' [175]

Criseyde made little response* to that, like someone who was so oppressed with sorrow that in effect she did not catch what he was saying, except now a word or two here and there. It seemed to her that her sorrowful heart would break in two, for when she made out her father in the distance she very nearly sank down off her horse. But nevertheless, she thanked Diomede for all his trouble and his kind welcome, and that he wished to offer her his friendship, and she accepted it civilly, and would gladly do whatever was pleasing and dear to him, and she would trust him, as well she might, she said—and she alighted from her horse.

Her father took her in his arms and kissed his sweet daughter twenty times and said:

'O my dear daughter, welcome!'

She too said she was glad to meet him again and stood there mute, mild-mannered, and meek. But here I leave her to remain with her father, and I will tell you further about Troilus. [196]

This unhappy man has returned to Troy in sorrow bitter beyond all sorrows, with sullen look and a cruel face. Then he suddenly jumped down from his horse and went through his palace to his room, his heart swollen with grief. (He took no notice of anything, and no one dared speak a word to him for fear.) And there he gave full vent to the sorrows that he had held in and cried out: 'Death!' And in his frantic mad throes he cursed Jove, Apollo, and also Cupid; he cursed Ceres, Bacchus,* and Venus, his birth, himself, his fate, and also Nature, and, except his lady, every created thing. He went to bed, and there writhed and turned about in furious agony, as Ixion* does in hell, and he remained in this state until it was nearly day. But then his heart began to grow a little less swollen because of the tears that welled up, and he piteously called out to Criseyde, and to himself he spoke just like this, and said:

'Where is my own, dear, dear lady? Where is her white breast? Where is it, where? Where are her arms and her bright eyes that were with me at this time last night? Now I may weep many a tear alone, and I may well reach out, but I find nothing to embrace here except a pillow! What shall I do? When will she come back? I don't know, alas, why I let her go. Would to God I had been killed then! O my heart, Criseyde! O sweet enemy! O my lady that I love and no others, to whom for ever more I dedicate my heart, see how I am dying, and you will not rescue me! Who sees you now, my true lodestar? Who is sitting or standing right now in your presence? Who is able to comfort now the conflict in your heart? Whom do you listen to, now I'm gone? Who speaks for me right now in my absence? Alas, no one—and that's the whole of my sorrow, for I know very well that you're suffering as badly as I am. How should I endure a full ten days like this, when I have all this grief the first night? How will she do, too, poor creature? She's so sensitive, how will she be able to bear such sorrow for me? O your fresh, feminine face will be pitifully pale and wan for distress before you return to this place!' [245]

Whenever he fell asleep, he would at once begin to groan and dream of the most frightening things that could be, such as: dream he were lamenting alone forever in some appalling place, or dream he was in the midst of all his enemies and fallen into their hands. And at that his body would jump, and with a start he would wake up very abruptly, and feel such a tremor round his heart that his body would quiver with fear. And at that he would cry out, and seem as though he was going to plummet down from a great height, and then he would weep, and feel so pitifully sorry for himself that it was astonishing to hear his imaginings. Another time he would greatly comfort himself, and say it was folly to endure such fear so causelessly; and then his bitter sorrows would begin again, so that anyone would feel sorry for his sorrows. [266]

Who could truly tell, or fully describe, his unhappiness, his lamenting, his distress, and his torment? Not all those who have been or are now alive. You, reader,* can divine very well for yourself that my wits are not up to describing such a sorrow. I should labour in vain to write it, when my mind is weary to think of it!

The stars were still visible in the sky, although the moon had grown very pale, and all towards the east the bright horizon was whitening, as it is wont to do. Soon afterwards Phoebus prepared to travel upwards with his rosy chariot,* and then Troilus sent for Pandarus.

The whole day before, Pandarus was not able to come to see Troilus—even if he had sworn by his head to do so—because he was with King Priam all day, so that it was not in his power to go anywhere. But in the morning he went to Troilus when he sent for him. For in his heart he could easily guess that Troilus had not slept all night for sorrow, and that he wanted to tell him of his suffering—he knew this well enough, and needed no book to tell him so. And so he made his way straight to the bedroom, and he then greeted Troilus gravely, and very soon sat down on the bed. [294]

'My Pandarus,' said Troilus, 'I can't endure for long the sorrow that I'm suffering. I don't believe I'll live until tomorrow, and so—both in case that happens and at any event—I wish to describe to you the form of my tomb.* As for my personal possessions, dispose of them as you think best. But I beg you, take good care that everything is well done with regard to the funeral fire and flame in which my body will be burned to glowing embers, and the feast and funeral games* at my wake. Offer my horse, my sword, and my helmet to Mars. And dear, dear brother, give my bright-shining shield to Pallas. I beg you to collect up the ashes into which my burnt heart shall turn and preserve them in a golden vessel that is called an urn. And give it to my lady, whom I serve, and for love of whom I am piteously dying like this, and do me this favour: ask her to keep it as a memento. For I do feel, by my illness and by my dreams now and long ago, that I must certainly die. The owl too which is called Ascalaphus* has screeched after me the whole of these last two nights. And O you god, Mercury,* may you now guide my soul and fetch it away when you please!' [322]

Pandarus replied:

'Troilus, my dear friend, as I've told you in the past, it's madness to sorrow like this and causeless—and so I can't say or do any more. I can't see any help for someone who won't believe advice or teaching—but let him remain with his delusions. But Troilus, I beg you, tell me now if you believe that before this any man was in love as passionately as you? Yes, God knows, and his lady has gone away from many an excellent knight for a fortnight, and yet he didn't make half this fuss! What need is there for you to grieve like this? You can see yourself day by day that of necessity a man must be parted from his love, or else from his wife—yes, even though he love her like his own life!—and yet he won't be at war with himself like this.

For you well know, my dear, dear brother, that friends can't always be together. How do these people do who see their loves wedded to others through the powerful influence of friends, as happens very often, and witness them put to bed* in their spouse's bed? God knows, they take it wisely, quietly, and without objection, because good hope keeps up their spirits; and because they can endure a time of sorrow, as time hurts them, a time heals them!* So should you bear up, and let the time pass by, and try to be cheerful and light-hearted. Ten days isn't so long to wait. And since she's promised you to come, she won't break her promise for anybody. Never fear that she'll find a way to come back—I'd bet my life on it! [357]

'Banish your dreams* and all such imaginings, and let them go to the devil! For they stem from your depression,* which makes you experience all this suffering in your sleep. A straw for all the significance there is in dreams! So help me God, I don't think they're worth a bean! No man knows correctly what dreams mean. For priests of the temple say dreams are the revelations of gods, and they say as well, indeed, that they're illusions from hell! And doctors say that they derive from people's temperaments, or from fasting, or from gluttony! So who knows in truth what they signify? Also, others say that some dreams come through mental impressions,* as when a person has a fixed idea in mind; and others say, as they find in books, that by nature men dream according to the seasons of the year,* and that the effect is determined by the moon. But don't believe any dream, for it's not worth doing. Dreams are all very well for old women, and truly, divination from the birds as well—such as the croaking of ravens, or screeching of these owls—for fear of which men think they'll lose their lives. Believing in it is both mistaken and shameful. Alas, alas, that such a noble creature as is man should fear such rubbish! [385]

'So I do implore you with all my heart to spare yourself all this. Get up, without any more talk, and let's consider how this time may best be spent, and also what a good time we may have when she comes back, which will be very soon. God help me, it's for the best! Get up, let's talk of the lively life we've led in Troy, to pass the time. And let's rejoice too at the coming time that will bring us happiness so soon now. And in that way we'll so forget or overcome the suffering of these ten days that it will scarcely cause us any hardship. This town is full of lords all around, and meanwhile a truce is lasting. Let's go and visit Sarpedon,* only a mile from here, and have fun in some lively company. This way you'll be able to wile away and pass the time until that blissful day that you see her who is cause of your sorrow. Now get up, my dear brother Troilus, for it certainly does you no honour to weep and take to your bed like this. For believe me about one thing, truly: if you lie like this for a day— or two, or three—people will say that you're pretending to be ill, out of cowardice, and that you daren't get up!' [413]

'O dear brother,' Troilus replied, 'those who have suffered pain know it's no wonder if someone who feels pain and anguish everywhere in his body weeps and behaves sorrowfully. And though I continually weep or lament, I'm in no way to blame, because I've lost the cause of all my happiness. But since I must get up, out of sheer necessity, I'll get up as soon as ever I can. And may God, to whom I sacrifice my heart, quickly send us the tenth day! For no bird was ever so glad of May as I'll be, when she who's the cause of my torment and my joy comes back to Troy. But where do you advise that we can amuse ourselves best in this whole town?'

'By God,' said Pandarus, 'my advice is to ride over and have a good time with King Sarpedon.'

Back and forth they discuss this at length, until Troilus at last agreed to get up, and off they went to Sarpedon. As someone who throughout his life was honourable and full of high generosity, Sarpedon fed them day by day with every delicacy that could be served at table, even though it cost a fortune, so that such magnificence, as everyone said, great and small, was never known before that day at any feast. Nor is there in this world, as far as anyone has ever travelled, any delightful-sounding wind or string instrument that tongue can tell of or heart remember, that was not heard played well in harmony at that feast. Nor was so lovely a company of ladies ever seen dancing before then. [448]

But what use was this to Troilus who, on account of his sorrow, cared nothing about it? For his piteous heart was continually seeking very anxiously for his lady, Criseyde. His heart was always thinking entirely about her, imagining now this, now that, so intently that certainly no festivity could make him happy. Since he saw his own lady was away, it was also a grief to him to see the ladies who were at this feast, or to hear instruments being played. Because she who held the key of his heart was absent, you see, this was his whim:

that no one should make music.* Nor was there an hour in the whole day or night, when he was where no one could overhear him, that he did not say:

'O most fair and lovely lady, how have you got on since you were here? Welcome, indeed, my own, dear lady!'

But alas, all this was only a delusion—Fortune intended to delude him even further, and arm him with a helmet made of glass!* The letters too that she had sent him in earlier times he would read alone a hundred times between midday and early next morning, picturing again in his heart her form and her womanliness, and every word and deed that was past. And so he passed the fourth day, and declared he wanted to leave, saying:

'Dear brother, do you intend us to stay here until Sarpedon invites us to leave? It would be more proper for us to take our leave of him. For the love of God, let's take our leave soon now, this evening, and let's return home, for truly, I won't stay on like this.' [483]

'Have we come here,' Pandarus replied, 'just to borrow a light and then run home again? So help me God, I can't tell where we could go, if I'm to speak truthfully, where anyone is more glad to see us than Sarpedon! And I consider it bad manners if we hurry away from here suddenly like this. Since we said we'd stay with him a week—and now, so suddenly, to take our leave of him on the fourth day—he'd truly be very surprised at it! Let's keep strictly to our plan. Since you promised him to stay, keep your promise now, and afterwards let's ride on our way.'

In this fashion, with much effort and misery, Pandarus made him stay, and at the end of the week they then took their leave of Sarpedon and hurried to depart on their way.

'Now Lord send me grace,' said Troilus, 'that when I get home I may find Criseyde returned!' And with that he started to sing.*

'Oh, fiddlesticks!'* thought Pandarus, and he said very softly to himself: 'God knows, all this hot stuff may cool down before Calchas sends Criseyde to Troilus!'

But he cracked jokes nevertheless, and played about, and swore, indeed, his heart assured him she would come as soon as ever she could. When they reached Troilus' palace, they dismounted from their horses and made their way to the bedroom, and until nightfall they spoke of the fair Criseyde. And after this, when they both wished, they hurried from supper to their rest. [518]

The next morning, as soon as day began to dawn, Troilus woke from his sleep and said very piteously to Pandarus, his own dear brother:

'For the love of God, let's go and see Criseyde's palace. For since we can't as yet have any greater pleasure, then at least let's see her palace.'*

And thereupon, to deceive the members of his household, he invented a reason to go into town, and they went to Criseyde's house. But Lord, how unhappy poor Troilus was! It seemed to him his sorrowful heart would break in two. For when he saw her doors all barred he nearly fell down for sorrow. And then, when he took note and observed how every window of the place was shut, it seemed to him his heart grew cold as frost; and so, with an altered, deathly pale face, he passed on by without a word, and, as God would have it, he rode so fast that no one caught sight of his face. [539]

'O deserted palace!'* he then said in this way, 'O house, once called the best of houses! O empty and cheerless palace! O you lantern, whose light is quenched!* O palace, that once was day and now is night! You certainly ought to fall in ruins, and I should die, since she has gone who used to guide us! O palace, once the crown of all houses, and lit up by the sun of all joy! O ring from which the ruby* has fallen out! O cause of misery, that has been cause of joy! Yet since I can't do better, I would gladly kiss your cold doors, if I dared to in front of this crowd. And farewell, shrine, from which the saint is absent!'

With that he looked at Pandarus, with changed face and pitiful to see. And when he could find the right time, as he rode along, he continually told Pandarus about his new sorrow and his former happiness too, so piteously and with such a deathly pale colour that anyone would have had compassion on his sorrow. After that, he rode up and down, and everything brought back memories to him, as he rode past places in the town in which he had once had his whole delight. [564]

'Look, over there I last saw my lady dance;* and in that temple my own, dear lady first captured me with her bright eyes. And over there I've heard my dear heart's peals of laughter. And over there too I once saw her enjoying herself, quite blissfully happy; and over there she once said to me: "Now, good sweetheart, I beg you, love me well!" And over there she looked at me so kindly that my heart is bound to her till death. And at that corner, in the house over there,

I heard my most beloved, dear lady sing so well, so beautifully, so clearly, and in such a feminine way in her melodious voice, that it seems to me I still hear the heavenly sound in my soul! And in that place over there my lady first took me into her favour.'

Then he thought:

'O blessed Lord Cupid! When I remember the whole process—how you have made war on me on all sides—a book could be written about it, like a story! What need is there for you to seek victory over me, since I am yours and wholly at your will? What pleasure do you have in destroying your own people? You have well avenged your anger on me, you mighty god and terrible to offend! Show mercy now, Lord! You well know I desire your favour most of all dear delights, and I will live and die in your faith,* for which I only ask one favour as a reward—you send me Criseyde again soon! Impel her heart to want to return as much as you make mine long to see her; then I know that she will not delay. Now, blessed Lord, don't be so cruel to the Trojans, I beg you, as Juno was to the Theban race,* through which the people of Thebes were destroyed!' [602]

And after this he went to the gates where Criseyde had ridden out at a good pace, and he took many a turn up and down there, and he very often said to himself:

'Alas, my bliss and my joy rode out from here! Blessed God, now grant, for his joy, that I might see her come back into Troy again! And I conducted her to the hill over there, alas, and there I took my leave of her! And over there I saw her ride to her father, for sorrow at which my heart will split in two! And I came home here when it was evening, and here I remain and ever shall, outcast from all happiness, till I can see her again in Troy.'

And he often imagined himself to be changed for the worse, and pale and thinner than he used to be, and that people were saying quietly:

'What can the matter be? Has anyone guessed the truth, why Troilus is so despondent?'

And it was only because of his depression that he had such delusions about himself. Another time he would imagine that everyone who went by in the street pitied him, and that they were saying:

'I'm very sorry Troilus is going to die.'

And, as you have heard, he spent a day or two like this. His life was such that he was like someone torn between hope and fear. And for this reason he liked to show in his songs, as best he could, the reason for his unhappiness. He composed a song of no more than a few words, to gladden his sorrowful heart somewhat. When he was out of everyone's sight, he sang in a quiet voice of his dear lady who was absent—as you may hear:

Troilus' Song*

'O star, whose light I have all lost! With grieving heart I ought indeed to lament that night after night, in torment and continual darkness, I sail towards my death, with the wind at my back. And because of this, if I am without the guidance of your bright beams for an hour on the tenth night, Charybdis* will swallow up my ship and me!' [644]

When he had sung this song like this, he soon fell back again into his former sighs. And every night, as was his custom, he stood looking at the bright moon; and he told all his sorrows to the moon, and said:

'Indeed, when you have your new horns* I shall be happy—if all the world be true! I saw your old horns too in the morning when my own dear lady rode from here, which is the reason for my torment and my sorrow. And so—O bright Latona,* shining one!—move quickly round your orbit, for the love of God! For when your new horns begin to show, she will then come who can bring back my bliss!'

It seemed to him then that the days were longer—and every night longer—than they used to be, and that the sun wrongly travelled its course by a longer way than it used to do. [662]

'Indeed,' he said, 'I'm continually afraid that the sun's son Phaethon* is alive, and that he's driving his father's chariot awry.'

He would also walk a lot on the walls, and look at the Greek host, and talk to himself just like this:

'Look, over there is my noble lady, or else over there, where those tents are! And from there comes this breeze* that is so sweet that in my soul I feel it does me good. And surely this wind that hour by hour blows stronger and stronger in my face is made up of my lady's deep, sad sighs! I prove it like this: for in no other place in this whole town, except in this place alone, do I feel any wind that sounds so like pain. It says: "Alas, why are we two parted?"'

He made this long time pass just like this, until the ninth night was completely gone by. And at his side always was Pandarus, who did his utmost to comfort him and make him more light-hearted, always giving him hope that she will come on the tenth day and bring all his sorrow to an end. [686]

On the other side* too was Criseyde, with a few women, amongst the powerful Greeks, and because of this she said many times a day:

'Oh, I wish I'd never been born! My heart may well long for death, for now I've lived too long. And I can't put things right, alas, because everything is worse now than I ever imagined before! My father won't allow me to return at any price, whatever I do to please him. And if I outstay my appointed time, my Troilus will think in his heart that I'm unfaithful, and so it may well seem. I'll be blamed on all sides like this—oh, how I wish I'd never been born! And if I put myself in jeopardy and steal away by night, and I happen to be caught, I'll be taken for a spy; or else—and this I dread most of all—if I fall into the hands of some man, I'm nothing but a lost woman, even though my heart's true! Now, almighty God, have pity on my sorrow!'* [707]

Her radiant looks had grown very pale, and her limbs were thin, like someone who stood all day, when she dared, and looked at the place where she was born, and where she had always lived. And all night, alas, she lay weeping. And so this sorrowful creature led her life like this, despairing of any help. Many times a day too she sighed for distress, and always went picturing to herself the great excellence of Troilus, and remembering all his gracious words since that day her love first began to grow. And so she set her sorrowful heart ablaze, through the memory of what she desired. In this whole world there is not so cruel-hearted a person that, if he had heard her lament in her sorrow, would not have wept for her painful sufferings, so tenderly did she weep, both evening and morning. She did not need to borrow any tears! And the worst part yet of all her suffering was that there was no one to whom she dared confide her sorrow. She looked back very ruefully towards Troy, and saw the tall towers and also the halls. [730]

'Alas,' said she, 'the pleasure and happiness that I've often had inside those walls over there is now all turned into bitterness! O Troilus, what are you doing now?' she said. 'Lord! Do you still think about Criseyde? How I regret that I didn't trust in your advice and go with

you as you advised me before this! Then I wouldn't have been sigh-
ing half so bitterly now. Who could have said that I'd acted wrongly
to steal away with such a one as he is? But the medicine comes all
too late when the body is being carried to the grave!* It's too late
now to talk of that. Alas, Prudence!* I was always lacking one of your
three eyes before I came here! I well remembered time past, and I
could well see present time too, but I couldn't see future time before
I was caught in the snare, and that's the cause of my sorrow now.
But nevertheless, come what may, tomorrow night I'll steal out of
this army on one side or the other, east or west, and go with Troilus
wherever he wishes. I'll hold to this purpose, and this is best. It
doesn't matter about wicked tongues' gossip, because wretches have
always been envious of love. For doubtless, those who'll take notice
of every word, or let themselves be ruled by everyone's opinion, will
never prosper. For, you see, the same thing that's always criticized
by some people, is praised by other kinds of people. And as far as
I'm concerned—despite all such differences of opinion—I call hap-
piness enough for me!* And so, without any more words, I shall
definitely go to Troy.'

But God knows, before two months were out,* she was very far
from that intention! Both Troilus and Troy shall slip through her
heart like a knotless string, for she will decide to stay. [770]

This Diomede (of whom I was telling you) now went around always
debating in himself, with all his cunning and all he can do, how he
might best, and with the shortest delay, bring Criseyde's heart into
his net. He could never cease from this purpose; he laid out hook
and line to fish for her. But nevertheless, he felt in his heart that
she was not without a lover in Troy, for never since he brought her
from there could he see her laugh or be happy. He did not know
how best to soothe her heart.

'But it does no harm to try,' he said, 'for nothing ventured, noth-
ing gained!'*

Yet he said to himself one night:

'Now aren't I a fool, knowing very well her sorrow is for love of
another man, and just now to go and try something with her? I might
know it won't do me any good, for wise folk express it in books:*
"A person in woe is not to be wooed." But whoever might win such
a flower from him for whom she mourns night and day, he might
say he were a conqueror.'

And straightaway, bold as always, he thought to himself:

'Come what may, even though it kills me, I'll try to win her heart! I shan't lose anything more than my words.'

This Diomede, as books tell us,* was prompt and courageous in whatever he needed to do; with a stern voice and powerful limbs, thick-set; in actions bold, impetuous, strong, and brave, like his father Tydeus. And some people say he was free with his tongue;* and he was heir to Calydon and Argos. [805]

Criseyde* was of average height;* there could not be a more beautiful creature in figure, in face, and also in manner. And this was often her custom: to go with her shining hair down over her collar at the back in plaits, which she would tie with a golden thread. And except that her eyebrows were joined together* in the middle, there was no flaw in her, as far as I can see. But to speak of her bright eyes—well, truly, those who saw her write that paradise stood mirrored in her eyes.* And love continually strove in her* with her rich beauty, as to which of them was greater. She was demure, unaffected too, and prudent as well, and also the best brought up that could be, and pleasant in all respects in her speech, kindly, dignified, vivacious, and generous; she never lacked for compassion; tender-hearted; irresolute.* But truly, I cannot tell her age. [826]

And Troilus* was well grown in height, and so perfectly formed in proportion that nature could not improve upon it: young, tireless, strong, and brave as a lion; true as steel in every aspect; one of the best endowed with good characteristics of all beings that there are, or shall be, while the world may last. And certainly, it is found in the stories that in his time Troilus was never in any way second to anyone in daring to do what befits a knight. Although a giant might surpass him in strength, his heart always stood fully equal with the first and the best in daring to do what pleased him. [840]

But to continue telling of Diomede: it happened afterwards that, on the tenth day* after Criseyde went out of the city, Diomede, as fresh as a branch in May, came to the tent where Calchas was staying, and pretended to have business to do with Calchas. But I shall soon tell you what he intended! To put it briefly, Criseyde welcomed him and sat him down beside her—and it was easy enough to make him stay! And after this, without any long delay, wine and spiced cakes* were brought to them, and they spoke further together of this and that, as friends do—some of which you shall hear.

He first fell into conversation about the war between them and the people of Troy, and he also begged her to tell him what was her opinion of the siege. From that request he proceeded to ask her if Greek manners and activities seemed strange to her; and why her father delayed so long to marry her to some worthy man? Criseyde, who was suffering deeply for love of Troilus, her own knight, replied to him then as far as she had the ability or strength to do so. But as to what was in his mind, it did not seem that she knew what he meant. [868]

But nevertheless, this same Diomede increased in self-confidence, and he said this:

'If I have observed you correctly, it seems to me—O my lady Criseyde*—that from the moment I first laid a hand on your bridle, when you came out from Troy in the morning, I have never been able to see you except in sorrow. I can't say what the cause may be, unless it were for love of some Trojan, and it would greatly grieve me that you should spill a quarter of a tear, or delude yourself so pitifully, for anyone who lives there—for without a doubt it's not worth your while. The people of Troy are, so to speak, in prison one and all, as you see for yourself; nor shall one escape alive out of there for all the gold between sun and sea. Trust me, and understand me clearly: not one shall receive mercy and escape alive, even though he were lord of ten worlds! Before we go from here, such vengeance shall be taken on them for the abduction of Helen that the Manes,* who are gods of pain, will be afraid that Greeks will injure them, and from henceforth until the end of the world men will fear to ravish any queen, so cruel shall our vengeance on them appear. And unless Calchas is misleading us with ambiguities—that's to say, with sly, double words, such as are called two-faced words—you'll certainly understand that I'm not lying, and see all this with your own eyes, and very soon at that—you won't believe how soon. Take all this in now, because it has to happen. What! Do you think your clever father would have exchanged Antenor for you, if he didn't know that the city was going to be destroyed? Why no, on my life! He knew very well that not one Trojan shall escape, and because of that great fear he daren't let you remain there any longer. What more do you want, dear, lovely lady? Let Troy and Trojan pass from your heart! Drive out that bitter hope, and be happy! Bring the beauty back again to your face, that you're defacing so with salt tears, for

Troy is in such jeopardy no remedy can save it now! And think to yourself that, before nightfall, you'll find among the Greeks a lover more perfect than any Trojan is, and more kind, and who will strive his utmost to serve you better. And if you agree, my fair lady, I'll be the one to serve you myself—indeed, rather than be king of twelve Greeces!' [924]

And with those words he turned red, and his voice trembled a little, and he turned his head a little aside, and stopped for a while. And afterwards he roused himself and gazed at her gravely, and said:

'I am, although it be no pleasure to you, as nobly born as any man in Troy. For Criseyde, if my father Tydeus* had lived, I would have been a king before now, of Calydon and Argos,' he said, 'and so I hope I shall be yet, indeed. But he was unluckily killed all too soon at Thebes—alas, more's the pity!—to the detriment of Polynices* and many others. But my heart, since I am your man—and you are the first from whom I seek favour—to serve you as wholeheartedly as I can, and always shall while I live, then before I leave this place I beg you, will you please grant that I may tell you of my sorrow at greater length tomorrow?' [945]

Why should I repeat the words he uttered? He spoke enough for one day at least, and indeed, this was borne out. He spoke to such effect that, at his request, Criseyde agreed at least to speak with him the next day—as long as he would not speak of such matters. And she spoke to him like this, as you may hear—like one who had her heart set so firmly on Troilus that none could uproot it. She spoke distantly, and said in this way:

'O Diomede, I love that same place where I was born, and may Jove, of his grace, deliver it soon from every cause of care! O God, of your might, let it prosper! I know very well indeed that Greeks would avenge their anger on Troy if they could. But it's not going to happen as you say, as God is my witness! Furthermore, I do know that my father is wise and resourceful, and I'm the more obliged to him that he's paid so dearly for me, as you've told me. I'm also well aware that Greeks are men of high character. But as worthy folk are certainly to be found inside the town of Troy: as knowledgeable, and as perfect, and as kind, as are between the Orkneys and India.* I also well believe that you could serve your lady well, in order to deserve her thanks.

'But as to speaking of love, indeed,' she said, 'I had a lord, to whom I was married, and to whom my heart entirely belonged until he died; and, as Pallas* help me now, there is no other love in my heart, nor ever was!

'And I've indeed heard it said, without a doubt, that you're of high and noble kindred. And that makes me so very much surprised that you will mock any woman so. Also, God knows, love and I are far apart! For the life of me, I'm more inclined to be sorrowful and lament until I die! What I'll do in the future, I can't say. But truly, as yet I've no thought of enjoyment. My heart's in tribulation now, and day by day you're involved in fighting. Sometime after this, when you've won the town, it may perhaps so happen that, when I see what I never yet saw, then I'll do what I never yet did! This ought to be enough for you. I'll gladly speak with you tomorrow too, provided that you don't touch on this subject, and you can come here again when you want. And before you go, I say this much to you here: so help me shining-haired Pallas, if I should ever take pity* on any Greek, it would be yourself, upon my word! I'm not saying therefore that I will love you, nor am I saying no, but in the end I mean well, by God above!'

And at that she looked down and sighed, and said:

'O town of Troy, I pray God I may yet see you in peace and quietness, or let my heart break!'

But to speak briefly and to the point, this Diomede pressed on again afresh, and begged intently for her mercy. And after this, to tell the truth, he took her glove,* which he was very glad about, and finally, when it was evening and everything was going well, he rose and took his leave. [1015]

Bright Venus* followed and showed the way where spreading Phoebus had set; and Cynthia reached over, urging on her chariot horses to whirl out of the sign of Leo if she could; and the Zodiac was displaying his bright candles, when Criseyde went to her bed inside her father's bright, handsome tent, always turning over in her soul, up and down, the words of this impetuous Diomede, his high rank, and the city's danger, and that she was alone and had need of friends' help; and thus began to develop, to tell the truth, the reason why she fully resolved to stay.

The morning came, and Diomede came to Criseyde—to give the spirit of it—and briefly, in case you interrupt my tale, he spoke so

well for himself that he laid all her bitter sighs to rest; and finally,
to tell the truth, he relieved her of the chief part of all her pain. And
after this, the story tells us,* she gave him the fine bay horse which
he once won from Troilus; and she also gave Diomede a brooch which
was Troilus' (and there was little need for that!); and also, the bet-
ter to relieve his sorrow, she had him wear her sleeve as a pennon
on his lance. I also find elsewhere* in the stories that, when Diomede
was injured, thrust through the body by Troilus, she then wept many
a tear, when she saw his wide wounds bleed, and that she took good
care to look after him; and in order to heal him of his painful sor-
rows, people say—I don't know—that she gave him her heart. But
truly, the story tells us that a woman never lamented more than she
did when she betrayed Troilus. [1053]

'Alas,' she said, 'for now my name for loyalty in love is completely
gone forever more! For I have betrayed the noblest man that ever
was, and the most deserving! Alas, no good word shall either be writ-
ten or sung about me until the end of the world, because these books
will ruin me.* O, my name will be rolled around on many a ton-
gue! Throughout the world my story will be spread! And women
will hate me most of all.* Alas, that such a thing should happen to
me! They will say that, in as much as it is my doing, I have brought
dishonour on them, alas! Even if I'm not the first that did wrong,
how does that help to remove my blame? But since I see there's no
better way, and that it's too late now for me to have regrets, I will
at any rate be true to Diomede.* But Troilus,* since I can do no
better, and since you and I part company like this, I still pray for
God's blessing on you, as truly the noblest I ever saw in serving loy-
ally, and can always best protect his lady's honour.'—And with that
word she at once burst out crying.—'And I shall certainly never hate
you, and you shall always have from me the love of a friend, and a
good word from me, even if I should live forever. And truly, I should
be sorry to see you in any adversity; and I believe you to be guilt-
less. But everything will pass away, and so I take my leave.'

But truly, I believe no author tells how long it was* before she
forsook him for this Diomede. Let everyone now consult his books;
he will certainly not find any specified period of time. For though
Diomede soon began to woo her, there was still more to do before
he won her. I do not wish to reproach this poor woman further than
the story devises. Her name, alas, is published so far and wide that it

ought to be sufficient punishment for her guilt. And if I might excuse her in any way, because she was so sorry for her faithlessness, I would certainly excuse her yet, out of pity. [1099]

As I have related before,* Troilus endured as best he could. But his heart often went hot and cold, and especially that ninth night, on the morning after which she had promised him to return. God knows, he had very little rest that night—he was not at all interested in sleeping!

The laurel-crowned Phoebus,* as he went ever upward in his course, was beginning to warm the wet waves of the eastern sea,* and the daughter of Nisus* sang with fresh endeavour, when Troilus sent for Pandarus, and they amused themselves on the town walls, to see if they could see anything of Criseyde. Until it was noon they stood to see who was coming there, and every sort of person who came from a distance they said was her—until they could recognize him properly. Now his heart was heavy, now it was cheerful. And thus deceived, Troilus and Pandarus stood staring about nothing.

'For all I know,' Troilus then said to Pandarus, 'Criseyde's certainly not coming into this town before noon. She surely has enough to do to get away from her father, so I believe. Her old father will yet make her dine before she goes—God give his heart pain!'

'It may well be so, certainly,' Pandarus replied, 'and therefore let's have dinner, I beg you, and then you can come again in the afternoon.'

And home they go, without any more talk, and come back again —but they will have to seek for a long time before they find what they are looking for. Fortune thinks to deceive them both! [1134]

'I see well now,' said Troilus, 'that she has delayed so with her father that it will be nearly evening before she comes. Come along! I'll go to the gate. These porters are always stupid, and I'll make them keep the gate open, as if there were nothing special about it, even though she arrive late.'

The day went quickly, and after that came evening, and still Criseyde did not come to Troilus. He looked out past hedge, tree, and grove, and craned his head far out over the wall; and at last he turned round and said:

'By God, I see what she means to do now, Pandarus! I almost had my sorrow all back again, for sure! Now undoubtedly, this lady knows what's best for her. I see she intends to ride back secretly. I take my

hat off to her wisdom! She doesn't want to have people gaping fool-
ishly at her when she comes, but she thinks to ride quietly into the
town by night. And dear brother, don't expect to have to wait very
long! We certainly don't have anything else to do. And Pandarus,
now will you believe me? Take my word for it! I see her! There she
is! Look up, man! Can't you see?'

'No, as I hope to thrive, I can't!' Pandarus replied. 'All wrong, by
God! What are you saying, man? Where are you? What I see over
there is only a cart!'* [1162]

'Alas, you're quite right,' said Troilus. 'But it's surely not for
nothing that I'm now so happy at heart like this. I think it presages
something good happening. I don't know how, but I never felt such
comfort since I was created, I dare say. She comes tonight—I'd dare
stake my life on it!'

'It may be, right enough,' Pandarus replied, and agreed with him
about everything he ever said. But in his heart he was thinking, and
laughed softly, and he said to himself very soberly:

'From never-never land, where merry Robin sported,* shall come
all that you're waiting for here! Yes, farewell to all the snows of
yesteryear!'*

The guard on the gates began to call the people who were outside
the gates, and told them to drive all their animals in, or they must
remain out there all night. And far into the night, with many a tear,
Troilus rode homewards, for he well saw it was of no use to stay.
[1183]

But nevertheless, he took comfort in this: he thought he had mis-
calculated his day, and said:

'I've completely misunderstood! For that night I last saw Criseyde
she said "I shall be here if I can, O sweet, dear heart, before the
moon, now in Aries, passes beyond the sign of Leo".* So she may
yet keep her promise!'

And in the morning he went to the gate, and he took many turns
on the walls, up and down, westwards and eastwards. But all in vain—
his hope was always deceiving him. And so at night, in sorrow and
with bitter sighs, he went home without more ado. His hope fled
quite clean out of his heart. He had nothing to hang on to any longer.
But so painful and amazingly severe were his sufferings, that it seemed
to him his heart was bleeding with the pain. For when he saw that
she stayed away so long, he did not know what to make of it, since

she had broken her promise to him. The third, fourth, fifth, and sixth days after those ten days I told of, his heart lay between hope and fear, still somewhat trusting in her old promises. But when he saw she would not keep to her appointed time, he could now see no other remedy than to prepare to die soon. [1211]

With that the wicked spirit—God bless us from it!—which is called mad jealousy began to creep into him in all this heaviness of heart; and so, because of his depression and because he wanted to die soon, he neither ate nor drank, and he also fled from all company—this was the life he led all this time. He was so disfigured that he was scarcely recognizable to anyone wherever he went. He was so thin, so pale and wan, and so weak that he walked with a crutch. He was destroying himself with his anger like this. But if anyone asked him what he was suffering from, he said his pain was all around his heart. Very often Priam, and his dear mother as well, and his brothers and sisters, asked him why his whole manner was so sorrowful, and what was the cause of all his suffering? But all for nothing. He would not reveal the cause of his trouble, but said he felt a grievous sickness around his heart, and he would be glad to die. [1232]

So one day he lay down to sleep, and it so happened that in his sleep he seemed to be walking in a dense forest to weep for love of her who caused him these sufferings. And as he explored the forest up and down, he dreamed he saw a boar* with large tusks, sleeping in the heat of the bright sun. And beside this boar, tightly clasped in his arms and continually kissing, lay his fair lady, Criseyde. For sorrow and resentment at this, when he saw it, he woke from out of his sleep with a start, and called loudly for Pandarus, and said:

'O Pandarus, now I know everything, root and branch. I'm a dead man; there's nothing else for it. My fair lady, Criseyde, has betrayed me, in whom I trusted most of anyone. Her heart has now found its fulfilment elsewhere. Through their great power, the blessed gods have shown it very exactly in my dream. In my dream I've seen Criseyde like this,' and he told Pandarus the whole thing.* [1253]

'O my Criseyde, alas, what guile, what new pleasure, what beauty, what knowledge, what justifiable anger comes between you and me? What guilt of mine, what dreadful experience, alas, has taken your thoughts away from me? O trust! O loyalty! O deep confidence! Who has taken Criseyde away from me, my whole delight? Alas, why did I let you leave here, because of which I'm very nearly going out of my mind? Who will ever believe in oaths again? God knows, O fair lady, Criseyde, I believed every word you said was gospel truth. But who is better able to deceive, if he chooses, than one in whom people think it best to trust? What shall I do, my Pandarus, alas? I now feel so sharp a new pain, since there's no remedy in this case, that it would be better if I killed myself with my own hands than always to be lamenting like this. For through death my unhappiness would have an end, where every day I now reproach myself with being alive.'* [1274]

'How I wish I'd never been born!' said Pandarus in reply. 'Haven't I said before this that dreams deceive* many kinds of men? And why? Because people interpret them wrongly. How dare you say your lady is unfaithful, on account of any dream, just because of your own fears? Forget this idea—you don't know how to interpret dreams. When you dreamed of this boar, it may perhaps signify that her father (who is old and white-haired) is lying in the sun on the point of dying, and she is weeping and crying for sorrow, and kisses him as he lies on the ground—that's how you should correctly interpret your dream!'

'What could I do then,' said Troilus, 'to learn the truth about this—yes, even if it were ever so trifling?'

'Now you're talking sense,' said Pandarus. 'This is my advice: that, since you know how to put things well in writing, you quickly write her a letter, through which you'll certainly manage to discover the truth of what you're now uncertain about. And now see why! For I dare say this: if she's unfaithful, I can't believe that she'll write back. And if she does write, you'll very soon see whether she has any freedom to return; or else, if she be prevented from coming, she'll reveal the cause in some clause! You haven't written to her since she went, nor she to you, and I'd dare to bet she has such good reasons in mind that you'll surely say yourself that her delaying is the best thing for both of you two. Now write to her then, and you'll soon find out the truth about everything. There's nothing else to be done.' [1309]

These same two lords are agreed on this decision, and that right away. And Troilus sat quickly down and turned over and over in his mind how he could best describe his unhappiness to her. And he wrote just like this to Criseyde, his own dear lady, and said as you may hear:

*Troilus' Letter**

'Freshest of flowers—in whose service I have been and shall be, with heart, body, life, desires, thought, and everything, and with no part of my service given elsewhere—I, unhappy man, commend myself to your noble favour, as constantly as space is filled with matter, and in every humble way that tongue can tell or heart imagine! May it please you to recall, sweet heart, as you well know, how long ago you left me in sharp and painful sufferings when you went away, for which as yet I have had no remedy, but from day to day I am ever more miserable, and so must remain as long as it please you, the source of my joy and woe. Therefore, as one driven to write by sorrow, with anxious, faithful heart, I am writing to you, lamenting my unhappiness, which every hour increases anew, as much as I dare or can express. And you can blame the fact that my letter is smudged* on the tears which rain from my eyes, and which would speak and lament if they could! [1337]

'I first beg you that you do not consider your bright eyes defiled by gazing upon this; and moreover that you, my dear lady, will agree to peruse this letter. And if I let anything amiss slip out, because my chill sorrows are overcoming my understanding—forgive me for it, my own sweet heart! If any servant dared or rightfully ought to complain* pitifully about his lady, then I suppose I ought to be that man, considering this: that you have delayed these two months,* whereas you said, to tell the truth, that you would only remain ten days with the Greeks—but in two months you have not yet returned! In as much as I must necessarily be content with all that pleases you, I dare not complain more; but humbly, with sick and sorrowful sighs, I write to you of my grievous, restless sorrows, desiring evermore from day to day to know, if it be your pleasure, how you have got on and all you have done while you have been there. May God increase your happiness and well-being in honour, such that it grow ever upward unceasingly! Just as your heart can imagine, my noble lady, I pray God that it may be so, and grant that you soon have pity upon me, as certainly as I am true to you in everything. [1365]

'And if you care to hear what state I am in—receptacle of every sorrow!—whose misery no wit can describe, I cannot say any more than that at the time of writing this letter I was alive, all prepared to drive out my unhappy spirit, which I am holding back and delaying until I see the content of your message. My two eyes, with which I see in vain, have become wells of sorrowful, salt tears. My song has turned into lamentation* for my adversity, and my good into harm; my ease into hell, my joy into woe. I can't say anything else to you, but that every joy or comfort is turned into its contrary, and because of that I curse my life. All of which, you may set right by your coming home again to Troy, and increase happiness in me a thousand times more than I ever had. For there was never yet a heart so happy to be alive as I shall be as soon as I see you. And even though no kind of compassion move you, yet think of your pledged word. [1386]

'And if my guilt has deserved death, or if you wish to see me no more, yet in reward of my past service I beg you, my own noble lady, my true lodestar, to write to me upon this matter, for the love of God, so that death can put an end to all my inward strife. If any other reason at all causes you to remain, I beg you to comfort me with a letter from you, for though your absence is a hell to me, I will bear my unhappiness with patience, and I will take hope and comfort from your letter. Now write, my sweet, and don't let me lament like this. With hope or death, deliver me from pain. I know indeed, my own dear, true heart, that when you next see me Criseyde will not be able to recognize me—I have so lost my health and my colour as well. Indeed, my heart's daylight, my noble lady, my heart so constantly thirsts to behold your beauty that I can hardly hold on to my life. [1407]

'I say no more, although I have much more to say to you than I can express. But whether you cause me to live or die, I still pray God to bless you! And farewell, my gracious, fairest, and freshest girl, as she who may command me to life or death! And to your faithfulness I always commend myself, in such a state of health that, unless you give me health,* I shall have none. In your power—when you wish that it should be—is the day on which my grave will enwrap me; in you is my life, in you power to save me from the distress of all bitter pains. And now farewell, my own sweet heart!

                                                         Your T.'*

This letter was sent to Criseyde, to which her reply essentially was this: she wrote back* in very pitiful vein and said that, as soon as she could, indeed, she would come and put right all that was amiss. And finally she wrote and said to him then that she would come, yes, but she did not know when. But in her letter she paid such compliments that it was most surprising, and swore she loved him best—in which he found only groundless promises. But Troilus, you can now go and whistle,* if you want! This is how the world goes! God shield us from misfortune and advance everyone who intends to be faithful! [1435]

Troilus' sorrow over Criseyde's delaying increased from day to night; and his hope and also his strength decreased, and for this reason he took to his bed. He neither ate, nor drank, nor slept, nor said a word, always imagining that she was untrue, and because of this he very nearly went out of his mind. He could never forget this dream, of which I have also told before. He thought all the time that he had lost his lady, and that, from his foreknowledge, Jove had shown him in his sleep a sign of her faithlessness and his misfortune, and that the boar had been shown to him as a symbol. He therefore sent for his sister, the sibyl, who was also universally known as Cassandra,* and told her all his dream before he would stop, and begged her to resolve his uncertainty about the great boar with strong tusks. And in the end, within a short while, Cassandra interpreted his dream to him just like this, first smiling and saying:

'O dear brother, if you wish to know the truth about this, you must listen to a few old stories* pertinent to the subject, how Fortune has overthrown ancient lords, through which you will indeed within a short time recognize this boar and from what family he comes, as is found in books.

'Diana was angry and enraged because the Greeks would not sacrifice to her or burn incense on her altar, and, because the Greeks neglected her so, she avenged herself in an astonishingly cruel way, for she caused all their corn and vines to be devoured by a boar as huge as an ox in stall. The whole country was raised to kill this boar and, amongst the people gathered, there came to see the boar one of the most celebrated maidens in this world, and Meleager, the lord of that country, fell so in love with that noble young maiden* that he would not cease until he had shown his manhood by slaying this boar, and sent her the head. And from this, as the old books tell us, there arose strife and great ill-will. And from this lord, Tydeus lineally descended,* or else old books are lying. But how this Meleager came to die through his mother's doing,* I will not tell you, because it would take far too long.' [1484]

Before she ceased, she also told* how Tydeus went to the powerful city of Thebes to claim the kingship of the city for his friend, Lord Polynices, whose brother Lord Eteocles very wrongfully held power in Thebes. This she related in due course and at length. She told too how Maeon,* son of Haemon, escaped when Tydeus slew fifty bold knights. She also related all the prophecies* by heart, and how seven kings with their army besieged the city all around. She told him all about the holy serpent,* and the well, and of the Furies;* and of the cremation of Archemorus* and the funeral games; and how Amphiaraus* was swallowed up by the earth; and how Tydeus, lord of the Argyves, was slain;* and how in a little while Hippomedon was drowned,* and Parthenopaeus died of his wounds;* and also how the proud Capaneus,* who boasted loudly, was slain by a thunderbolt. She told him too how each of the brothers, Eteocles and Polynices, slew the other* in a skirmish, and of the weeping of Argia,* and her unhappiness. And she also then told how the town was burnt;* and so proceeded from old histories to Diomede, and she spoke like this:

'This same boar symbolizes Diomede, Tydeus' son, who is descended from Meleager, who made the boar bleed. And your lady, wherever she is, indeed, Diomede has her heart, and she his. Weep if you will, or leave off, for, without a doubt, this Diomede's in, and you're out!' [1519]

'You're not telling the truth,' said he, 'you sorceress, with all your false spirit of prophecy! You think you're a great prophetess! Now, don't you see, this victim of delusions takes pains to tell lies about ladies? Off with you!' said he, 'may Jove send you sorrow! You will be proved wrong, perhaps, even by tomorrow! You might as well tell lies about Alcestis,* who was, unless men lie, the kindest and the best of beings that ever were! For when her husband was in danger of dying himself unless she would die, she chose to die for him and go to hell, and died at once, as the books tell us.'

Cassandra left, and with savage heart he forgot his unhappiness out of anger at what she had said. He suddenly leaped from his bed, as though a doctor had completely restored him to health. Day by day he enquired and sought after the truth of this most diligently. And so he endured his lot. [1540]

Fortune*—to whom the permutation of things is committed through the foresight and arrangement of high Jove, as to how kingdoms shall be transferred from people to people or when they shall be disgraced*—began from day to day to pluck away the bright feathers of Troy until they were bare of joy. In the midst of all this, the end of Hector's time on earth was approaching marvellously swiftly. Fate willed that his soul should leave his body and had devised a means to drive it out, against which fate it was no use for him to struggle. But he went out to fight one day, and there—alas!—he met his end. Therefore it seems to me that every sort of man who is used to bearing arms ought to lament the death of him who was so noble a knight, for, in an unguarded moment, as he was dragging a king along by the neckguard* of his armour, Achilles stabbed him through the chain-mail and through the body, and in that way this excellent knight was brought to his end. For him, as old books tell us, such lamentation was made that tongue may not tell of it, and especially the sorrow of Troilus, who, next to Hector, was the fount of excellence. And in this misery Troilus remained, so that, what for sorrow, and love, and a troubled mind, he many times a day bade his heart to break. But nevertheless, though he began to despair, and always dreaded that his lady was unfaithful, yet his heart always returned to her. And, as these lovers do, he always sought to get Criseyde back again, with her radiant looks. And he went on inwardly making excuses for her, that Calchas caused all her delaying. And he often seriously intended to disguise himself as a pilgrim,* so as to see her. But he could not pass himself off so as to be unrecognized by people in the know, nor devise an excuse that would do if he were recognized when among the Greeks, and so he very often wept a great many tears. [1582]

He still wrote to her often—he did not neglect it out of idleness— piteously imploring her, since he was faithful, that she should come back again and keep her pledge. And so Criseyde one day, out of pity—so I take it—regarding all this matter, wrote to him in reply, and said as you shall hear:

*Criseyde's Letter**

'Cupid's son, model of excellence! O sword of knighthood, fount of nobility! How could a person in torment* and in fear, and devoid of well-being, as yet send you happiness? I, disheartened! I, sick! I, in distress! Since you may not have any dealings with me, nor I with you, I can send you neither heart nor health.

'My heart's compassion has understood your copious letters,* the paper all written over with lamentations. I have also seen your letter all stained with tears, and how you request me to come back again, which as yet cannot be. But, out of fear, I make no mention now as to why, in case this letter were discovered.

'God knows, your distress and your impatience are painful to me, and that it seems you do not take for the best what the gods ordain. Nor is there anything else in your mind, it seems to me, except your own pleasure. But don't be angry, I beg you! The reason why I delay is all because of wicked talk. For I have heard a great deal more than I expected, concerning us two and how things have stood, which I will put right by dissimulation. And—don't be angry—I have also come to understand how you are only leading me on. But it doesn't matter now. I cannot imagine anything in you but all faithfulness and all nobility. [1617]

'I will come, but I am still in such a difficult situation just now that I cannot specify what year or what day that it will be. But essentially, I beg you, as well I may, for your good opinion and for your friendship always, for truly, while life may last, you can count on me as a friend. Yet I beg you not to take it amiss that what I have written to you is brief.* I dare not write letters where I am, and I have never been good at putting things in writing. And things of great consequence are written in few words—the intention is everything, and not the length of the letter. And now farewell, and may God keep you in his grace!

Your C.'

When he looked at it, Troilus thought this letter very distant, and he sighed sadly. It seemed to him like the beginnings of change.* But in the end he could not completely believe that she would not keep to what she had promised him. For he who is very much in love is most reluctant to believe in such a case, even though he may be troubled.

But nevertheless, they say that in the end, in spite of everything, people will see the truth. Such an event occurred, and very soon at that, so that Troilus well understood that she was not as kind as she ought to be. And at last he knew without a doubt that all was lost that he had been about. [1645]

One day, as Troilus was standing there, depressed and suspicious of her for whom he thought he would die, it so happened, as the story says, that a sort of tunic* embroidered with a heraldic device was being borne up and down throughout Troy in front of Deiphebus, as the custom was, as a sign of his victory—the which tunic, as Lollius* relates, Deiphebus had ripped from Diomede the same day. And when Troilus saw it, he looked at it intently, studying the length and the breadth, and all the workmanship. But as he looked, his heart very suddenly went cold, for he found inside on the collar a brooch* that he gave Criseyde that morning that she had to depart from Troy, in remembrance of him and of his sorrow. And she pledged her faith to him to keep it always! But now he knew full well his lady was no longer to be trusted. [1666]

He went home and very soon sent for Pandarus, and told him from beginning to end about all this latest event and this brooch, complaining of her heart's changeableness, his long love, his faithfulness, and his suffering. And without more words, he begged urgently for death, to restore his rest to him. Then he spoke like this:

'O my lady, Criseyde, where is your pledged word, and where is your promise? Where is your love? Where is your faithfulness?' he said. 'Is it Diomede who makes you happy now? Alas, I would at least have thought that, since you didn't want to be faithful to me, you wouldn't have led me along like this! Who will ever believe in oaths again? Alas, I would never have supposed, before this, that you, Criseyde, could have changed so, nor—unless I had offended and acted wrongly—did I believe your heart could be so cruel, indeed, to kill me like this! Alas, your reputation for faithfulness is now destroyed, and that is the reason for all my grief.

'Was there no other brooch you cared to let go, with which to endow your new love,' said he, 'but that very brooch that I gave you, with my tears, as a memento of me? You had no reason, alas, unless out of spite, and also because you meant to display your intentions quite openly. Through which I see that you have cast me clean out of your mind—and I can't for anything find it in my heart to un-love* you for a quarter of a day! I was born in an accursed time, alas, that you, who make me endure all this unhappiness, I still love best in all creation! [1701]

'Now God,' said he, 'send me yet the grace that I may encounter this Diomede! And truly, if I have strength and opportunity, I hope

I'll make the sides of his body bleed yet! O God,' said he, 'who ought to take good heed to promote fidelity and to punish wrongs, why won't you take vengeance upon this wrong? O Pandarus, who've often blamed and reproached me for trusting in dreams, you can see for yourself, if you will, how true your fair niece Criseyde is now! In various forms, God knows,' he said, 'the gods reveal both joy and grief in sleep, and this is now seen by my dream. And certainly, without any more talk, from henceforth, as far as I can, I'll seek my own death in battle—I don't care how soon be the day! But truly, Criseyde, my sweet girl—whom I've always served with all my might—I haven't deserved that you should do this!' [1722]

Pandarus—who heard all this and well knew that he was speaking the truth about it—did not answer a word to him, for he was sorry for his friend's sorrow, and ashamed because his niece had acted wrongly, and dumbfounded for these two reasons he stood stock-still —not one word could he say. But at last he spoke like this and said:

'My dear brother, I can do no more for you. What should I say? I hate Criseyde, indeed; and God knows, I'll hate her for evermore! And all that you once begged me to do, I did just as you wanted, having no regard at all to my honour nor to my ease. If I did anything that gave you pleasure, I'm glad; and God knows that this treachery now is a grief to me! And certainly, to relieve your feelings, I'd very gladly make things better, if I knew how. And I pray to Almighty God to deliver her soon from out of this world!* I can say no more . . .'

Great was the sorrow and lamentation of Troilus, but Fortune always kept onwards to her course. Criseyde loved the son of Tydeus, and Troilus had to weep in chill misery. Such is this world, whoever knows how to regard it—in each station of life the heart finds little rest. God grant us to take it for the best! [1750]

In many a cruel battle, without doubt, was seen the knighthood and great might of Troilus, this same noble knight, as can be read in these old books; and undoubtedly, the Greeks paid very cruelly day and night for his rage; and most of all he sought out Diomede. And I find that they often met, with bloody strokes and great words, testing how their spears were sharpened. And God knows, Troilus rained blows upon Diomede's helmet with much savage fury! But nevertheless, Fortune did not wish that either should die at the other's hand.

And if I had undertaken to write about this same brave man's feats of arms, then I would compose lines about his battles. Whoever wishes to hear of his valiant deeds, read Dares,* he can tell them all together. But because I first began to write about his love, I have said what I can, beseeching every lady of radiant looks, and every gentlewoman, whoever she be, that—although Criseyde was unfaithful—they not be angry with me because of her guilt. Her guilt is there for you to see in other books, and I will write more willingly, if you like, about Penelope's faithfulness, and good Alcestis.* Nor am I saying this solely for the sake of these men, but most of all for the sake of women who are betrayed by treacherous folk—God give them sorrow, amen!—who through their great cunning and subtlety betray you. And this moves me to speak, and essentially I beg you all: beware of men, and listen to what I say! [1785]

Go, little book!* Go, my little tragedy! May God yet send your maker before he die the power to compose some comedy! But, little book, do not vie with any other composition, but be humble before all poetry; and kiss those footsteps where you see Virgil, Ovid, Homer, Lucan, and Statius* pass by. And because there is such great diversity in English, and in the writing of our tongue, I pray to God that no one mistranscribe you, nor ruin the metre on account of any deficient command of the language.* And wherever you may be read, or else sung,* I beseech God that you may be understood! But now back to the point of what I was saying before.

As I began to tell you, the Greeks paid dearly for the wrath of Troilus, for thousands died at the hands of one who was without any equal in his time, except Hector, as far as I can hear. But alas—except that it was God's will—fierce Achilles slew him pitilessly! [1806]

And when he was thus slain, his weightless spirit ascended* most blissfully up to the concave inner surface of the eighth sphere* of the heavens, leaving every planetary sphere* behind him on the reverse side, and there he saw with unimpeded vision the wandering stars,* while hearkening to the harmony* of sounds full of celestial melody. And down from there he contemplated intently this little speck* of earth that is embraced by the sea, and came utterly to despise this wretched world, and held everything to be vanity in comparison with the complete felicity that is in heaven above; and finally he directed his gaze down at the place where he had been slain, and in himself he simply laughed outright at the grief of those who wept so much for his death, and condemned all our actions that are so much in pursuit of blind pleasure, which cannot endure, when we should turn our whole heart towards heaven. And, to be brief, he went forth to the place where Mercury* assigned him to dwell. [1827]

See! Such an end had Troilus for love! Such an end had all his great worth! Such an end had his royal splendour! Such an end had his desire, such an end his nobility! Such an end had the fickleness of this deceptive world! So began his loving of Criseyde, as I have related, and so he died.

O all you fresh young people, he or she,* in whom love grows as you yourselves grow up, come back home from worldly vanity, and turn your heart's face up to that God who made you after his own image, and think all this world is nothing but a carnival,* that passes away as soon as fairest flowers. And give your love to Him who, for pure love, to redeem our souls, first died upon a cross, and rose again and sits in heaven on high. For He will not play false with anyone, I dare to say, who will lay his heart wholly on Him. And since He is best to love, and most meek, what need is there to seek for loves that are pretended and not real?

Here you see the accursed old rites of pagans! Here you see what use all their gods can be! Here you see these wretched worldly hungers! Here you see the end and rewarding of effort given by Jove, Apollo, Mars, and suchlike rabble! Here you see all the form and substance of what the ancients say in poetry if you look through their books! [1855]

O moral Gower,* I dedicate this book to you, and to you, philosophical Strode,* that you may agree to correct* it where necessary out of your kindness and excellent zeal. And to that true Christ, that died upon the cross, I continually pray for mercy with all my heart, and to the Lord I speak and say this:

You one, and two, and three, eternally living, who ever in three, and two, and one, reign uncircumscribed, and yet all-circumscribing,* defend us from visible and invisible enemies, and, of your mercy, Jesus, make us each one worthy of your mercy, for love of her, Blessed Virgin and your mother most benign. Amen.

Here ends the Book of Troilus and Criseyde.

related, and so he died.

[1855]

EXPLANATORY NOTES

ABBREVIATIONS

Hassell   J. W. Hassell, *Middle French Proverbs, Sentences, and Proverbial Phrases* (Toronto, 1982)

MED   *Middle English Dictionary*, ed. H. Kurath and S. M. Kuhn (Ann Arbor, 1954–)

Walther   H. Walther, *Proverbia Sententiaeque Latinitatis Medii Aevi*, 9 vols. (Göttingen, 1963–9)

Whiting   B. J. and H. W. Whiting, *Proverbs, Sentences, and Proverbial Phrases from English Writings Mainly Before 1500* (Cambridge, Mass., 1968)

3   *double sorrow*: perhaps recalling Dante's reference to Statius, author (in his *Thebaid*) of 'the double sorrow of Jocasta' (*Purgatorio*, 22.56); cf. also Troiolo's 'double sorrow' over the fainted Criseida (*Filostrato*, 4.118), and Orpheus' 'love that doublide his sorwe' (*Boece*, 3.m.12.26).

   his fortunes . . . rose and fell: cf. the definition of tragedy in *Boece*, 2.pr.2.67–72; see Introduction, p. xix.

   Tisiphone: one of the Furies, invoked in Statius, *Thebaid*, 1.56–9, 85–7; for the Furies as both tormenting and suffering, cf. *Boece*, 3.m.12.33–7 ('And the thre goddesses, furiis and vengeresses of felonyes, that tormenten and agasten the soules by anoy, woxen sorweful and sory, and wepyn teeris for pite'). For the 'verses that weep', cf. *Filostrato*, 1.6 ('my tearful verses') and *Boece*, 1.m.1.1–2 ('Allas! I wepynge, am constreyned to bygynnen vers of sorwful matere').

   sad companion . . . sorrowful tale: rhetorical commonplace; see *Squire's Tale*, v. 103, and Whiting W254.

   serving the servants: alluding to the papal title 'servus servorum Dei' (servant of the servants of God). Language of love-as-service and of lovers as servants will be pervasive in *Troilus*.

   And pray for those: the ensuing exhortations to prayer imitate the form of the 'bidding prayer' in which the priest requests prayers for particular categories of people.

   despair: the sin against the Holy Ghost.

   malicious tell-tales: fear of gossips is a motif of medieval courtly literature; cf. the role of Male Bouche ('Wikked Tunge') in the *Roman de la rose*.

4   *a thousand ships . . . ten years*: see Virgil, *Aeneid*, 2.198, and Ovid, *Heroides*, 13.97.

   Helen: wife of Menelaus; her abduction by Paris led to the siege of Troy.

   Calchas: in Homer a Greek (*Iliad*, 1.69); in medieval tradition a Trojan, taking the place of Homer's Chryses.

4 *Phoebus . . . Delphic Apollo*: for Calchas' visit to the oracle of Apollo at Delphi (not in *Filostrato*) Chaucer returns to Benoît (*Troie*, 5817- 92) and Guido (*Historia*, p. 98). Warned by the oracle, Calchas defects to the Greeks.

calculations . . . lots: his astrological calculations and divination by casting of lots; with a play on Calchas/calculation, as too on Troy/destroyed.

without any friend: emphasis on Criseyde's isolation is added to *Filostrato* (1.11), despite her uncle Pandarus, three nieces, and other company.

Hector: eldest son of Priam and Hecuba; Chaucer later adds his principled opposition to Criseyde's exchange (iv. 176–82, p. 94; not in *Filostrato*); his death in battle is lamented (v. 1548–63, p. 148).

5 *children*: although *Filostrato* (1.15) plainly says she had no children.

Fortune . . . her wheel: for the commonplace of Fortune's wheel, see the proem to Book IV (p. 91) and *Boece*, 2.pr.2.51–4 ('I torne the whirlynge wheel with the turnynge sercle; I am glad to chaungen the loweste to the heyeste, and the heyeste to the loweste'); cf. Whiting F506, Hassell F123, R85.

Dares . . . Dictys: on Dares the Phrygian and Dictys of Crete, see Introduction, p. xiv. Homer's *Iliad* would not be known directly to Chaucer.

Palladium: a sacred image of Pallas, upon which Troy's safety depended, until betrayed by Antenor (iv. 204–5, p. 94).

temple: first sight of the beloved in church or temple is a convention; cf. especially Benoît's account of how Achilles fell in love with Polyxena (*Troie*, 17489 ff.).

our first letter is now an A: perhaps a compliment to Anne of Bohemia, married to Richard II in January 1382.

6 *this Troilus*: the demonstrative 'this' with the name Troilus is used some 42 times, 11 times with Pandarus, 16 times with Diomede, never with Criseyde. It has sometimes but not always been kept in translation.

peacock: 'as proud as a peacock' is proverbial (Whiting P280).

blind world: cf. *Filostrato*, 1.25 ('O blindness of worldly minds!') and Dante's references to the 'blind world' (*Inferno*, 27.25, *Purgatorio*, 16.66). The ensuing excursus on love is added; Chaucer returns to following *Filostrato* with 'This Troilus . . .' (i. 267, p. 7).

proud Bayard: traditionally the bay steed given by Charlemagne to Renaud, but the name became associated with rashness (see *Canon's Yeoman's Tale*, viii. 1413–14: 'Ye been as boold as is Bayard the blynde | That blondreth forth and peril casteth noon'). Horses were proverbially proud (Whiting H521; Walther 16856, 19031*a*), and traditionally an emblem of fleshly lusts, as also of lack of reason.

7 *Love can bind everything*: see Troilus' song (iii. 1744–71, p. 89); cf. also *Boece*, 3.m.12.53–5 ('Love is a grettere lawe and a strengere to hymself thanne any lawe that men mai yyven'), and *Knight's Tale*, i. 1163–8.

greater intelligence: for Solomon, Virgil, and Aristotle as love's 'wise' victims in medieval tradition, see Gower, *Confessio amantis*. 6.78 99.

strongest: for Samson and Hercules, see *Wife of Bath's Prologue*, iii. 721–6; cf. *Romaunt*, 4757–64, and Whiting M224.

This was . . . will see it yet: echoing the *Gloria Patri* ('as it was in the beginning, is now, and ever shall be').

Love has often appeased . . . disgrace: the morally improving effects of love are emphasized at i. 1076–85, iii. 24–6, 1786–1806 (pp. 22, 57, 90).

not among the shortest: cf. *Filostrato*, 1.27 ('she was tall').

8 *from her looks . . . impression . . . his heart*: the lady's appearance imprinted in the lover's heart is a commonplace; on how 'alle figures most first comen fro thinges fro withoute into soules, and ben emprientid into soules', see *Boece*, 5.m.4.6–20.

beams of her eyes: as medieval physiology had it, an effluence passed from Criseyde's eyes through Troilus' eyes into his heart.

vital spirit: the rays from Criseyde's eyes affect the 'vital' spirit in his heart, which controlled pulse and breathing. (The other two 'spirits' in medieval physiology were the 'natural' spirit in the liver, and the 'animal' in the brain).

your "order" . . . good "rule": alluding to lovers as members of a religious order, with its observances and devotions.

9 *lime his feathers*: birds were caught by liming the twigs of trees.

make a mirror out of his mind: cf. *Boece*, 5.m.4.6–20 (the belief that the soul, like a mirror or parchment, is imprinted with images it receives); *Romaunt*, 2804–8 (thought makes the lover's mind a mirror in which he sees his lady's person).

get the better of his sorrow: from 'on his sorwe for to wynne' (i. 390); see *OED*, s.v. *win* 10.

Lollius: see Introduction, p. xvii.

10 *Troilus' Song*: Boccaccio simply reports that Troiolo sings (*Filostrato*, 1.37); Chaucer inserts his adaptation of Petrarch's sonnet 132 (*Canzoniere*, ed. G. Contini and D. Ponchiroli (Turin, 1964), 184), of which the following is a literal translation: 'If this is not love, what is it that I feel then? But if it is love, by God, what kind of thing is it? If it is good, whence comes this bitter mortal effect? If it is evil, why is every torment so sweet? If I am burning by my own will, whence comes the weeping and lamentation? If against my will, what use is there in lamenting? O living death! O delightful harm! How can you have so much power over me if I do not consent to it? And if I do consent to it, I complain very wrongly. Amid such contrary winds I find myself at sea in a fragile boat, so light of wisdom, so laden with error, that I myself do not know what I want; and I shiver in midsummer, burning in winter.' (Among Chaucer's added motifs are the continual thirst, the strange illness, and the sensation of dying.)

If harm is agreeable to me: possibly mistranslating 'S'a mal mio grado' (if against my will), but Chaucer's manuscript may have read 'Se mal mi agrada' (if evil gives me pleasure).

10 *I die . . . I am cold!*: translating 'For hete of cold, for cold of hete, I dye' (i. 420), itself resembling Petrarch, *Rima* 182.5: 'Trem'al più caldo, ard'al più freddo cielo.'

goddess or woman: the uncertainty is from *Filostrato*, 1.38; cf. *Knight's Tale*, i. 1101 (Palamoun is uncertain whether Emelye is goddess or woman).

11 *the nearer the fire, the hotter it is*: proverbial; for how the lover will burn, the nearer he is to his lady, cf. *Romaunt*, 2478.

Polyxena: daughter of Priam and Hecuba, beloved of Achilles.

his sleep . . . his food . . . his colour: typical symptoms of love sickness; cf. Andreas Capellanus, *De amore*, rules 23 and 15: 'He whom the thought of love vexes eats and sleeps very little', 'Every lover regularly turns pale in the presence of his love'; see also *Knight's Tale*, i. 1355–76.

12 *dance*: cf. the Wife of Bath: 'Of remedies of love she knew per chaunce, | For she koude of that art the olde daunce' (*General Prologue*, i. 475–6).

that fool: unidentified.

nearly drowned in salt tears: a courtly commonplace; see iv. 510, 930 (pp. 100, 107).

Pandarus: with Pandaro's entry Boccaccio here begins the second part of *Filostrato*, the opening scene of which Chaucer absorbs into his Book I, which thus ends later, with Pandarus' agreement to help Troilus in his suit.

O mercy, God!: of over 200 oaths in *Troilus*, Pandarus swears over 80, Criseyde over 60, and Troilus about 40; see R. W. V. Elliott, *Chaucer's English* (London, 1974), 251.

14 *How the devil*: from 'How devel . . .' (i. 623), but possibly addressing Pandarus ('How, devel . . .').

though I may be foolish: cf. Ovid, *Ars amatoria*, 2.547–8 ('I confess I am not perfect in this art—what am I to do? I am less than my own counsels').

a whetstone . . . tools: proverbial; cf. Horace, *Ars poetica*, 304–5 ('so I shall play a whetstone's role, which makes steel sharp, but of itself cannot cut').

wise men . . . fools: not recorded as a proverb before Chaucer.

Everything is known . . . by its opposite: proverbial; cf. also *Boece*, 3.m.1, 4.pr.2.10–12, and *Roman de la rose*, 21573–82.

how could sweetness . . . bitterness?: proverbial; cf. *Roman de la rose*, 21559–72.

Oenone . . . a lament: alluding to Oenone's letter to Paris (Ovid, *Heroides*, 5) after he deserted her for Helen. Criseyde later echoes Paris' vow of loyalty to Oenone (iv. 1548–53, p. 118).

cure his sorrows: Oenone laments that her own medical knowledge cannot cure her of love (*Heroides*, 5.145 ff.). For Phoebus Apollo as the inventor of medicine who cannot cure himself of his love for Daphne, see Ovid, *Metamorphoses*, 1.521–4. In love with the daughter of King Admetus (husband of Alcestis), Apollo served him as a shepherd for seven years. For the physician who cannot cure himself, cf. Luke 4: 23.

15 *to mistrust everyone or else believe everyone*: cf. Seneca, *Epistles*, 3.4 ('Either is a fault, to trust everyone or to trust no one').

"Woe to him that is alone ... rise": cf. Ecclesiastes 4: 10, attributed to the 'wise man', Solomon.

Niobe: wife of Amphion, king of Thebes, she was turned to stone as she wept for her seven sons and seven daughters, slain in punishment for her offending of Latona, mother of Apollo and Diana, 'and even to this day tears trickle from the marble' (Ovid, *Metamorphoses*, 6.312).

pleasure in seeking out misery: cf. Ovid, *Metamorphoses*, 7.720 ('I am set on seeking out something I may grieve over'), and Seneca, *Epistles*, 99.26 ('For what is worse than to chase after pleasure in grief itself, indeed from grief, and even to seek out what gives pleasure amid tears').

no more bad luck ... room!: cf. Ovid, *Ex Ponto*, 2.7.41–2 ('so wounded am I by the continual blows of Fortune that there is scarcely room upon me for a new wound').

16 *sleeping sickness*: from 'litargie' (i. 730); cf. *Boece*, 1.pr.2.19–21 ('he is fallen into a litargye, whiche that is a comune seknesse to hertes that been desceyved').

a donkey at the sound of a harp: cf. *Boece*, 1.pr.4.2–3; also proverbial.

to seem to flee from a thing ... hunted eagerly: cf. *Roman de la rose*, 7557–8; *Romaunt*, 4783–4.

brother: first of many occasions when Troilus and Pandarus so address each other.

17 *Tityus*: for his punishment, see *Boece*, 3.m.12.41–3.

never yet has he kissed his lady's mouth!: cf. *Roman de la rose*, 20889–92.

What? ... can deserve: cf. Hope's speech to the Lover in Machaut, *Remède de Fortune*, 1636–51.

18 *Fortune is common*: Pandarus' speech on Fortune echoes Philosophy's to Boethius; see *Boece*, 2.pr.1, pr.2, pr.3.

uncover his wound: cf. *Boece*, 1.pr.4.4–6; Ovid, *Remedia amoris*, 125–6; also proverbial.

Cerberus: three-headed canine porter of hell; cf. *Boece*, 3.m.12.31–3.

my sister: cf. Troilus' offer of his sisters (iii. 407–13, p. 64).

19 *a noble and well-ordered nature ... himself*: cf. Seneca, *Epistles*, 2.1, and *Boece*, 2.pr.4.134–8.

nothing but good in loving well: cf. Dante, *Purgatorio*, 17.97–9 ('while [love] is directed on the primal good and on the secondary keeps right measure, it cannot be the cause of sinful pleasure').

it follows that there is some pity ... other virtues: cf. Machaut, *Remède de Fortune*, 1671–83.

love-sickness: translating 'blanche fevere' (i. 916), a form of love-sickness that turns its victims pale (see Gower, *Confessio amantis*, 6.239–40).

19 *sure method ... everywhere*: cf. *Roman de la rose*, 21551–2.

beat your breast: like a priest Pandarus invites Troilus to confess and repent.

20 *For that same ground ... the end of sorrow*: cf. Ovid, *Remedia amoris*, 43–6 (the former teacher of love now offers to heal its wounds: 'the same earth fosters healing herbs and noxious, the nettle is often nearest the rose'). For the series of antitheses, see Whiting G478, N108, Walther 22030.

He that is divided ... is nowhere whole: cf. *Roman de la rose*, 2245–6 (*Romaunt*, 2367–8); Seneca, *Epistles*, 2.2–3; *Boece*, 3.pr.11.62–9.

like planting a tree ... it never thrives: proverbial; cf. Seneca, *Epistles*, 2.3 ('a plant that is often moved can never flourish').

the wise and learned: unidentified, but cf. Dante, *Purgatorio*, 17.91–3 ('Neither Creator nor creature ... was ever without love, either natural or of the spirit'). Boccaccio's Pandaro here expresses the view that Criseida, like all women, is amorous (*Filostrato*, 2.27).

21 *for appearances' sake ... her uncle*: translating 'for the manere | Of the, hire em, she nyl no swich thyng here' (i. 1021–2). Troiolo fears Criseida will not listen to Pandaro 'in order to show you how respectable she is' (*Filostrato*, 2.30). But an alternative meaning may be: 'because of the behaviour of you, her uncle, she won't hear of any such thing.'

Man in the Moon: for a Middle English lyric in which the Man in the Moon fears he will fall, see Carleton Brown (ed.), *English Lyrics of the XIIIth Century* (Oxford, 1932), 160; also Whiting M138.

22 *For everyone ... first of all*: from the rhetorical handbook, Geoffrey of Vinsauf's *Poetria nova* (43–5), describing the necessary premeditation before the poet begins his work: 'If anyone has a house to build, his impetuous hand does not rush into action; the inward plumb line of his heart measures out [praemetitur] the work beforehand' (Chaucer may have read 'praemittitur' or 'praemittetur', i.e. 'will be sent out'). See E. Faral (ed.), *Les Arts poétiques du xiie et du xiiie siècle* (Paris, 1924), 198; but this passage circulated excerpted in various compilations. Cf. also Luke 14: 28–30; *Boece*, 4.pr.6.86–93; Walther 29021.

23 *to sail ... the ship of my skill*: from *Purgatorio*, 1.1–3 ('To course over better waters the little boat of my wit now hoists her sails, leaving behind her so cruel a sea ...'), although the figure of a voyage for poetic composition was a commonplace.

first days ... hope: translating 'of hope the kalendes' (ii. 7); used again, by contrast, when Criseyde's letter seems 'a kalendes of chaunge' to Troilus (v. 1634, p. 149).

Clio: the muse of history; i.e. the writer's purported role is confined to versifying historical report, and he needs no other inspiration or art.

out of any personal feeling: translating 'of no sentement' (ii. 13); to compose 'de sentement' is the claim of Machaut (*Remède de Fortune*, 407–8) and Froissart (*Paradys d'amours*, 1604–6; *L'Espinette amoreuse*, 919–21, 3925–30).

translating . . . from Latin: i.e. continuing the fiction of a classical source.

change in the forms of speech: cf. Dante, *Convivio*, 1.5, 55–66: 'Hence in the cities of Italy, if we will look attentively back over some fifty years, we see that many words have become extinct and have come into existence and been altered; wherefore, if a short time so changes the language, a longer time changes it much more. Thus I say that if those who died a thousand years ago were to return to their cities, they would believe that these had been occupied by some foreign people, because the language would be at variance with their own.' See also Dante's *De vulgari eloquentia*, 1.9, and Horace, *Ars poetica*, 60–72 (cited in *Convivio*, 2.14, 83–9, and John of Salisbury's *Metalogicon*, 1.16; 3.3).

every person who travels to Rome . . . one way: proverbial; cf. Chaucer's *Treatise on the Astrolabe*: 'right as diverse pathes leden diverse folke the righte way to Rome' (Prol. 39–40).

24 *the white Bull*: either that white bull in whose shape Jupiter ravished Europa (*Metamorphoses*, 2.852), and taken by medieval commentators as the origin of the zodiacal sign Taurus, or a recollection of Virgil's 'candidus . . . Taurus' (*Georgics*, 1.217–18).

third day of May: also the date of Chauntecleer's capture by the fox (*Nun's Priest's Tale*, vii. 3189-90) and of Palamoun's escape from prison (*Knight's Tale*, i. 1462–3).

Procne: wife of Tereus, she was metamorphosed into a swallow, and her sister Philomela into a nightingale, after they avenged Tereus' rape of Philomela by killing the son of Tereus and Procne and feeding Tereus a meal of the child's flesh. Ovid tells the tale in *Metamorphoses*, 6.412–674, retold by Chaucer in his *Legend of Good Women*, 2228–2393. Chaucer's allusion probably recalls Dante's in *Purgatorio*, 9.13–15; at the close of the day here beginning with Pandarus' awakening, Criseyde falls asleep to the song of the nightingale (ii. 918–24, p. 40).

astrological forecast: the Middle English 'and caste' (ii. 74) may suggest that Pandarus checked the day of the lunar month in a *lunarium* or moon-book to see if it was propitious.

Janus: Roman god of thresholds and doorways, represented with two faces, looking in opposite directions. See Ovid, *Fasti*, 1.125–7, 139.

parlour: a smaller room apart from the main hall, affording some privacy for private conversation.

reading . . . siege of Thebes: in this scene of reading aloud as a domestic pastime, Chaucer includes a representation of how *Troilus and Criseyde* may well have been enjoyed by its early audiences. The story   Middle English 'geste' (ii. 83)—of Thebes is then specified as 'this romaunce is of Thebes' (ii. 100), which may suggest Criseyde is listening to a version of the Old French *Roman de Thèbes*, itself based on the twelve-book Latin *Thebaid* of Statius, to which Pandarus apparently refers. (A contrast may be intended with the ladies' vernacular romance reading matter.) An outline summary or *argumentum* of the *Thebaid* in Latin is included in most manuscripts of *Troilus* after v. 1498

(p. 147). For other references by Chaucer's Trojans to the earlier fated city of Thebes: v. 601–2, 937, 1485–1509 (pp. 131, 137, 147).

25 *Laius died through his son Oedipus*: narrated in *Roman de Thèbes*, 175–224, more fully than in *Thebaid*, 1.57 ff.

rubric: Criseyde refers to 'thise lettres rede' (ii. 103), i.e. the rubrication or headings (often beginning 'How . . .') used to set off titles, chapters, or sections of works in the page layout of medieval manuscripts.

Bishop Amphiaraus: his death is narrated at the close of *Thebaid*, book 7, and in *Roman de Thèbes*, 4711–842. Amphiaraus is termed *vates* in *Thebaid* (7.815) and *evesque* or *arcevesques* in *Thèbes* (4791, 5053). In his spelling *Amphiorax* (ii. 105), Chaucer follows the French spelling of the classical name.

veil: translating 'barbe' (ii. 110; some manuscripts read 'wimpel'). Worn by nuns, and by widows as a sign of mourning, the 'barbe' was a piece of pleated white linen worn over or under the chin and reaching to the breast.

any life for a widow: on widowhood as a pious life, see 1 Timothy 5: 5- 6. Criseyde pictures herself like the penitent Mary Magdalene in her cave.

26 *second Hector*: on Troilus as second only to Hector (as he had been described by Benoît and Guido), see ii. 740, iii. 1775, v. 1804 (pp. 37, 89, 152).

power and moral virtue . . . together: from Lucan, *Pharsalia*, 8.494 5, as cited in *Roman de la rose*, 5660–2. Cf. Whiting E148.

swarm of bees: a traditional figure (Whiting B167).

27 *stood at a distance*: Chaucer represents his romance as taking place in the circumstances of a medieval household, where privacy is the exception and must be deliberately sought.

Minerva: Roman goddess of wisdom. Troilus also invokes her, when about to compose his letter to Criseyde (ii. 1062, p. 42).

not including mistresses: translating 'withouten paramours' (ii. 236), where 'paramours' may also mean more generally 'amorous relations, courtly love-making'.

28 *the end is the strong point . . . tale*: a traditional commonplace, cited in English in Whiting (E75, E78, E81, W598), in Latin in Walther (9536), and in French in Hassell (F89).

sensitive minds . . . trickery: cf. *Squire's Tale*, v. 221–4; Whiting W411.

29 *beautiful gem*: powers (particularly of healing) were attributed to gems.

if there is no pity in you as well: cf. Pandarus' earlier argument to Troilus that Criseyde's virtuousness must include pity (i. 897–900, p. 19).

30 *Think too . . . your beauty*: cf. Ovid, *Ars amatoria*, 2.113–18; *Filostrato*, 2.54.

31 *highly coloured story*: the Middle English 'paynted proces' (ii. 424) suggests the 'colours' of rhetoric, deceptively painted.

Pallas: cf. v. 977, 999 (p. 138). A virgin goddess, Pallas is defender of Troy.

O cruel god . . . Furies of hell: cf. *Teseida*, 1.58, 3.1; also the fourth proem (see p. 91).

32 *The other day*: in *Filostrato* Pandaro specifies (2.61–2) that this episode occurred before he came across Troiolo lamenting alone in his room (cf. i. 549, p. 12). Chaucer leaves open the possibility that it is all Pandarus' invention.

beside a well . . . garden: a typical setting; in *Roman de la rose* the Lover rests beside a well in the garden (*Romaunt*, 1456).

33 *I confess*: Chaucer here (ii. 525) has Troilus exclaim in Latin 'mea culpa', from the *Confiteor*.

ordain . . . by just providence: cf. Boethius' discussion of providence (*Boece*, 4.pr.6).

despair: suggesting despair as the Christian sin against the Holy Ghost; see the first two proems (i. 36–42, ii. 6, pp. 3, 23).

wounded me . . . my heart: see i. 295–308 (p. 8). Beams from the lady's eyes strike through the lover's eyes into his heart; cf. *Roman de la rose*, where Love shoots his arrow through the Lover's eye into his heart (*Romaunt*, 1727–9).

all the hotter . . . ashes: proverbial; cf. *Metamorphoses*, 4.64, and *Legend of Good Women*, 735.

hung his head . . . began to mutter: gestures of a figure at confession.

pine with longing: cf. Troilus' earlier mockery of lovers, i. 328–50 (pp. 8–9).

34 *netted . . . without using a net*: cf. iv. 1370–1 (p. 115); on binding without a cord, see iii. 1358 (p. 82).

the ruby's well set in the ring: from *Filostrato*, 2.43. See iii. 1371, v. 549 (pp. 82, 130).

the whole of you: translating 'whan ye ben his al hool' (ii. 587).

thought like this: Boccaccio's Criseida here debates with herself whether to love (2.69–78), then gazes at Troiolo and Pandaro from her window as they walk by (2.82). Chaucer inserts Troilus' first ride past before Criseyde's monologue, perhaps recalling Hector's triumphant return from battle (*Troie*, 10201–18) and Lavinia's sight of Aeneas in the *Roman d'Eneas*, ed. J. J. Salverda de Grave (Paris, 1925–9), 8047–8126, 8381–98.

Gate of Dardanus: in Guido the first of Troy's six gates (*Historia*, p. 47), in Benoît the second (*Troie*, 3148). Barrier chains were used to close off gates and streets to horsemen.

35 *the body and the strength for it . . . vigorous*: translating 'a body and a myght | To don that thing . . . weldy' (ii. 633–4, 636). 'The verb *weelden* has, inevitably, a common sexual sense in Middle English, and "that thing" seems a probable euphemism' (E. T. Donaldson, *Speaking of Chaucer* (London, 1970), 66 n.).

it was heaven to look at him: cf. *Squire's Tale*, v. 558.

Who gave me a drink?: possibly referring to a love-potion (as in the tale of Tristan and Iseult), but perhaps simply any intoxicating drink.

all red at her own thought: cf. *Shipman's Tale*, vii. 111.

seventh house: a 'house' is one of the twelve divisions of the celestial sphere, formed by great circles passing through the north and south points of the

horizon; the seventh house (just above the western horizon) is especially asso-
ciated with questions of love and marriage. As an evening star in the seventh
house, with Jupiter and Mercury standing in favourable aspect to her, Venus
is here auspiciously placed, as she also was in Troilus' horoscope at the time
of his birth.

36 *as my author . . . set it down*: Chaucer is actually working very freely with *Filostrato*
here (2.69–78).

drunkenness . . . drink forever!: cf. *Roman de la rose*, 5744–5 ('Because I forbid
drunkenness, I don't wish to forbid drinking'); also proverbial.

no boaster: on the evils of lovers' boasting, see Pandarus' argument (iii. 295–
322, pp. 62–3).

37 *"checkmate"*: use of the chess figure was a commonplace (Whiting C169; Hassell
E15); cf. *Book of the Duchess*, 659.

to drink . . . our own woes: for the notion of drinking up unhappy experience,
see iii. 1035, 1214–16 (pp. 76, 79); and *House of Fame*, 1879–80.

too keen a beginning . . . in the end: proverbial; one *Troilus* MS (S1) has in Latin
here the gloss 'Those very keen in the beginning are broken in the end'.

38 *What was nothing . . . nothing*: see *Boece*, 5.pr.1.43–4; also proverbial.

nothing ventured, nothing gained: proverbial; Diomede later cites the same proverb
(v. 784, p. 134).

now hot, now cold: the god of Love warns the Lover he will feel now hot, now
cold (*Roman de la rose*, 2278; *Romaunt*, 2398).

she then went . . . into the garden: this garden scene, and Antigone's song, are
not in *Filostrato*.

Flexippe, Tharbe, Antigone: Chaucer would know the name Antigone from the
story of Thebes, but the origin of the other two names is unexplained.

This garden: Criseyde's garden has the features of a typical medieval English
garden, with sanded paths railed by palings (generally painted), and with benches
(made of earth, with wooden or walled sides, topped with turf). See T. McLean,
Medieval English Gardens (London, 1981), 103–19, 160–1, which also describes
'a little staircase down from the Queen's apartments to her garden' at Guildford
Palace, 'a popular device also used at the royal palace at Kennington, and in
many noble houses' (102–3).

Antigone's Song: the song (which responds point for point to Criseyde's
hesitations about love) has general similarities to Machaut's lay *Le Paradis
d'amours*, and to various of his lyrics, especially *Mireoir amoureux*, in which
ladies sing in praise of love and their loves. Cf. Chaucer's *Complaint of Venus*.

Apollo: 'god of science and of lyght' (*House of Fame*, 1091).

39 *Love's bow . . . for them*: cf. the proverb 'Many men speak of Robin Hood that
never bent his bow' (Whiting R156). Two *Troilus* MSS (H4Ph) refer to 'Robin
Hood' here.

a head of glass . . . in battle!: the proverb 'People who live in glass houses shouldn't throw stones' is unrecorded before Chaucer (Whiting H218), but for the notion of a glass helmet as delusive protection, see v. 469 (p. 129).

40 *all this I call the sun*: cf. *Franklin's Tale*, v. 1017–18.

A nightingale: cf. the earlier allusion to the Procne story, ii. 64–70 (p. 24).

she dreamed: Criseyde's dream of the white eagle (a creature unknown to nature) is not in *Filostrato*, but may be influenced by Troiolo's later dream (7.23–4) of the boar (Diomede) tearing out Criseida's heart with his tusks, to her apparent pleasure (cf. v. 1233–42, p. 142). The exchange of hearts is a commonplace conceit of courtly poetry.

41 *keep your shirt on*: translating 'don thyn hood' (ii. 954), a phrase of uncertain meaning; perhaps 'call it a day', 'get ready to sleep', 'relax', with 'hood' as a nightcap or hood for a falcon.

sir: the only occasion when Pandarus so addresses Troilus.

one foot's lamed . . . dogging you!: apparently conceiving of Troilus' sorrow as a hound that is pursuing him; less probably referring to Criseyde as prey, now half captured.

as flowers . . . bright sun: from *Filostrato*, 2.80, itself following *Inferno*, 2.127–32.

there's a time for everything: proverbial; deriving from Ecclesiastes 3: 1.

42 *ride past the place*: this second, contrived ride past is not in *Filostrato*.

to make your ears glow: a traditional notion (cf. Whiting E12).

Regarding your letter . . . artfully: recalling the advice in Ovid, *Ars amatoria*, 1.455 ff. (e.g. the lover should address his lady with coaxing words; he is not to address her as he would the senate or a judge; only a fool would declaim at his lady (463–5)).

Blot it with your tears: cf. Ovid, *Heroides*, 3.3 ('Whatever blots you see, tears have made').

to harp on one string: Horace advises against this (*Ars poetica*, 355–6).

if a painter . . . just a joke: cf. the opening lines of Horace, *Ars poetica* (partly quoted in John of Salisbury, *Policraticus*, 2.18): 'If a painter chose to join a human head to the neck of a horse, and to spread feathers of many a colour over limbs picked up now here, now there, so that what at the top is a beautiful woman ends up below in a black and ugly fish, could you . . . refrain from laughing?' (1–5).

Minerva: goddess of wisdom.

43 *wrote exactly in this way*: the following summary replaces Boccaccio's verbatim presentation of Troiolo's eleven-stanza letter (2.96–106).

his niece's palace: Chaucer adds to *Filostrato* the description of Criseyde's house as a 'paleis' (ii. 1094).

a jolly woe, a cheerful sorrow: i.e. the traditional oxymorons of the language of love (cf. Troilus' song, i. 400–20, p. 10).

43 *love's dance*: the expression 'old daunce' is unrecorded in English before Chaucer, who always associates it with questions of love and sex (*General Prologue*, i. 476; *Physician's Tale*, vi. 79). In French the phrase suggested artfulness and shrewdness, not originally confined to sexual matters.

44 *Strike . . . with a thunderbolt*: the fate of Capaneus; see v. 1504–5 (p. 147), and *Thebaid*, 10.888–939.

45 *sew up the letter*: when sent, a letter 'was folded to form a small packet and secured by stitching with string or by passing narrow paper tape through the slits and sealing the ends with wax . . .' (N. Davis (ed.), *Paston Letters and Papers of the Fifteenth Century* (Oxford, 1971), vol. i, p. xxxiv).

   the first letter I ever wrote: Criseyde is not illiterate; she reads Troilus' letter alone, and Troilus later reads through all her letters to him during their affair (v. 470–2, p. 129). Helen of Troy claims to be a novice at letter-writing in Ovid, *Heroides*, 17.143–4.

46 *Disdain's prison*: the lady's reserve or standoffishness (her 'daunger') is a traditional aspect of the lover's difficulties in courtly literature; cf. *Merciles Beaute*, a roundel doubtfully attributed to Chaucer: 'For Daunger halt [holds] your mercy in his cheyne' (16).

   the gist of it briefly: Boccaccio's verbatim account of the letter (2.121–7) is again replaced with a summary here, but Chaucer will draw on the Italian letters for his lovers' letters in Book V (see pp. 144, 148, 149).

   gold-embroidered cushion . . . jasper: Criseyde's palace is richly decorated.

   something started . . . in the end: unrecorded elsewhere, Pandarus' proverb modifies the common proverb 'An evil beginning has a foul ending' (Whiting B199; Hassell F90).

   "Slight impressions . . . very quickly": unrecorded elsewhere as an English proverb; one *Troilus* MS (H4) glosses in Latin: 'light impression, light recession'.

47 *a thorn she will not pull out*: cf. 2 Corinthians 2: 17, and iii. 1104–5, p. 77.

   Because of talk: translating 'for speche' (ii. 1291), although many *Troilus* MSS read 'shame' instead of 'speche' here.

   two years!: this was sometimes considered an appropriate period of widowhood before remarriage.

48 *the more wood . . . greater the fire*: from *Filostrato* (2.85), but also proverbial.

   the luck of the dice: dicing might be used for divination in love affairs; cf. Gower, *Confessio amantis*, 4.2792–5.

   paced himself . . . progress: translating 'held after his gistes ay his pas' (ii. 1349), where 'gistes' probably means stopping or resting places (*MED*, s.v. *giste*).

49 *the sturdy oak*: cf. the proverbs 'An oak falls all at once' and 'The oak is feeble that falls at the first stroke' (Whiting O8, T471).

   Deiphebus: third of the five sons of Priam and Hecuba (*Troie*, 2939); Virgil alludes to the tradition that he married Helen after the death of Paris (*Aeneid*, 6.511–12).

50 *Poliphetes*: Chaucer may derive the name from a Trojan priest (Polyphoetes or Polyboetes), seen by Aeneas in the underworld (*Aeneid*, 6.484) shortly before he meets Deiphebus, who tells how Helen betrayed him at the fall of Troy.

Antenor and Aeneas: in one tradition, the betrayers of Troy (see iv. 203–4, p. 94).

51 *saved by your faith, in truth!*: cf. Luke 8: 48, 18: 42.

a sort of trick: the device of the feigned illness may derive (C. Muscatine, *Modern Language Notes*, 63 (1948), 372–7) from the story of Amnon and Tamar (2 Samuel 13: 1–20), itself cited in medieval treatises on friendship as an example of what one friend ought not to do for another.

52 *at ten o'clock*: 10.00 a.m. was the hour of dinner.

avoid being prolix: cf. *Squire's Tale*, v. 404–5; Whiting P408.

54 *bier*: i.e. funeral bier (here with the bawdy innuendo of something Troilus will lie on).

55 *two crowns*: now obscure and unexplained, but the two crowns may refer to pity and bounty, or justice and mercy. Cf. *Complaint unto Pity*, 58, 71–7 (where pity is 'coroune of vertues alle', 'annexed ever unto Bounte ... | Ye be also the corowne of Beaute'), and *An ABC*, 137–44 (addressing the Virgin: 'Soth is that God ne granteth no pitee | Withoute thee ... | ... and he represseth his justise | After thi wil; and therfore in witnesse | He hath thee corowned in so rial wise').

56 *predicament*: a translation, inferred from the context, of the unexplained word 'kankerdort' (ii. 1752).

57 *proem*: the third proem is brought forward from *Filostrato*, 3.74–9, part of Troiolo's song, itself derived in part from Boethius, *De consolatione*, 2.m.8. (At the close of his third book, Chaucer substitutes for his Troilus a song adapted directly from *Boece*, 2.m.8; see iii. 1744–71, p. 89). Troiolo's song to Venus after his union with Criseida thus becomes the proem to Book III of *Troilus*; Venus is invoked both as planet, with benefic astrological influence, and as pagan goddess of love, while love is invoked both as sexual attraction and as that cosmic love which binds together the universe.

third sphere ... beloved of the sun ... daughter of Jove: Venus is addressed both astrologically and mythologically: as planet of the third sphere (reckoned outwards from the earth, after the moon and Mercury); as Jove's daughter; and as beloved of the sun, because Venus accompanies the sun through the heavens both as morning and evening star (cf. Dante, *Paradiso*, 8.11–12).

always ready ... in noble hearts!: closer than the corresponding line in *Filostrato* (3.74) is Guido Guinizelli's line 'Al cor gentil rempaira sempre Amore' (Love always repairs to noble hearts), *Poeti del Duecento*, ed. G. Contini (Milan, 1960), ii.460, cited by Dante in *Convivio*, 4.20.

You first moved Jove: in *Filostrato* (3.76) Venus' influence moves Jove to mercy on mankind's offences against him; the 'thousand forms' recalls Jove's amorous escapades, e.g. with Europa (see iii. 722, p. 70).

57 *You appease fierce Mars*: in astrology Venus offsets Mars' malefic influence, and in mythology Mars, god of wrath and contention, becomes lover of the goddess of love, as Troilus later recalls (iii. 725, p. 70).

you make hearts noble . . . reject vice: one of the recurrent references to the morally improving and ennobling effects of love (e.g. i. 1076–85, iii. 1786–1806, pp. 22, 89–90).

Calliope: muse of epic poetry, perhaps recalled (like the opening lines of Book II) from the opening of Dante's *Purgatorio* (1.7–9). Medieval commentators interpreted Calliope as the 'best voice' among the muses.

58 *not presumptuous . . . flattering words*: translating 'Al nere he malapert, or made it tough, | Or was to bold to synge a fool a masse' (iii. 87–8).

(as old books teach): the following scene of the lovers' meeting is actually invented by Chaucer.

59 *made a heart of stone to feel pity*: proverbial; cf. *Legend of Good Women*, 1841–2.

as if he would turn to water: proverbial; cf. *Squire's Tale*, v. 496.

60 *feast of Jupiter, god of nativities*: translating 'natal Joves feste' (iii. 150), with 'natal' referring to Jove's presiding over nativities, but the sense is obscure and unexplained.

held his hands up high: a gesture of prayer.

every bell . . . of its own accord: instances of bells ringing 'without hand' recur in ballads, romances, and saints' lives at special moments.

61 *take first place*: translating 'bere the belle' (iii. 198), which may mean 'take the prize' or 'lead the flock' (as a bellwether); cf. Whiting B230.

When everyone had left: Chaucer here resumes following *Filostrato* with Pandaro's speech on confidentiality (3.4–10), but changes the setting from the temple where Pandaro finds Troiolo lost in thought, which Chaucer will use later for his Troilus' added soliloquy on free will (iv. 953–1078, pp. 107–9).

this year: Troilus first saw Criseyde in April (i. 156, p. 5); Pandarus visited Criseyde in early May (ii. 50, p. 24).

62 *betrayer*: Chaucer's 'traitour' (iii. 273) mistranslates Boccaccio's 'trattator' (3.8), (procurer, go-between).

to us young folk: translating 'to us yonge' (iii. 293) which, alternatively, may mean 'to us when young'.

"The first virtue is to hold one's tongue": proverbial, from the pseudo-Cato, *Disticha*, 1.3 (*Troilus* MSS Dg and S2 have a gloss 'Cato' here). Cf. *Manciple's Tale*, ix. 332–3, and *Roman de la rose*, 7037, 7041–5, 7055–7.

63 *out of any distrust of you . . . silly fools*: since Pandarus is alone with Troilus, any fools must be among the audience.

the wise take warning from fools' misfortune: proverbial; see also *Roman de la rose*, 8003–4.

for exchanging contracts: translating 'the chartres [agreement, deeds] up to make' (iii. 340).

in April last: reference to 'this year' (iii. 241, p. 61) suggests Troilus means the April of the current year, unless he concealed his love for a year.

64 *may Achilles cleave my heart*: Troilus is indeed to be killed by Achilles (v. 1806, p. 152).

Differentiate things: cf. Thomas Aquinas, *Summa theologica*, 1–1.31.2 ('Diversity requires a distinction').

65 *as is written in the story*: again, the pretension to a source precisely where one is not being followed.

66 *as my author says*: as Chaucer is not following *Filostrato*, this account of omissions in his sources is invented; some MSS read 'a hundred lines' instead of 'nearly half this book'.

things then happened: Chaucer's account of how Troilus and Criseyde meet secretly is independent of *Filostrato* until the lovers are in bed together (iii. 1310, p. 81), and has points in common with the lovers' meeting in Boccaccio's *Filocolo* (2.165–83), including the role of the go-between, the concealment of the lover, the incidence of jealousy, the exchange of vows and rings. See K. Young, *The Origin and Development of the Story of 'Troilus and Criseyde'*, Chaucer Society, 2nd ser. 40 (London, 1908), 139–61.

downwind . . . magpie: translating 'cler in the wynd | Of every pie . . .' (iii. 526–7). For the chattering magpie, see *Parliament of Fowls*, 345, and *House of Fame*, 703.

This timber frame: referring to the construction of a medieval timber-frame house; cf. the earlier parallel between the love affair and building a house (i. 1065–71, p. 22).

67 *lightless*: i.e. an especially dark night, both moonless and cloudy.

My author does not care to state in full: the reticent source here is another of Chaucer's invented references to an author.

I must trust you: translating 'moste' in 'I moste on yow triste' (iii. 587) as 'must' rather than the adverb 'most', but the construction in the original is—perhaps designedly—ambiguous.

by stocks and stones: a phrase applied contemptuously to pagan idols, i.e. gods of wood and stone.

68 *Tantalus*: doomed in Hades to stand up to his chin in water that receded whenever he tried to quench his thirst (see Ovid, *Metamorphoses*, 4.458–9).

small room: translating 'stewe' (iii. 601), a small room, usually with a fireplace. Troilus has been hiding here since the previous night.

Wade: there are various references in medieval literature to Wade as a celebrated hero, but his story is now lost and this allusion remains unexplained.

Fortune, executrix of the fates: cf. *Boece*, 4.pr.6.42–196; 5.m.1.18–23.

Saturn, and Jupiter: occurring in 1385, for the first time since AD 769, the rare conjunction of Saturn and Jupiter in the sign of Cancer, with the crescent moon appearing in the evening, may be dated to 9 or 10 June 1385, although the contemporary chronicler Walsingham reports the conjunction of Saturn and Jupiter in Cancer as occurring in May 1385. Conjunctions of Saturn and Jupiter were held to be portents of great events (including Noah's Flood) and associated with heavy rain. The lovers' union during a rainstorm (in *Filostrato* the night is simply dark and cloudy (3.24)) may be an echo of that of Dido and Aeneas (cf. Virgil, *Aeneid*, 4.160–2).

69 *my little room*: i.e. 'my litel closet' (iii. 663), a small room adjoining, at the dais end, the hall where they have been dining; a curtain will be drawn across the hall, forming for her women a 'middle' chamber nearest the room where she is to sleep, and an outer room where Pandarus is to sleep. How Pandarus moves through the house, the location of Troilus' hiding-place, and if or when Pandarus leaves Criseyde's room, remain unexplained.

The wine, at once!: wine was drunk as a nightcap; cf. *General Prologue*, i. 819–20.

old game: translating 'olde daunce' (iii. 695); cf. ii. 1106 (p. 43).

70 *make a complete mess*: proverbial; translating 'casten al the gruwel [gruel] in the fire' (iii. 711).

time of my birth: Troilus prays to Venus as goddess of love (and a benefic planet in astrology) to intercede with her father Jupiter (also astrologically benefic) to avert any harm if at his birth the malefic planets, Mars and Saturn, were in unfavourable aspect. If too near the sun, Venus lost influence.

Adonis: beloved of Venus, killed by a boar; see Ovid, *Metamorphoses*, 10.503–739.

Jove: excluding the malefic Saturn, Troilus now prays to the gods in the descending order of their distance from the earth as planets in medieval cosmology: Jupiter, Mars, Phoebus (the sun), Mercury, Diana (the moon). Venus, positioned between the sun and Mercury, has already been invoked first.

Europa: for Jove's abduction of Europa, see Ovid, *Metamorphoses*, 2.833–75.

Daphne: fleeing from Phoebus, Daphne was metamorphosed into the laurel; see Ovid, *Metamorphoses*, 1.452–567.

Aglauros: she incurred the enmity of Pallas, who caused her to envy her sister Herse, for which Mercury (enamoured of Herse) turned Aglauros to stone; see Ovid, *Metamorphoses*, 2.708–832. But Chaucer is mistaken in suggesting that Pallas' enmity towards Aglauros was caused by Mercury's love for Herse.

Diana: goddess of chastity.

fatal sisters: i.e. the three Fates, Clotho, Atropos, and Lachesis. Clotho spins the thread of life (as a gloss in MS H4 notes), and it was a commonplace that a child's fate was spun before his first clothes were made (cf. Whiting D106).

hem of his clothes: just as Pandarus had led Criseyde to Troilus' bedside (iii. 59, p. 58).

71 *via a secret route, by a gutter*: from 'thorugh a goter, by a pryve wente' (iii. 787); 'goter' may here mean a window leading to the eavestrough (*MED* s.v. goter 4; cf. *Legend of Good Women*, 2705), but it could mean a sewer (*MED* s.v. goter 2(a)).

Orestes: Chaucer spells the name 'Horaste' (iii. 797); the motif of the lover's jealousy may be borrowed from Boccaccio's *Filocolo*, 1.247–89.

72 *wicked spirit*: Boccaccio uses the phrase 'wicked spirit of jealousy' (*Filostrato*, 7.18; *Filocolo*, 1.259–60).

'*O God,*': Criseyde's monologue (down to 'worth very little') is drawn from Boethius, although the sentiments were commonplaces; see *Boece*, 2.pr.4.75–8, 118–27, 150–62.

care a bit: translating 'sette a myte' (iii. 832); a 'myte' was a small Flemish coin, often mentioned in expressions of worthlessness (cf. Whiting M596–611).

a bean: translating 'an hawe' (iii. 854), a hawthorn berry, proverbially worthless (Whiting H193).

There's a time for everything: proverbial; deriving from Ecclesiastes 3: 1.

73 *the bird has flown*: translating 'fare-wel feldefare!' (iii. 861), a proverbial expression for 'All is over' (Whiting F130); the 'frosty feldefare' (*Parliament of Fowls*, 364) is a species of thrush which migrates northwards at the end of winter.

blue ring: blue is proverbially the colour of constancy; cf. Whiting B384 ('Blue is true'), Hassell B112.

Fiddlesticks!: rendering 'ye, haselwodes shaken!' (iii. 890); the sense is uncertain, but the context suggests incredulity, as in Pandarus' two later references to hazelwood (v. 505, 1174, pp. 129, 141).

a stone . . . dead men alive again: cf. Pandarus' earlier reference to the power of gems (ii. 344, p. 29).

lost time . . . slothfulness: cf. the proverb 'Lost time cannot be recovered' (Whiting T307).

he won't say any jealous words: because Troilus is not privy to Pandarus' invention of his jealousy of Orestes.

74 *the horns of a dilemma*: translating 'at dulcarnoun' (iii. 931). Derived from the Arabic term for 'two-horned' (referring to the shape of the diagram), 'Dulcarnoun' was a name for the 47th proposition of the first book of Euclid's geometry, and hence a term for a puzzle or perplexing difficulty. In reply, Pandarus evidently confuses 'Dulcarnoun' with the 5th proposition of Euclid's first book, known as the 'Fuga Miserorum', which he translates as 'flemyng of wrecches' (iii. 933), i.e. the banishment or putting to flight of weak students.

beans: translating 'fecches' (iii. 936), i.e. vetch-seeds, proverbially worthless (cf. Whiting V27).

how red: cf. the blushing, tongue-tied Troilus, when visited by Criseyde (iii. 82–4, p. 58).

75 *But O Jove*: cf. *Boece*, 1.m.5; *Knight's Tale*, i. 1313–14.

76 "*. . . jealousy is love!*": not recorded as a proverb before Chaucer.

drinks up . . . distress: for experience as a bitter drink, see iii. 1214–16 (p. 79).

ordeal . . . oath . . . lots: on trial by ordeal and purgation by oath, see F. Pollock and F. W. Maitland, *The History of English Law* (Cambridge, 1898), ii. 595–9.

76 *misty morning . . . victories*: proverbial lore (cf. Whiting W693, W372, S277, S278).

77 *spirits*: for the three spirits in medieval physiology, see i. 307 (p. 8). Cf. the Lover's faint in Machaut, *Remède de Fortune*, 1490–3.

fell down in a faint: the swoon is partly modelled on Troiolo's later swoon in *Filostrato*, 4.18–19, when the Trojan council agrees to Criseida's exchange (Chaucer omits the swoon from the corresponding scene in *Troilus*; see iv. 218, p. 95).

pull out the thorn: see the earlier references to thorns in the flesh (ii. 1272–4, p. 47).

78 *redeemed*: from 'bought' (iii. 1165); some MSS instead read 'wrought', i.e. created.

79 *Pandarus . . . lay down to sleep*: but whether in the 'outer room' he mentioned earlier, or in the same room as the lovers, remains unclear.

lark . . . sparrowhawk . . . talons: cf. Whiting L84, and Boccaccio's *Filocolo*, 2.165–6.

sweet or bitter: translating 'sucre or soot' (iii. 1194), sugar or soot (proverbially bitter; cf. Whiting S480, Hassell S123).

like an aspen leaf: cf. *Legend of Good Women*, 2648, and *Summoner's Tale*, iii. 1667; and, for later instances, Whiting A216.

the seven bright gods: i.e. the seven planets.

drink a very bitter drink: cf. the proverb 'A bitter drink heals a fever' (Whiting D393).

sweetness seems sweeter . . . before: proverbial; cf. *Boece*, 3.m.1.5–6.

honeysuckle: tree and vine, tree and creeper, are commonplace similes for lovers (e.g. Ovid, *Metamorphoses*, 4.365).

80 *Cytherea*: i.e. Venus, named after Cythera, where she arose from the sea.

Hymen: god of marriage.

Gracious Love . . . what we deserve: lines borrowed from St Bernard's prayer to the Virgin Mary in Dante's *Paradiso*, 33.14–18, so that pagan Troilus expresses an understanding of love in terms of the Christian language of grace. The *sacred binding force of things* translates 'holy bond of thynges' (iii. 1261); for the Boethian notion, see Troilus' song (iii. 1744–71, p. 89).

so high a place: Troilus' idea of himself at this high point comes at the mid-point, the 4119th of the poem's 8239 lines.

mercy surpasses justice: proverbial; cf. Machaut, *Remède de Fortune*, 1686; *Knight's Tale*, i. 3089; *Prologue to the Legend of Good Women*, F162.

81 *fulfilment*: translating 'suffisaunce' (iii. 1309), on which see *Boece*, 3.pr.9.

experienced the great excellence of love: from 'Felten in love the grete worthy-nesse' (iii. 1316), itself translating 'D'amor sentiron l'ultimo valore' (*Filostrato*, 3.32).

82 *exchange of their rings*: this 'playful' exchange is unlikely to represent a form of clandestine marriage as this was known in Chaucer's England, i.e. legitimate albeit disapproved by canon law.

inscriptions on the rings: for inscriptions on medieval rings, see J. Evans, *English Posies and Posy Rings* (London, 1931).

brooch: perhaps the same brooch that Troilus later gives Criseyde (v. 1661–5, p. 150). Heart-shaped pins were evidently fashionable in late-medieval England, and a number survive.

silver, and gold: translating 'white and . . . rede' (iii. 1384).

Midas . . . Crassus: stock examples of covetousness, associated together in Dante, *Purgatorio*, 20.106–8, 116–17, and added by Chaucer to the censure of avarice in *Filostrato* here (3.39). Midas, granted his wish that all he touched should turn to gold, was punished for his folly by growing ass's ears (see Ovid, *Metamorphoses*, 11.100–93); Crassus, notorious for love of gold, was killed on an expedition against the Parthians (53 BC) who poured molten gold into his mouth.

83 *communal astrologer*: the epithet is from Alanus de Insulis, *De planctu naturae* (ed. N. Häring, *Studi Medievali*, 19 (1979)), 2.163–4, ('vulgaris astrologus'), which six *Troilus* MSS cite in Latin as a gloss, and one MS (H4) refers to Alanus.

the morning star Venus: translating 'Lucyfer' (iii. 1417), which five *Troilus* MSS gloss 'stella matutinal' (morning star). This differs from the actual sky in 1385, where until at least September Venus was an evening star (J. D. North, *Chaucer's Universe* (Oxford, 1988), 381).

Fortuna major: a figure in the occult art of geomancy, associated with the sun and with Aquarius, and with the form of a four of diamonds placed above a two of diamonds (a figure also corresponding to a group of six stars in the constellations of Aquarius and Pisces, which would have been rising in the east at dawn in mid-May 1385). Cf. *Purgatorio*, 19.4–5 ('when the geomancers see in the east before dawn their *Fortuna Major*'), where Dante, like Chaucer here, may refer either to the group of stars or the sun rising.

alas, that day must separate us: the lovers' laments at dawn—'O black night' (iii. 1429, p. 83), 'O cruel day' (iii. 1450, pp. 83–4), 'But cruel day' (iii. 1695, p. 88)—are much expanded from *Filostrato* in the tradition of the lyric dawn-song (the French 'aube' or 'aubade', the Provençal 'alba').

Alcmena: when Jupiter lay with Alcmena and Hercules was conceived, the night was miraculously lengthened; see Ovid, *Amores*, 1.13.45–6; Statius, *Thebaid*, 6.288–9, 12.300–1; Boccaccio, *Teseida*, 4.14, *De genealogia deorum*, 13.1.

well may beasts complain: cf. Ovid, *Amores*, 1.13.15–34.

84 *small seals*: cf. Ecclesiasticus 38: 27, 28.

Titan: i.e. the sun, frequently confused with Tithonus, the mortal lover of Aurora (the dawn); see Ovid, *Heroides*, 18.111–14.

84 *two worlds such as this one*: translating 'thise worldes tweyne' (iii. 1490). *Filostrato* has 'dearer to me than the Trojan realm' (3.47), and Chaucer possibly meant 'the realms of both Greece and Troy'.

sooner shall Phoebus fall . . . its place: see Criseyde's later list of 'impossibles' (iv. 1534–54, pp. 117–18).

85 *In the morning*: in *Filostrato*, where the consummation occurs at Criseida's house, there is no morning visit by Pandaro.

86 *God forgave his death*: cf. Luke 23: 34.

Phlegethon: the infernal river of fire; see Virgil, *Aeneid*, 6.551, and Dante, *Inferno*, 14.116, 131.

the worst kind of misfortune: cf. *Boece*, 2.pr.4.5–9; Dante, *Inferno*, 5.121–3; also proverbial.

87 *keeping is as great a skill as winning*: proverbial; cf. *Roman de la rose*, 8261–4, and Ovid, *Ars amatoria*, 2.11–14.

88 *perfect felicity*: cf. *Boece*, 3.pr.2.8–11.

Pyrois: the sun's other three horses were Eous, Aethon, and Phlegon (see Ovid, *Metamorphoses*, 2.153–4).

89 *Troilus' Song*: having drawn on Troiolo's song at this point (*Filostrato*, 3.74–9) for the proem to Book III (see p. 167 n.), Chaucer substitutes a song adapted from *Boece*, 2.m.8.

knits together law of companionship: cf. *Boece*, 2.m.8.23–4, which instead reads: 'knytteth sacrement of mariages of chaste loves'.

90 *Dione*: mother of Venus (cf. Virgil, *Aeneid*, 3.19; Ovid, *Ars amatoria*, 2.593, 3.3, 3.769; *Amores*, 1.14.33).

blind and winged son: on the tradition of Cupid's blindness, see Whiting C634 and E. Panofsky, *Studies in Iconology* (Oxford, 1939), ch. 4.

you nine sisters: i.e. the Muses. The invocation of Dione, Cupid, and the Muses seems to mingle recollections of Boccaccio's *Teseida*, 1.1, 11.63, and Dante, *Paradiso*, 8.7–8.

Helicon: actually a mountain rather than a spring (as Chaucer erroneously takes it here and in *House of Fame*, 521–2) and not near Parnassus, but confusion was common, and Boccaccio takes Helicon first as a mountain but later as a spring in *Teseida* (1.1; 11.63).

91 *Fortune*: for Fortune as most deceptive when seeming truest, see *Boece*, 2.pr.1, m.1; as blinding her victims and as traitor, see *Book of the Duchess*, 620, 647, 813; for Fortune's bright face, see *Monk's Tale*, vii. 2765–6.

Furies: translating 'Herynes' (iv. 22), i.e. Erinyes. For the Furies as daughters of Night, see Ovid, *Metamorphoses*, 4.451–2; and as tormenting and suffering pain, see i. 8–9, p. 3.

Quirinus: i.e. Romulus, mythical founder of Rome. Pandarus has already linked Mars and the Furies (ii. 435–6, p. 31); Troilus mentioned the malefic Mars of astrology (iii. 716, p. 70).

fourth book . . . both life and love: possibly indicating *Troilus* was once planned in four books; two MSS (H3 H4) have 'and last' after 'fourth'.

in the first part of the sign of Leo: translating 'Upon the brest of Ercules lyoun' (iv. 32), which associates the sign Leo with Hercules, who killed the Nemean lion (cf. Ovid, *Ars amatoria*, 1.68). The sun being in Leo from around 12 July to early August, the 'breast' of the lion may suggest the earlier part of this period. Boccaccio gives no date for the episode.

92 *in spite of Polydamas . . . Riphaeus*: in *Filostrato* (4.3) all those mentioned here are taken captive; with his 'in spite of' ('Maugre', iv. 51) Chaucer follows the account in Benoît and Guido (*Troie*, 12551–65; *Historia*, p. 159), where only Antenor is captured. By omitting 'Maugre' one *Troilus* MS (H3) may retain a detail from Chaucer's drafts. The name 'Phebuseo' is Chaucer's invention.

request of the Greeks: in *Filostrato* (4.4) Priam requests the truce, but in Benoît and Guido the Greeks send Ulysses and Diomede as envoys to seek a truce (*Troie*, 12822–13120; *Historia*, p. 160). In a variant line in MS H3 Priam requests the truce.

93 *Apollo and Neptune*: for the story of the withheld wages (unmentioned in *Filostrato* here), see Ovid, *Metamorphoses*, 11.194 ff.; Servius, *Comm. in Aeneida*, 2.610; Boccaccio, *De genealogia deorum*, 6.6; Bode (ed.), *Scriptores rerum mythicarum*, 1.43–4, 138, 174.

Thoas: in *Filostrato* Antenor is exchanged for Criseida, without mention of Thoas, but in Benoît and Guido Thoas is exchanged for Antenor, and Priam also agrees that Briseida be sent to her father (*Troie*, 13079–120; *Historia*, pp. 160–1).

parliament: the sources depict a council or parley; Chaucer presents a parliament more in the English sense.

94 *An outcry . . . blaze of straw*: possibly referring ironically to the traditional phrase 'Vox populi, vox Dei' (the voice of the people is the voice of God), perhaps with a pun on the name of Jack Straw, a leader of the Peasants' Revolt of 1381.

Juvenal, your maxim: Juvenal, *Satires*, 10.2–4; Walther 20873.

Antenor: for Antenor's betrayal of Troy, in removing the Palladium, see *Troie*, 24397–5713; *Historia*, pp. 228–9.

95 *Troilus sped*: in *Filostrato* at this point (4.18–21) Troiolo faints at the parley which agrees to Criseida's exchange.

as in winter the leaves . . . branch: from Dante, *Inferno*, 3.112–14, itself derived from *Aeneid*, 6.309–12.

bark: cf. the metamorphosis into trees of Daphne and Myrrha, cited in *Troilus* (see iii. 726–7, iv. 1138–9, pp. 70, 111).

Just as the wild bull . . . his death: from *Filostrato*, 4.27, itself borrowing from Dante, *Inferno*, 12.22–4, which derives from Virgil, *Aeneid*, 2.222–4.

96 *fallen from a place of honour into misery*: cf. *Monk's Tale*, vii. 1973–7, and Introduction, p. xix.

96 *Oedipus*: the living death of Oedipus, who blinded himself on discovering that he had unwittingly killed his father Laius and married his mother Jocasta, would be known to Chaucer from Statius' *Thebaid*, and the *Roman de Thèbes*.

be useless: translating 'Stonden for naught' (iv. 312), with a possible pun on 'naught' as zero, the shape of an eye (cf. Dante, *Purgatorio*, 23.32).

her light is quenched: translating 'she is queynt' (iv. 313), perhaps a pun (see v. 543, p. 130).

my tomb: cf. Ovid's epitaph (*Tristia*, 3.3.73–6), echoed in Boccaccio's *Teseida*, 11.91; also the lover's epitaph in Boccaccio's *Filocolo*, 1.266.

97 *with his arms folded*: a traditional gesture of melancholy.

98 *in common*: on the 'common' nature of Fortune's gifts, see Pandarus (i. 843–4, p. 18), and *Boece*, 2.pr.2.9–14, 84–6.

If one can sing . . . All are valued: cf. Ovid, *Amores*, 2.4.9–48.

Zanzis: unexplained; perhaps referring to Zeuxis, the ancient Greek painter, described as valuing different qualities in different ladies (Cicero, *De inventione*, 2.1; *Roman de la rose*, 16155 ff.).

"The new love often drives out the old": probably from Ovid, *Remedia amoris*, 462 ('every love is vanquished by a new successor'), a line that became proverbial; cf. also Andreas Capellanus, *De amore*, Rule 17 ('a new love compels the old to leave').

a new situation requires new consideration: cf. Chaucer's *Melibee*, 1225: 'For the lawe seith that "upon thynges that newely bityden bihoveth newe conseil".'

in one ear and out of the other: cf. the Lover's indifference to Reason's speeches in the *Roman de la rose* ('For al yede [went] out at one ere | That in that other she dyd lere [teach]', *Romaunt*, 5151–2).

99 *first the nettle . . . dock-leaf soothes*: translating 'Nettle in, dok out' (iv. 461), part of a charm to be repeated while applying dock-leaves, traditional cure for nettle-stings (cf. Whiting D288).

"Don't think about pain, and you won't feel any": a commonplace; cf. Seneca, *Epistles*, 78.13, and *Boece*, 2.pr.4.109–13.

Proserpina: queen of the underworld, wife of Pluto.

who once said to me: see Pandarus' earlier advice (iii. 1625–8, pp. 86–7).

100 *happy is the death . . . pain*: cf. *Boece*, 1.m.1.18–20.

like liquor distilling . . . from an alembic: cf. Reason's mockery of the Lover's misery: 'Many times I see you crying as an alembic does into an aludel' (*Roman de la rose*, 6382–3).

because of the abduction of women: Telamon abducted Hesione, Priam's sister; in reprisal, Paris abducted Helen (*Troie*, 2793–804, 3187–650, 4059–68; *Historia*, pp. 42, 74–5).

asking for her from my father: presumably in marriage; Boccaccio's Troiolo knows his father would object to Criseida's low birth (4.69).

101 *care a jot*: translating 'sette at a grote' (iv. 586); a groat was a fourpenny piece.

too scrupulously: translating 'preciously' (iv. 590); many *Troilus* MSS read 'courteously'; cf. *Filostrato*, 4.72: 'Love does not make such subtle distinctions as you seem to do.'

It isn't a rape: cf. *Filostrato*, 4.73 ('You don't have to carry off a woman whose wishes are far from your own . . .'). Most *Troilus* MSS instead read: 'It is no shame unto yow' (iv. 596).

Fortune helps the bold man: proverbial; cf. Virgil, *Aeneid*, 10.284.

102 *Laws are broken all the time through love*: cf. *Boece*, 3.m.12.52–5: 'But what is he that may yeven a lawe to loverys? Love is a grettere lawe and a strengere to hymself thanne any lawe that men mai yyven'; *Knight's Tale*, i. 1163–8; also proverbial.

on a throw of the dice: translating 'on six and sevene' (iv. 621), an unexplained phrase, presumably from dicing.

martyr: a martyr's death was believed to ensure entry to heaven.

'Why,' said Pandarus . . . 'all this time!': five *Troilus* MSS have a variant reading: 'Pandarus answered: "As to that, be as it may"' (iv. 638).

Swift Rumour . . . on swift wings: from *Filostrato*, 4.78, in turn deriving from Virgil, *Aeneid*, 4.174, 180, 188.

103 *headache*: *Filostrato* has 'itch' in the head instead of ache (4.85).

104 *born under an unfavourable constellation*: i.e. her 'nativity', the state of the planets at her birth; for Troilus' 'nativity', see ii. 684–6 (p. 36).

Argia: the name of Criseyde's mother is not mentioned by Benoît, Guido, or Boccaccio; Chaucer may derive the name from that of Polynices' wife, mentioned by Cassandra (v. 1509, p. 147).

unsheath my soul: perhaps recalling Apollo's flaying of Marsyas 'out of the sheath of his limbs' (Dante, *Paradiso*, 1.20–1).

the observance of my "order": in Troilus' absence Criseyde imagines herself as a nun.

I bequeath my heart: for the lover's testament, see *Romaunt*, 4609–11; *Knight's Tale*, i. 2768–70; and Troilus' testament (v. 298–322, p. 126).

105 *the field of compassion . . . Elysian Field*: translating 'the feld of pite, out of peyne, | That highte Elisos' (iv. 789–90), which may derive from 'arva piorum' (fields of the pious) in Ovid's allusion to how Orpheus went there to rescue his wife Eurydice from the underworld (*Metamorphoses*, 11.61–6; lines 61–4 appear as a gloss in *Troilus* MS H4). Chaucer may also have been influenced by the *Ovide moralisé*, and possibly knew an etymology connecting Elysium with the 'Kyrie eleison' (Lord have mercy upon us) of the liturgy (MS R reads 'eleisos' for 'Elisos'). A Latin gloss on Lucan, *Pharsalia*, 3.12, by Arnulf of Orleans reads: '*Elysian*: "Eleison," that is, "to pity," hence "Elysian Fields," as it were "fields of pity" where the pious rest; or *Elysian*: placed "beyond injury"', B. M. Marti (ed.), *Arnulfi Aurelianensis glosule super Lucanum* (Rome, 1958), 156.

105 *read or sung*: a formula, also used by Criseyde (v. 1059, p. 139) and near the poem's close (v. 1797, p. 152), this is not evidence that *Troilus* was sung in performance.

shame: in *Filostrato* (4.96) Criseida hides her face 'per vergogna' (for shame); three *Troilus* MSS read 'for shame', but the rest read 'for sorrow', which may be Chaucer's emendation.

primary cause: translating 'cause causyng' (iv. 829), i.e. the 'causa causans' or primary cause in logic. MS H4 has a gloss 'causa causans'.

Sorrow always takes possession of the end of bliss: cf. Proverbs 14: 13 (partly cited in a Latin gloss here by MS H4); also proverbial.

107 *the flat of the blade, not the cutting edge*: perhaps alluding to the sword with which Achilles wounded Telephus, which had the power to heal the wound it inflicted (see Ovid, *Metamorphoses*, 12.112, 13.171–2; *Tristia*, 5.2, 15; *Remedia amoris*, 44–8; also Dante, *Inferno*, 31.4–6; and *Squire's Tale*, v. 156–65, 239–40).

how you may come back again soon after you've gone: this is the course of action later proposed to Troilus by Criseyde (iv. 1307–20, p. 114).

Women are clever at quick thinking: found as a proverb after Chaucer.

108 *everything that happens, happens by necessity*: resembling Wyclif's '[nec] omnia que eveniunt de necessitate eveniunt' (not all things that come about come about from necessity), as noted in J. A. W. Bennett, *Chaucer at Oxford and at Cambridge* (Oxford, 1974), 63 n. Troilus' soliloquy derives closely from Chaucer's translation of Boethius (*Boece*, 5.pr.3), but has been given a more predestinarian slant. In its original context the speech is answered by Philosophia's explanation of how God's foreknowledge does not preclude man's free will.

great scholars who prove predestination: cf. the reference to Augustine, Boethius, and Bradwardine, in *Nun's Priest's Tale*, vii. 3241–2.

109 *now listen*: although alone in the temple, Troilus speaks as if responding to an interlocutor, recalling Boethius' dialogue form in the *Consolation*.

110 *Juno*: Roman goddess, wife of Jupiter. Pandarus' prayer for her grace is not in *Filostrato* here (4.111–12).

111 *lign-aloes*: the aloe was, like gall, proverbially bitter (cf. Walther 33629; Whiting G8).

Myrrha: daughter of Cinyras, king of Cyprus, who was metamorphosed into a myrrh tree, and whose continuing tears exude through the bark as aromatic gum (see Ovid, *Metamorphoses*, 10.298–502).

spirits: from 'goostes' (iv. 1142), itself from 'spiriti' (*Filostrato*, 4.116), but Boccaccio meant the physiological spirits, not the lovers' souls.

112 *Minos*: the ancient judge of the dead (cf. Virgil, *Aeneid*, 6.431–3), who sits at the entrance of Dante's hell (*Inferno*, 5.4–6) and later judges the suicides (13.94–6).

Atropos: third of the three Fates, who cuts the thread of life apportioned by the second Fate, Lachesis (see v. 7, p. 121). Criseyde calls on Atropos to break the thread of her life (iv. 1546, p. 117).

Venus: translating 'Cipride' (iv. 1216), i.e. the Cyprian Venus, to whom the island of Cyprus was sacred.

for even a few minutes: translating 'a forlong wey' (iv. 1237), i.e. the time it takes, reckoned at two and a half minutes, to walk a furlong (an eighth of a mile).

113 *nightlight*: translating 'morter' (iv. 1245), a float-wick lamp.

I've made my mind up all of a sudden: cf. Pandarus' earlier remark on women's quick thinking (iv. 936, p. 107).

114 *he who serves love ... happiness*: cf. *Roman de la rose*, 2601–2; *Romaunt*, 2740–2.

as thick as bees fly from a hive: a commonplace figure (cf. Whiting B167, and see ii. 193, p. 26).

115 *I can catch him, without a net!*: cf. ii. 583 (p. 34).

"it's hard to have the wolf full and the sheep unharmed": i.e. you cannot have your cake and eat it, but unrecorded as a proverb elsewhere.

worth next to nothing at all: translating 'avayleth nought thre hawes' (iv. 1398), a proverbial expression of worthlessness.

"Fear first invented gods ...": proverbial in Latin; a version in Petronius (Fragment 27) is quoted in Statius, *Thebaid*, 3.661, and thence by Servius, *Comm. in Aeneida*, 2.715, and is variously quoted by many medieval commentators.

when he fled in fright from Delphi: on Calchas' defection, see i. 64–84 (p. 4).

And truly, I find it written: this paragraph has no equivalent in *Filostrato* here (4.136, 137).

116 *love-making*: from 'th'amorouse daunce' (iv. 1431). See *MED* s.v. *amorous* 2.

Argus: a mythical monster with one hundred eyes, of proverbial cunning (Whiting A180). For women's capacity to outwit Argus, see *Wife of Bath's Prologue*, iii. 358–60, and *Merchant's Tale*, iv. 2111–13.

117 *to exchange the substantial reality ... attribute*: from 'For accident his substaunce 4ay to lese' (iv. 1505). For the distinction, see *Pardoner's Tale*, vi. 538–9.

Athamas: see Ovid, *Metamorphoses*, 4.416–562, where 'Saturnian Juno' crosses the Styx to request the fury Tisiphone to drive Athamas, king of Thebes, to madness; cf. also *Inferno*, 30.1–12, where Dante includes Athamas among the 'falsifiers'.

in Styx, the pit of hell: Styx is one of the rivers of hell, but the pit of hell is a medieval commonplace.

on every nymph ... on satyrs and fauns: cf. Ovid, *Metamorphoses*, 1.192–3: 'I have demigods, rustic divinities, nymphs, fauns and satyrs, and forest deities upon the mountain slopes.'

Atropos: the Fate who cuts the thread of life; see above (iv. 1208, p. 112).

118 *Simois*: cf. Ovid, *Amores*, 1.15.10 ('as long as Simois will roll its swift waters to the sea'); but Simois, a tributary of the ancient Scamander, does not flow through Troy.

you flow backwards to your source: cf. Ovid, *Metamorphoses*, 13.324 ('sooner will Simois flow backwards . . . than . . .'), and Oenone's letter to Paris: 'If Paris can go on breathing, having abandoned Oenone, the water of the Xanthus shall run backwards to its source' (Ovid, *Heroides*, 5.29–30, also cited in *Roman de la rose*, 13225–8; cf. *Troilus*, i. 652–65, p. 14).

Make a virtue of necessity: proverbial in French, but unrecorded in English before Chaucer; cf. *Knight's Tale*, i. 3041–2, and *Squire's Tale*, v. 593.

before Phoebus' sister . . . passes the sign of Leo: i.e. before the moon (Lucina), sister of the sun (Phoebus), passes from its present position in the sign of Aries, through Taurus, Gemini, and Cancer, and beyond Leo.

Juno, queen of heaven: translating 'Juno, hevenes quene' (iv. 1594), which applies to Juno the title of the Virgin Mary.

119 *Cynthia*: the moon, emblem of change, with whose movements Criseyde has linked her return.

"love is something always full of anxiety": cf. Ovid, *Heroides*, 1.12; also proverbial.

For rely on it: in the equivalent speech in *Filostrato* (4.164–6), it is Troiolo who explains to Criseida why he loves *her*.

120 *the mind of man cannot imagine . . . nor tongue tell*: cf. 1 Corinthians 2: 9.

121 *The fatal destiny was approaching*: from *Teseida*, 9.1 ('Now approached the dolorous fate').

entrusts to you three sisters: i.e. Clotho who spins, Lachesis who apportions, and Atropos who cuts the thread of life; but the roles were often confused, and here Lachesis spins. On the Fates as instruments in the execution of Jove's decrees, see Statius, *Thebaid*, 1.212–13; *Boece*, 4.pr.4; *Knight's Tale*, i. 1663–5.

Golden-tressed: may derive from Valerius Flaccus, *Argonautica*, 4.92, Martianus Capella, *De nuptiis*, 1.12. The passage from 'Phoebus' to 'green leaves' derives from Boccaccio, *Teseida*, 2.1.

three times: three springs have passed since Troilus fell in love with Criseyde.

Zephyrus: the west wind.

Queen Hecuba's son: i.e. Troilus.

prime: the first division of the day, from 6.00 to 9.00 a.m.; here perhaps 9.00 a.m.

122 *son of Tydeus*: i.e. Diomede; for Tydeus, see v. 1485, 1493 (p. 147).

knew more than the rudiments: from 'koude more than the crede | In swich a craft' (v. 89–90), where knowledge of the creed represents elementary knowledge.

seized the reins of Criseyde's horse: from 'by the reyne hire hente' (v. 90), perhaps mistranslating *Filostrato*, 5.13, where Diomede is taken with love for Criseida, or following *Troie*, 13529 ('And the son of Tydeus leads her').

He's a fool . . . himself: not recorded as a proverb before Chaucer.

123 *Diomede . . . struck up a conversation*: Boccaccio does not record a conversation here between Criseida and Diomede, whose courtship begins when he visits her four days later. Chaucer adapts Benoît's account (*Troie*, 13529–712) of how Diomede immediately declares his love as they ride from Troy.

Give me your hand: at this point Benoît's Diomede takes Briseida's glove (*Troie*, 13709–12), which Chaucer delays to a later meeting (v. 1013, p. 138).

124 *Criseyde made little response*: Benoît's Briseida replies composedly that it is not the time to promise love; many women are deceived in love; she has just left her friends and home; it would be unfitting to embark on a love affair in an armed camp; but she knows Diomede's qualities; no lady could refuse him, if inclined to love, and nor is she refusing him; but she does not intend or desire to love anyone at present, although if she decided to do so, she would prefer no one over him (*Troie*, 13619–80).

Apollo . . . Ceres, Bacchus: Apollo is the god responsible for Calchas' flight to the Greeks; Ceres and Bacchus, gods of food and wine, are associated with Venus in *Parliament of Fowls*, 275–7 (from *Teseida*, 7.66), but the association was a commonplace (cf. Terence, *Eunuchus*, 4.5.732, and Whiting C125, W359).

Ixion: tied to an ever-turning wheel in hell (sometimes associated with Fortune's wheel) for attempting to lie with Juno (cf. *Boece*, 3.m.12.37–8).

125 *You, reader*: this unique reference to a reader in *Troilus* does not derive from *Filostrato*.

The stars . . . with his rosy chariot: from a stanza of time-description in *Teseida*, 7.94; cf. also *Boece*, 2.m.3.1–5.

126 *my tomb*: Troilus' instructions for his tomb and funeral are added to *Filostrato*, recalling details of the death and pagan funeral of Arcita in Boccaccio's *Teseida*, 10–11, especially the funeral games (7.27) and the cremated ashes collected in a golden urn (11.58).

funeral games: translating 'pleyes palestral' (v. 304); cf. *Teseida*, 7.27: 'palestral gioco' (athletic contest).

Ascalaphus: metamorphosed into an owl by Proserpina (see Ovid, *Metamorphoses*, 5.539–50, 6.431–2). For the owl as a bird of foreboding, see *Parliament of Fowls*, 343; *Legend of Good Women*, 2254.

Mercury: guide of souls ('psychopomp'), who will indeed guide Troilus' soul after death (v. 1827, p. 153).

127 *witness them put to bed*: for the custom of blessing the wedding chamber and bed, see *Merchant's Tale*, iv. 1818–20.

your dreams: expanding on *Filostrato*, 5.32, where Pandaro attributes Troiolo's dreams to melancholy. Much dream lore was common knowledge, and discouragement of belief in dreams was proverbial (cf. Whiting D387; Hassell S106; Walther 30025*b*, 30026–8*a*).

your depression: Troilus' dream is a 'somnium naturale', lowest of the dream types, caused by physiological disturbance through the melancholic humour. See *Nun's Priest's Tale*, vii. 2922–39.

127 *impressions*: see *Parliament of Fowls*, 99–105; *House of Fame*, 36–40; *Squire's Tale*, v. 371–2.

seasons of the year: on variation of dreams with the seasons, see Vincent of Beauvais, *Speculum naturale*, 26.63, as cited by W. C. Curry, *Chaucer and the Mediaeval Sciences* (2nd edn., New York, 1960), 211.

128 *Sarpedon*: king of Lycia, kinsman of Priam (cf. *Troie*, 6685–90).

129 *no one should make music*: Arcite, in his lover's melancholy, cannot hear music without tears (*Knight's Tale*, i. 1367–8).

helmet made of glass!: cf. Antigone's reference to a head of glass (ii. 867–8, p. 39); also Whiting H624.

started to sing: not in *Filostrato* (5.48).

Oh, fiddlesticks!: translating Pandarus' exclamation 'Ye, haselwode' (v. 505); cf. iii. 890, v. 1174 (pp. 73, 141).

130 *palace*: Boccaccio calls Criseida's home a 'casa' (house) (5.50).

O deserted palace: Troilus' address to the beloved's house expands on *Filostrato* (5.53) in the tradition of the 'paraclausithyron' (address to the door), of which there are many classical examples.

quenched: translating 'queynte' (v. 543), past participle of 'quenchen', which may be a bawdy pun (cf. *Miller's Tale*, i. 3276: 'And prively he caughte hire by the queynte').

ruby: cf. Pandarus' remark 'The ruby's well set in the ring!' (ii. 585, p. 34).

dance: the remembered haughtiness and changeable moods of Criseida (5.55) are replaced by memories of Criseyde's dancing and singing.

131 *in your faith*: translating 'in thy byleve' (v. 593).

as Juno was to the Theban race: perhaps recalling Dante, *Inferno*, 30.1–2. Juno's enmity to Thebes arose from the affairs of Jove, her husband, with the Theban women Semele and Alcmena (cf. Statius, *Thebaid*, 1.250–82; *Knight's Tale*, i. 1329–31).

132 *Troilus' Song*: replacing Troiolo's five-stanza song (*Filostrato*, 5.62–6).

Charybdis: whirlpool opposite Scylla's rock between Italy and Sicily (Virgil, *Aeneid*, 3.420; Ovid, *Metamorphoses*, 14.75).

when you have your new horns: cf. iv. 1590–6 (p. 118). Criseyde left Troy when the moon was in Aries, and the sun in Leo. The moon was thus in its last quarter phase; when passed beyond Leo, the 'new horns' of its crescent would appear.

Latona: mother of Diana (and perhaps here confused by Chaucer with the moon). For the moon as 'Latonia', see Virgil, *Aeneid*, 9.405, 11.534; Ovid, *Metamorphoses*, 1.696, 8.394.

Phaethon: allowed by his father, the sun, to drive his chariot for a day, he lost control and was killed by Jove's thunderbolt (see Chaucer's account in *House of Fame*, 940–56).

this breeze: for the motif of feeling the wind softer from where the beloved is, cf. *Filostrato*, 5.70 and proem; also Boccaccio's *Filocolo*, 1.120, and *Teseida*, 4.32.

133 *On the other side*: with this transition Boccaccio opens Part 6 of *Filostrato*, but Chaucer, making no division, here begins to fashion a single fifth book from Parts 5–8 of *Filostrato*.

'Oh, I wish . . . my sorrow!': a speech expanded from *Filostrato*, 6.1, allowing Criseyde to admit her mistaken judgement and express her fears.

134 *medicine comes all too late . . . grave*: proverbial; cf. *Knight's Tale*, i. 2759–60.

Prudence: cf. *Purgatorio*, 29.130–2, interpreted by early commentators on Dante as the three-eyed Prudence that regards past, present, and future. For the tripartite nature of Prudence, see Cicero, *De inventione*, 2.53; Aquinas, *Summa theologica*, 1–2.57.6; Dante, *Convivio*, 4.27.5.

happiness enough for me: from 'Felicite clepe I my suffisaunce' (v. 763). On 'suffisaunce', see *Boece*, 3.pr.2, pr.3, pr.9. Cf. also iii. 1309 (p. 81).

before two months were out: the time span is not specified here in *Filostrato*, (6.8).

nothing ventured, nothing gained: proverbial; Criseyde used the same proverb (ii. 807–8, p. 38).

wise folk . . . in books: not identified, but cf. Ovid, *Ars amatoria*, 1.361–2 ('when hearts are glad, and not bound fast by grief, then they lie open, and Venus steals in with persuasive art').

135 *Diomede, as books tell us*: although Dares, Benoît, and Guido all provide a series of portraits of the chief figures of the Trojan War, including Diomede, Briseis, and Troilus, Chaucer's portraits are based on Joseph of Exeter's *Frigii Daretis Ylias* (itself based on Dares), and lines from the *Ylias* occur as marginal glosses in the *Troilus* MSS Gg and J. For the portrait of Diomede, cf. Joseph, *Ylias*, 4.124–7: 'His voice was fierce, his temper violent. His brains boiled and his rage was daring; his limbs were massive and he stood foursquare. His mighty deeds made him the worthy son of his father, Tydeus—such were the lightning bolts leaping from his spirit, his savage voice, and his arms' (*The Iliad of Dares Phrygius*, trans. G. Roberts (Cape Town, 1970), 43).

free with his tongue: from 'of tonge large' (v. 804).

Criseyde: for her portrait, cf. *Troie*, 5275–88, and Joseph, *Ylias*, 4.156–62: 'Briseis was of medium height, and displayed a noble countenance. Her golden hair was plaited into coils of equal length. Her eye suspends in a joined arch the delights of a lesser shade. The riches of her beauty were rivalled only by the excellence of her character—sober simplicity, courteous modesty, never-failing compassion, and a kindly and gentle manner of speech' (Roberts, 43).

average height: this accords with Dares (ch. 13), Benoît (5276), and Guido (p. 85), although Boccaccio, as followed by Chaucer earlier, implied Criseyde was tall (i. 281, p. 7).

eyebrows were joined together: considered a blemish by Benoît and Guido (*Troie*, 5279–80; *Historia*, p. 85), although a sign of beauty in the ancient world. Medieval physiognomic treatises held joined brows to signify a range of undesirable characteristics.

135 *paradise stood mirrored in her eyes*: cf. Beatrice's remark in Dante, *Paradiso*, 18.21: 'For not only in my eyes is Paradise.'

love continually strove in her: probably deriving from a misreading of 'morum' (of good character) as 'amorum' (of loves) in Joseph's portrait (a misreading found in the MS J gloss).

irresolute: from 'slydynge of corage' (v. 825); cf. Benoît, 5286 ('but her purpose wavered in her'), and Guido, p. 85 ('she had not maintained constancy of mind').

Troilus: for Troilus' portrait, cf. *Troie*, 5393–446; *Historia*, p. 86; and Joseph, *Ylias*, 4.61–4: 'Troilus was broad and tall. In spirit he was a giant, but in age he was a boy. He was second to none in venturing upon brave deeds. Pride graced his noble features, more pleasing because it was blended with manly vigour' (Roberts, 41).

tenth day: the fourth day in *Filostrato* (6.9).

wine and spiced cakes: from 'the spices and the wyne' (v. 852). Spices were taken with wine, but 'spices' could also mean 'spiced cakes'.

136 *my lady Criseyde*: omitting Diomede's address to Criseida as 'young lady' (*Filostrato*, 6.14).

Manes: gods of the underworld.

137 *Tydeus*: see v. 1485, 1493 (p. 147).

Polynices: see v. 1488 (p. 147).

the Orkneys and India: i.e. the furthest points of the world.

138 *Pallas*: protectress of Troy; Criseyde invoked her before (ii. 425, p. 31).

if I should ever take pity: cf. *Troie*, 13674–8 ('I have no intention nor desire to love you or anyone else at present, but be assured that if I decided to do so, I should hold no one dearer than you'), and *Historia*, p. 164 ('the offers of your love I at present neither repudiate nor admit').

her glove: in *Troie* (13709–11) and *Historia* (p. 165) Diomede takes the glove at the end of the ride from Troy.

Bright Venus: as an evening star Venus follows the sun in setting; the moon is in Leo and hence not visible, so that the stars shine more brightly. Criseyde promised (iv. 1590–4, p. 118) to return before the moon passed out of Leo.

139 *the story tells us*: Chaucer here refers to some incidents in *Troie*: after Diomede has been unhorsed Briseida returns to him the horse he had earlier won from Troilus and presented to her (15079–186); Briseida gives Diomede her silk sleeve as a pennon (15176–9).

I also find elsewhere: see *Troie*, 20202–28, and *Historia*, p. 198.

these books will ruin me: cf. Benoît's Briseida: 'Nothing good will ever be written or sung about me' (*Troie*, 20238–9); Criseyde's soliloquy (not present in *Filostrato* or *Historia*) is drawn from that of Briseida (*Troie*, 20238–340).

women will hate me most of all: Briseida foresees the women of Troy will talk of the shame she has brought them (*Troie*, 20257–60) and later finds herself hated by women (20678–9).

I will at any rate be true to Diomede: cf. *Troie*, 20277–8.

But Troilus: Chaucer much expands Briseida's parting tribute and farewell to Troilus (*Troie*, 20317–20).

no author tells how long it was: although in Benoît's account of events, the period between Briseida's arrival in the camp and her acceptance of Diomede can hardly be less than two years.

140 *related before*: Part 7 of *Filostrato* begins here.

laurel-crowned Phoebus: cf. Ovid, *Ars amatoria*, 3.389 ('laurel-adorned Phoebus').

eastern sea: Chaucer may have thought the sea lay to the east of Troy, as in *Legend of Good Women*, 1425–6.

daughter of Nisus: Scylla, who (gazing out from her city's walls) fell in love with its besieger Minos, to whom she betrayed the city, but was then betrayed by him. See Ovid, *Metamorphoses*, 8.6–151, and *Legend of Good Women*, 1902–21. She was changed into the bird 'ciris', which Chaucer may have found glossed as 'lark'.

141 *cart*: from 'fare-carte' (v. 1162), i.e. a cart for sending outside the manor, a rustic vehicle inappropriate for Criseyde.

From never-never land, where merry Robin sported: translating 'From haselwode, there joly Robyn pleyde' (v. 1174). On hazelwood and expression of a sense of futility, see iii. 890, v. 505 (pp. 73, 129); 'joly Robyn' was a generic name for a shepherd or rustic, but Pandarus may refer to Robin Hood.

snows of yesteryear!: cf. the refrain 'Mais ou sont les neiges d'antan!' (But where are the snows of yesteryear), 'Ballade des dames du temps jadis', in A. Mary (ed.), *Œuvres de François Villon* (Paris, 1970), 31–2.

beyond the sign of Leo: this would give Criseyde an extra day.

142 *he dreamed he saw a boar*: in *Filostrato* Troiolo dreams the boar tears out Criseida's heart with its tusks, to her apparent pleasure (7.23–4). Cf. Criseyde's dream (ii. 925–31, p. 40).

he told . . . the whole thing: in *Filostrato* here (7.27–8) Troiolo himself interprets the boar as signifying Diomede.

143 *I now reproach myself with being alive*: Troiolo's attempted suicide with a knife, frustrated by Pandaro, is here omitted (cf. *Filostrato*, 7.33–9).

dreams deceive: cf. Pandarus' reproof on this subject earlier in Book V (p. 127). The deceptiveness of dreams was proverbial (Whiting D387).

144 *Troilus' Letter*: rewritten from the letter in *Filostrato* (7.52–75), using some standard epistolary formulas found in French and fifteenth-century English letters, including: the respectful opening address; a humble commendation of the writer to the recipient; a wish to hear of the recipient's welfare, with a prayer for the continuation and increase of that welfare; a deferential offer of

news of the writer's welfare and good health at the time of writing. (See N. Davis, *Review of English Studies*, NS 16 (1965), 233–44.)

144 *smudged*: cf. Ovid, *Heroides*, 3.3–4 ('whatever blots you see, her tears have made').

If any servant dared . . . complain: cf. Ovid, *Heroides*, 3.5–6 ('if it is right for me to utter brief complaint about my master and my beloved, of you I will utter brief complaint').

two months: Criseida has stayed away forty days (*Filostrato*, 7.54).

145 *turned into lamentation*: for the contraries and antitheses of love, see *Book of the Duchess*, 599–616, and *Romaunt*, 4703 ff. (Reason speaks against love.)

unless you give me health: cf. Ovid, *Heroides*, 4.1 ('with wishes for the well-being which she herself, unless you give it her, will ever lack . . .').

Your T.: Chaucer's Troilus signs himself 'le vostre T.' (v. 1421), reflecting the strong influence of French epistolary conventions on English letter-writing.

she wrote back: Criseida does not reply immediately (*Filostrato*, 7.76).

146 *go and whistle*: from 'Pipe in an ivy lef!' (v. 1433), also used of futile activity in *Knight's Tale*, i. 1838, and proverbial after Chaucer (Whiting I72).

the sibyl . . . Cassandra: like some other medieval writers, Chaucer evidently takes 'Sibille' (v. 1450) as another proper name for Cassandra, one of Priam's three daughters and traditionally the prophetess of disaster. In *Filostrato* Troiolo has already interpreted his dream and is overheard lamenting by Deiphebus, who sends his sisters and other ladies to console his brother. Cassandra taunts Troiolo with Criseida's low birth, and an altercation ensues (7.77–106).

a few old stories: for the story of Meleager and the boar, see Ovid, *Metamorphoses*, 8.270–525, and Boccaccio, *De genealogia deorum*, 9.15, 19.

maiden: Atalanta.

Tydeus lineally descended: as Boccaccio's *De genealogia deorum* (9.21) correctly states, Tydeus was a half-brother of Meleager, but in *Filostrato* (7.27) Meleager is described as Diomede's grandfather.

his mother's doing: Meleager's presentation of the boar's head to Atalanta starts a quarrel among the huntsmen and Meleager slays his two uncles. His mother avenges her brothers on her son by burning the piece of wood, given her by the Fates, upon which Meleager's life depends.

147 *she also told*: in this paragraph (cf. *Troilus*, v. 1485–1512) Cassandra summarizes the events of Statius' *Thebaid*. Polynices and Eteocles, sons of Oedipus, were to rule Thebes alternately, but Eteocles expelled Polynices. King Adrastus of Argos came to the aid of Polynices, and with Tydeus, Amphiaraus, Capaneus, Hippomedon, and Parthenopaeus, fought the war of the Seven against Thebes. All except Adrastus perished, and Creon, who took power in Thebes, refused burial to their bodies (see *Anelida and Arcite*, 50 ff.; *Knight's Tale*, i. 931 ff.).

Maeon: one of fifty warriors sent by Eteocles to waylay Tydeus, who single-handedly slew all except Maeon (*Thebaid*, 3).

prophecies: possibly those of Maeon, Amphiaraus, or Laius (*Thebaid*, 3.71–7; 3.640–5; 4.637–44).

holy serpent: sent by Jove, it stings to death Archemorus, infant son of King Lycurgus, while his nurse Hypsipyle guides the Argive army to the River Langia (termed a 'welle' by Chaucer; v. 1497). Cf. *Thebaid*, 5.505–40.

Furies: who incited the women of Lemnos to kill every male on the island except one. At this point in the text (after v. 1498) all *Troilus* MSS except two (H4R) include a twelve-line Latin 'argument' summarizing the twelve-book *Thebaid* of Statius. For Cassandra's summary, Chaucer draws on both this argument and a series of fuller arguments for each book of the poem, and on the *Thebaid* itself.

cremation of Archemorus: described, along with the funeral games, in *Thebaid*, 6. Although the Latin argument records the cremation, only two *Troilus* MSS refer to the 'burning' of Archemorus; the rest read 'burying'. The *Roman de Thèbes* tells only of burying, not cremation (2621–30).

Amphiaraus: for his death, see *Thebaid*, 6.794–823.

Tydeus . . . was slain: see *Thebaid*, 8.716 ff.

Hippomedon was drowned: see *Thebaid*, 9.526 ff.

Parthenopaeus . . . wounds: see *Thebaid*, 9.841 ff.

Capaneus: struck dead by Jove's thunderbolt for his blasphemous, defiant cries against the gods; see *Thebaid*, 10.907 ff.

each of the brothers . . . slew the other: see *Thebaid*, 11.389 ff.

Argia: wife of Polynices.

the town was burnt: the burning of Thebes is not described in Statius' *Thebaid*; Chaucer may recall the *Roman de Thèbes*, 10131–9, or Boccaccio's *Teseida*, 2.81.

Alcestis: wife of Admetus, king of Pherae; see Hyginus, *Fabulae*, 51; Boccaccio, *De genealogia deorum*, 13.1; Gower, *Confessio amantis*, 7.1917–43; *Legend of Good Women*, Prologue F 510 ff.

Fortune: cf. Dante, *Inferno*, 7.78–82 ('He ordained a general minister and guide who should in due time change vain wealth from race to race and from one to another blood, beyond the prevention of human wits, so that one race rules and another languishes'). With Hector's death, Part 8 of *Filostrato* begins.

148 *disgraced*: from 'smytted' (v. 1545), meaning either 'sullied' or 'smitten'.

neckguard: translating 'aventaille' (v. 1558), a chain-mail strip forming the lower part of the helmet and serving to protect the neck.

as a pilgrim: a not infrequent wartime disguise in both medieval literary and historical texts.

Criseyde's Letter: Boccaccio gives only a summary here of Criseida's replies: 'From her he had only fine words and large but unfulfilled promises' (*Filostrato*, 8.5). Chaucer invents Criseyde's letter, making some use of earlier letters between Troiolo and Criseida (2.96, 122, 126), omitted from *Troilus*, Book II.

148 *How could a person in torment*: cf. the opening of Troiolo's first letter to Criseida: 'How can he who is placed in torment, in heavy sorrow, and in dreadful state, as I am for you, O lady, give salutation to anyone?' (*Filostrato*, 2.96).

149 *your copious letters*: cf. Criseida's reply to Troiolo's first letter: 'I have received those pages covered with your writing in which I have read of your life in misery; and, as I hope for joy, I was not unmoved. And although they are adorned with tears, I have pondered them carefully' (*Filostrato*, 2.122).

brief: cf. *Filostrato*, 2.126: 'of little value, as you can see, is the writing and art in this letter, which I would wish might give you more pleasure.'

the beginnings of change: from 'a kalendes [calends] of chaunge' (v. 1634).

150 *tunic*: translating 'cote-armure' (v. 1651), a garment embroidered with a heraldic device, often worn over armour; see *Knight's Tale*, i. 1016–19.

Lollius: Chaucer is actually adapting *Filostrato* here.

brooch: unmentioned at the lovers' parting, but perhaps the brooch Criseyde gave Troilus (iii. 1370–2, p. 82); her gift of the brooch to Diomede was recorded earlier (v. 1040–1, p. 139).

to un-love you: from Chaucer's 'unloven' (v. 1698).

151 *out of this world*: Pandarus' hatred of Criseyde and prayer for her death replace Pandaro's less vehement disapproval (*Filostrato*, 8.23–4).

152 *Dares*: Chaucer probably means Joseph of Exeter's *Frigii Daretis Ylias*.

Penelope's faithfulness, and good Alcestis: traditional instances of womanly constancy.

Go, little book!: a formula since classical times; cf. Ovid, *Tristia*, 1.1.1., and Boccaccio's address to 'my little book' in the envoy to *Filocolo*, 2.376–8.

Statius: prologues and epilogues deprecating envy are a conventional device; see Chaucer's *Treatise on the Astrolabe*, Prologue, 59–64. For the kissing of footprints, see the close of Statius' *Thebaid*, 12.816–17 ('nor try to match the divine *Aeneid*, but follow from afar and evermore worship its footprints'). For the list of poets, cf. Boccaccio's envoy to *Filocolo*, which mentions Virgil, Lucan, Statius, Ovid, and Dante (2.376–8); see also *Inferno*, 4.88–90 (Dante, guided by Virgil, meets Homer, Horace, Ovid, and Lucan), and *House of Fame*, 1456–1512.

deficient command of the language: as sources of manuscript corruption Chaucer probably refers to dialectal variation in English and to neglect of the final *-e* upon which the metre of many *Troilus* lines depends. Criticism of scribes was conventional; cf. Chaucer's poem to his scribe, *Adam Scriveyn*.

read, or else sung: see iv. 799 (p. 105).

his weightless spirit ascended: this paragraph translates three stanzas (v. 1807–27) borrowed from Boccaccio's description of the ascent of Arcita's soul in *Teseida*, 11.1–3 (an episode omitted from the *Knight's Tale*). Principal sources for the *Teseida* passage are Lucan, *Pharsalia*, 9.1–14 (the ascent of Pompey's soul); the *Somnium Scipionis*; Boethius, 2.pr.7, 152–7, 4.m.1; Dante, *Paradiso*, 22.

eighth sphere: although all but two *Troilus* MSS (JR) read 'seventh', *Teseida*, 11.1, reads 'cielo ottava' (eighth sphere), which is probably what Chaucer wrote, although what he (or Boccaccio) meant by this remains disputed. The context does not make clear whether Chaucer is here numbering the spheres outwards from the earth, or from the outside towards the earth (and, in this case, with which sphere the numbering would begin). The former suggests Troilus' destination is the sphere of the fixed stars (as in *Somnium Scipionis* or *Paradiso*); the latter suggests the sphere of the moon (as in *Pharsalia*). If Troilus leaves behind the planetary spheres in his ascent (see next note) he may reach the fixed stars; if he leaves behind the four elements he may reach the moon. In either sphere his soul has risen above the realm of sublunary change.

planetary sphere: translating 'element' (v. 1810), as is probably also meant in *Teseida*, 11.1, where the soul ascends 'leaving behind the convex [i.e. outer] surfaces of the *elementi*', although the four elements of earth, water, air, and fire may be meant.

wandering stars: from 'erratik sterres' (v. 1812), i.e. the planets.

harmony: the harmony of the spheres; see *Parliament of Fowls*, 59–63.

this little speck: cf. Dante, *Paradiso*, 22.133–5 ('with my sight I returned through every one of the seven spheres, and I saw this globe such that I smiled at its paltry semblance').

153 *Mercury*: the 'psychopomp' or guide of souls; the final destination of Troilus' soul is unspecified.

he or she: *Filostrato* addresses only young men (8.29).

carnival: from 'faire' (v. 1840); cf. the proverb 'all is nothing but a fair' (Whiting W662).

Gower: John Gower (*c*.1330–1408), author of the Anglo-Norman moral poem *Mirour de l'omme* (*c*.1374–8) and of the Latin poem *Vox clamantis* (*c*.1385), a denunciation of contemporary society. In his English poem *Confessio amantis* (begun *c*.1386) Gower salutes Chaucer (8.2941–57), a passage later excised (cf. G. C. Macaulay (ed.), *The English Works of John Gower*, EETS, ES 81 (1900), pp. xxvi–xxviii). On the friendship of Gower and Chaucer, see J. H. Fisher, *John Gower: Moral Philosopher and Friend of Chaucer* (London, 1965), 27–36.

Strode: the Ralph Strode recorded as a Fellow of Merton College, Oxford, before 1360 is thought to be the same Ralph Strode subsequently recorded as a lawyer in London (d.1387). Strode's chief logical treatise is lost, but fragments of his logical system survive in his treatises *Consequentiae* and *Obligationes*. He engaged in amicable controversy with Wyclif, although Strode's position is now only known through Wyclif's rejoinders. Strode contested Wyclif's doctrine of predestination as depriving man of hope and denying free will. Strode was Common Sergeant of the City of London 1373–85, and Standing Counsel for the City from 1386. In 1382 Strode and Chaucer were both sureties for the peaceful behaviour of John Hende, a well-to-do London draper. A 1422 Latin Catalogue of Fellows of Merton declares of Strode: 'he was a noble poet, and he composed a book in elegiac meter called "Ralph's

Vision".' See the article by Sir Israel Gollancz in the *Dictionary of National Biography* and A. B. Emden (ed.), *A Biographical Register of the University of Oxford to AD 1500* (Oxford, 1959), iii. 1807–8.

153 *correct*: the request for correction was a convention; in his *Ameto, De genealogia deorum, Vita di Dante*, and *De casibus*, Boccaccio variously requests correction.

You one . . . all-circumscribing: from the song of the spirits in Dante, *Paradiso*, 14.28–30 ('That One and Two and Three who ever lives and ever reigns in Three and Two and One and uncircumscribed circumscribes all . . .').

INDEX OF PROVERBS

This index lists the occurrence in *Troilus and Criseyde* of proverbs and proverbial phrases, with references to the relevant entries in the following standard collections of French, Latin, and English proverbs of the Middle Ages:

Hassell   J. W. Hassell, *Middle French Proverbs, Sentences, and Proverbial Phrases* (Toronto, 1982)

Walther   H. Walther, *Proverbia Sententiaeque Latinitatis Medii Aevi*, 9 vols. (Göttingen, 1963–9)

Whiting   B. J. and H. W. Whiting, *Proverbs, Sentences, and Proverbial Phrases from English Writings Mainly Before 1500* (Cambridge, Mass., 1968)

BOOK ONE

6 *There's not one of you that can take warning from another's example*: Whiting F449; see also pp. 14, 63

   fools' expectations are disappointed all the time: Whiting F448

7 *The sapling that will bow and bend is better than the one that breaks*: Whiting B484

8 *to draw in his horns*: Whiting H491

10 *tossed to and fro, I am in a rudderless boat*: Whiting S247; Hassell N9

11 *the nearer the fire, the hotter it is*: Whiting F193

14 *a fool can often guide a wise man*: Whiting F404

   a whetstone is no cutting instrument, yet it sharpens cutting tools: Whiting W217

   wise men often take warning from the example of what happens to fools: Whiting M340

   Everything is known for what it is by its opposite: Whiting C415, T110

   how could sweetness ever have been known to him who never tasted bitterness?: Whiting S943

   Nor can any man be completely happy who was never in some distress or sorrow: Whiting M236

   white by black, nobility beside disgrace: Whiting W231

   there's one lesson to be learned from two contraries: Whiting C415

   all his skill could not cure his sorrows: Whiting L171

15 *both things are faults: either to mistrust everyone or else believe everyone*: Walther 32756c

   To a miserable person it's consolation to have a companion in his pain: Whiting W715; Hassell S111; Walther 29943

16 *are you like a donkey at the sound of a harp*: Whiting A277; Hassell A137; Walther 27969

  A man often makes a rod for his own back: Whiting S652

17 *Unknown is unkissed*: Whiting U5

18 *whoever wants to be healed by his doctor must first uncover his wound*: Whiting L173

20 *He hastens well who can wait prudently*: Whiting H171

  like planting a tree or herb in various ways, and next morning pull it up right away! No wonder it never thrives: Whiting T474; Walther 17403a

BOOK TWO

23 *a blind man cannot judge well between colours*: Whiting M50; Walther 2208a, 2214a

  To win love in different times and different places, customs differ: Whiting T63

  every person who travels to Rome does not keep to one route or always to one way: Whiting P52, T63; Walther 14873

29 *you've landed a fine catch of fish*: Whiting F240

  It's a good idea to think carefully before the need arises: Whiting A62

30 *Aware too late, said Beauty, when it's passed*: Whiting B155

32 *One must choose the lesser of two evils*: Whiting E193

  if the cause stops, the illness always stops: Whiting C121; Hassell C17

33 *all the hotter are the glowing coals because people cover them with pale, dead ashes*: Whiting G154

34 *what will occur of necessity cannot be prevented*: Whiting N160

35 *everything must have a beginning*: Whiting E164

36 *there should be moderation in all things*: Whiting M464

  although drunkenness may be banned, I don't suppose this requires everyone to go without a drink forever!: Whiting D423

37 *harm that's done is done*: Whiting H134

  too keen a beginning often leads to break-up in the end: Whiting B200, 201; Hassell A48; Walther 18425

38 *What was nothing before turns back into nothing*: Whiting N151; Walther 8299

  who can stop every wicked tongue?: Whiting T399

  nothing ventured, nothing gained: Whiting N146; Hassell A17, A218, E53

41 *there's a time for everything*: Whiting T88

43 *what kind of winds now guide you here?*: Whiting W343

46 *something started reluctantly very often turns out well in the end*: Whiting T150

  Slight impressions are always ready to fade very quickly: unrecorded elsewhere as an English proverb

47 *felt the iron was hot, and he began to strike*: cf. 'Strike while the iron is hot';
   Whiting I60

48 *the more wood or coal there is, the greater the fire*: Whiting W560

   an oak tree comes from a little shoot: Whiting O7, G418, K12; Walther 5105

49 *A reed that bends with every gust will straighten up very easily if the wind should
   drop*: Whiting R71

51 *people think a man they see sweating is hot*: unrecorded elsewhere as a proverb;
   cf. Whiting H553

BOOK THREE

59 *might have made a heart of stone to feel pity*: Whiting H277

   as if he would turn to water: Whiting W81

62 *The first virtue is to hold one's tongue*: Walther 33716; Whiting V41

   A boaster and a liar are the same thing: Whiting A244

63 *the wise take warning from fools' misfortune*: Whiting F449, W47, W391, W400,
   C161; Hassell C101; Walther 8952, 8927

68 *everything comes to an end*: Whiting T87

70 *make a complete mess*: Whiting G484

71 *It's not a good idea to wake sleeping dogs*: Whiting H569

72 *Danger is introduced by delay*: Whiting P145; Walther 31436-8

   There's a time for everything: Whiting T88; Hassell C198

75 *jealousy is love!*: Whiting J22

78 *Light isn't good for sick folk's eyes*: Whiting L260

79 *sweetness seems sweeter, because bitterness was experienced before*: Whiting S944;
   Walther 6407

80 *mercy surpasses justice*: Whiting M508

86 *the worst kind of misfortune is this: for a man to have been in good times and to
   remember them when they're past*: Walther 6534, 31586

87 *keeping is as great a skill as winning*: Whiting C518; Walther 16215

   happiness in this world only holds on by a thread: Whiting W671

BOOK FOUR

98 *The new love often drives out the old*: Whiting L547; Walther 30604

101 *a wonder only ever lasts nine nights*: Whiting W555

   Fortune helps the bold man: Whiting F519; Hassell F120; Walther 1687-8

102 *Laws are broken all the time through love*: Whiting L579; Walther 25383

   lie dead in a street like dogs: Whiting D329

104 *How should a fish last out of water?*: Whiting F233

THE TROJAN WAR:
AN INDEX OF NAMES

Achilles, son of Peleus and Thetis, a nereid or sea nymph. Greatest of Greek warriors at the siege of Troy, he slew both Hector and Troilus in battle. In some ancient traditions he felt an unreciprocated passion for Troilus, and, after an ambush, slew him in a temple.

Aeneas, prominent Trojan, son of Anchises and Aphrodite; in medieval tradition he was associated with Antenor in the betrayal of Troy to the Greeks.

Agamemnon, king of Mycenae and elder brother of Menelaus; the latter's wife, Helen, was carried off by Prince Paris of Troy, so causing the Trojan War. Commander-in-chief of the Greek forces besieging Troy.

Antenor, prominent Trojan; in a medieval tradition beginning with Dares Phrygius and Dictys Cretensis he was the betrayer of Troy, handing over to the Greeks the Palladium, a sacred relic upon which Troy's safety depended.

Briseis, i.e. Hippodamia, daughter of Brises; concubine of Achilles, taken from him by Agamemnon, so causing the quarrel between them in the *Iliad*.

Calchas, in Homer a diviner who accompanied the Greek army to Troy; in medieval tradition, a Trojan, taking the place of Homer's Chryses, priest of Apollo.

Cassandra, daughter of Priam, sister of Troilus. To win her love, Apollo gave her the power of prophecy; but, when cheated by her, he turned the blessing into a curse by causing her always to be disbelieved.

Chryseis, daughter of Chryses, priest of Apollo. Taken as a concubine by Agamemnon, who, when forced by Apollo to return her to her father, took Briseis from Achilles, so starting the quarrel between them.

Criseyde, daughter of Calchas; first appears as the character of Briseida, in Benoît de Sainte-Maure's *Roman de Troie*, taking the name of the classical Briseis. In his *Filostrato* Boccaccio names her Criseida.

Dardanus, ancestor, or possibly grandfather, of Priam.

Deiphebus, son of Priam, brother of Troilus; a prominent participant in the Trojan War. After Paris' death he married Helen, who betrayed him at the fall of Troy.

Diomedes, son of Tydeus; a leading Greek warrior at the siege of Troy in both classical and medieval accounts.

Hector, eldest son of Priam and Hecuba, brother of Troilus; greatest and bravest of Trojan warriors, but eventually slain by Achilles.

Hecuba, queen of Troy, wife of Priam, mother of Troilus. According to Homer, mother of nineteen of Priam's fifty sons.

Helen, wife of Menelaus, younger brother of Agamemnon. Immediate cause of the Trojan War, she was carried off to Troy by Paris, who there made her his wife. Her appearance in *Troilus* is Chaucer's addition to *Filostrato*. Of legendary beauty, she was the daughter of Zeus and Leda in classical tradition.

Hesione, sister of Priam; carried off to Greece by Telamon. Priam sent Antenor as his ambassador to demand her return from the Greeks, who refused to give her up. In reprisal, Paris abducted Helen, which then led to the siege of Troy.

Laomedon, king of Troy, father of Priam. The gods Neptune and Apollo built the walls of Troy for him, but Laomedon withheld their wages and they departed angry with Troy and its king.

Oenone, a nymph of Mount Ida, loved by Paris, who deserted her for Helen.

Pandarus, a Lydian archer in the *Iliad*, eventually killed by Diomedes. The name is borrowed by Boccaccio for his invented character of Pandaro in *Filostrato*.

Paris, son of Priam and Hecuba, brother of Troilus; he carried off Helen, wife of Menelaus, so causing the siege of Troy.

Penelope, faithful wife of Ulysses, who resisted all suitors in his prolonged absence at the siege of Troy and during his subsequent wanderings.

Polyphoetes, or Polyboetes, a Trojan priest mentioned by Virgil (*Aeneid*, 6.484).

Polyxena, daughter of Priam and Hecuba, sister of Troilus. In early tradition she was sacrificed to the ghost of Achilles, prompting later stories that Achilles fell in love with her. From Benoît de Sainte-Maure's *Roman de Troie* Chaucer would know a very full account of the love affair of Achilles and Polyxena.

Priam, son of Laomedon, king of Troy at the time of its siege and destruction by the Greeks. Homer's Priam is an old man, as he is in *Troilus* (iv. 141–2). He was slain during the sack of Troy by Neoptolemus, son of Achilles.

Troilus, son of Priam and Hecuba, slain by Achilles in battle according to Virgil (*Aeneid*, 1.474–8), but in earlier classical tradition ambushed by Achilles at a fountain, pursued, and slaughtered on a temple altar of Apollo. Tradition gave Achilles two motives for the murder: an unreciprocated passion for Troilus, and a prophecy that Troy would fall if Troilus did not reach the age of 20. In medieval tradition from Dares Phrygius, Troilus becomes a prominent Trojan warrior. He is first linked with Briseida/Criseyde in Benoît de Sainte-Maure's *Roman de Troie*.

A SELECTION OF   OXFORD WORLD'S CLASSICS

The Bhagavad Gita

The Bible Authorized King James Version
With Apocrypha

The Koran

The Pañcatantra

Upaniṣads

AUGUSTINE   **The Confessions**
               On Christian Teaching

BEDE   **The Ecclesiastical History**

HEMACANDRA   **The Lives of the Jain Elders**

ŚĀNTIDEVA   **The Bodhicaryàvatàra**

	Oriental Tales
WILLIAM BECKFORD	**Vathek**
JAMES BOSWELL	**Boswell's Life of Johnson**
FRANCES BURNEY	**Camilla**
	Cecilia
	Evelina
	The Wanderer
LORD CHESTERFIELD	**Lord Chesterfield's Letters**
JOHN CLELAND	**Memoirs of a Woman of Pleasure**
DANIEL DEFOE	**Captain Singleton**
	A Journal of the Plague Year
	Memoirs of a Cavalier
	Moll Flanders
	Robinson Crusoe
	Roxana
HENRY FIELDING	**Joseph Andrews and Shamela**
	A Journey from This World to the Next and The Journal of a Voyage to Lisbon
	Tom Jones
	The Adventures of David Simple
WILLIAM GODWIN	**Caleb Williams**
	St Leon
OLIVER GOLDSMITH	**The Vicar of Wakefield**
MARY HAYS	**Memoirs of Emma Courtney**
ELIZABETH HAYWOOD	**The History of Miss Betsy Thoughtless**
ELIZABETH INCHBALD	**A Simple Story**
SAMUEL JOHNSON	**The History of Rasselas**
CHARLOTTE LENNOX	**The Female Quixote**
MATTHEW LEWIS	**The Monk**

GEORGE ELIOT	Adam Bede
	Daniel Deronda
	Middlemarch
	The Mill on the Floss
	Silas Marner
ELIZABETH GASKELL	Cranford
	The Life of Charlotte Brontë
	Mary Barton
	North and South
	Wives and Daughters
THOMAS HARDY	Far from the Madding Crowd
	Jude the Obscure
	The Mayor of Casterbridge
	A Pair of Blue Eyes
	The Return of the Native
	Tess of the d'Urbervilles
	The Woodlanders
WALTER SCOTT	Ivanhoe
	Rob Roy
	Waverley
MARY SHELLEY	Frankenstein
	The Last Man
ROBERT LOUIS STEVENSON	Kidnapped and Catriona
	The Strange Case of Dr Jekyll and Mr Hyde and Weir of Hermiston
	Treasure Island
BRAM STOKER	Dracula
WILLIAM MAKEPEACE THACKERAY	Barry Lyndon
	Vanity Fair
OSCAR WILDE	Complete Shorter Fiction
	The Picture of Dorian Gray